THE WORLD ENCYCLOPEDIA OF
FIRE ENGINES

HINO
多摩800
そ・136

THE WORLD ENCYCLOPEDIA OF
FIRE ENGINES

AN ILLUSTRATED GUIDE TO FIRE TRUCKS AROUND THE WORLD AND A HISTORY OF FIREFIGHTING IN 700 PHOTOGRAPHS

NEIL WALLINGTON

LORENZ BOOKS

NOTE

In describing various fire engines throughout this book, a fire engine may be described, for example, as a 1990 Dennis F127/Saxon/Simon ST240 24m/78ft aerial platform ladder. The first reference (a Dennis F127) refers to the make of the fire engine's chassis/cab; the second to the bodybuilding company; and the third reference is to the manufacturer of the aerial ladder assembly and mechanism fitted.

The alphabetic A–Z listing includes a few companies that actually build a complete fire engine, those that supply the chassis/cab element, and a number that construct the bodywork and firefighting/rescue fitments and equipment, to the specification of the fire brigade concerned.

The listing also includes a number of companies that have long since disappeared from the scene but have clearly made an important contribution to fire engine design and development over the years.

Contents

INTRODUCTION

It is something of a paradox that throughout history fire has been and remains both a friend and an enemy of humans. In the twenty-first century, uncontrolled fire is just as deadly as it was in Roman times. In many ways and despite a plethora of fire safety messages and sophisticated technology, society around the world appears as vulnerable as ever to fire and its immediate threat to life and property.

Against this background, the men and women of the world's fire brigades train, equip themselves to stand ready around the clock in all weathers to tackle the worst fire tragedy or emergency that might befall their local community, business or commercial district.

Modern firefighting and rescue is a hazardous business. After all, when the fire service is called to a dangerous situation, members of the public are usually fleeing in the opposite direction.

An essential part of the firefighting provision in an urban or rural country area, industrial plant, or airport is the fire engine. Not only is it a means of getting a firefighting crew safely and quickly to the scene of the fire or other emergency situation, but it also carries hundreds of items of firefighting equipment. For example, modern fire engines pump water and foam, provide on-board power for a wide range of cutting and lifting tools at

■ BELOW LEFT *This c.1900 American Amoskeag horse-drawn, steam-driven pump makes an impressive sight as it thunders towards a fire call.*

■ BELOW *New Orleans fire crews put their powerful water jets to work during a major fire.*

■ BOTTOM *A nineteenth-century London street scene as firemen set their steam pump to work amid crowds of excited onlookers.*

■ ABOVE *This 2021 Pierce Tiller 32.6m/107ft articulated aerial ladder is a good example of twenty-first century American fire engine development and technology.*

the scenes of accidents, have ladders that can reach the upper floors of high-rise buildings, and carry specialist protective clothing and decontamination equipment for its crew to use at incidents involving toxic and hazardous chemicals.

The development of the fire engine stretches back to the seventeenth century. It is also a story inextricably interwoven with the dramatic history of organized firefighting and the work of fire brigades who constitute the world's premier rescue and emergency organizations.

■ RIGHT *This Rosenbauer Panther airport foam tender is equipped with a roof-top telescopic boom, carrying a device which is capable of penetrating the fuselage of a burning aircraft, and projecting a cooling water/foam spray inside.*

TOWER
MACK
T 2

SECTION ONE

THE WORLD OF FIRE ENGINES AND FIREFIGHTING

Fire engines are among the most glamorous and high-profile vehicles on the public highway. Bright conspicuous colours, strobe warning lights and various warning wailers and hooters make these firefighting machines truly awesome pieces of equipment. The highly trained crews that operate these machines inhabit an exciting and often dangerous world, as they tackle a range of emergencies and disasters both minor and major. This section explores the history and development of the fire service and firefighting skills, from the first makeshift attempts at organized firefighting to the high-tech systems and specialized machines and equipment of today.

■ OPPOSITE *A 29m/95ft Baker Aerialscope tower ladder on a Mack chassis of Brockton, Massachusetts, gets to work at a big mill fire in New England.*

■ LEFT *Bush fires present firefighters with diverse and enormous challenges. Here, two American pumpers face a wall of flames during a serious outbreak.*

The Story of Firefighting

As soon as human beings discovered fire it became necessary to find ways of fighting the devastating flames whenever they got out of control. The first organized attempts at firefighting began at the time of the Roman Empire, albeit in a primitive way, but it was not until the seventeenth century, despite some devastating fires, that firefighting methods really started to develop. Manually pumped fire engines, pulled at first by hand, then drawn by horses, were soon followed by steam power and the emergence of properly organized fire brigades. The arrival of the internal-combustion engine heralded huge strides in both engine evolution and firefighting methods. Today, firefighting keeps abreast of a rapidly changing world and new technology, and the service has evolved into the world's major rescue organization.

The Nature of Fire

Through the ages human beings have regarded fire with a combination of awe and terror. It has always been an essential part of human existence, and for millennia people relied on it for warmth, for cooking their food and for keeping wild and predatory animals at bay, at least while the flames burned bright during the darkest hours. The flames also provided light and a relatively comfortable area around which families and other groups could gather. Fire was also important in the development of the use of metals, for it had the power to transform them into all manner of useful tools and equipment. Conversely, fire could also be used as a weapon of war to strike panic and destruction in an opponent's camp.

With all its inherent power, it is hardly surprising that from the earliest times, the almost magical properties of fire gave rise to many myths and much folklore. The Greek god of fire, especially of the blacksmith's fire, was Hephaestus, and his symbol was a fan of flickering flames. In due course, the Romans adopted Hephaestus as one of their own gods, attaching to him the myth and cult of fire under the title of Vulcan.

■ ABOVE *Vulcan, the Roman god of fire and blacksmiths, held the secret of working metal.*

■ BELOW *In the past, fire has been used as a weapon of war.*

■ BELOW *The awesome power of fire figures prominently in this dramatic impression of Hell by Hieronymus Bosch (1450–1516).*

■ ABOVE *To continue burning fire relies on fuel, heat and oxygen being present.*

■ RIGHT *Ceremonial fire walkers overcome the pain of burning embers in this early engraving.*

■ BELOW *Constable recorded the magnitude of this major fire in nineteenth-century London, viewed from Hampstead Heath.*

The way that fire behaves and spreads is what makes it so dangerous. From a purely scientific standpoint, for a fire to occur three separate factors must be present: fuel, which is something that will burn, a high-temperature source of ignition, and oxygen. Once a fire has been started, it can spread easily and quickly in a number of ways. Direct burning is when flames spread to combustible material directly alongside and in contact with what is already on

fire. Heat generated from a fire can travel laterally through the air (radiation) and be sufficient to ignite material remote from the original outbreak. When heat travels along solid materials (conduction), such as metal beams and joists, it can ignite combustible materials well away from the initial fire. Finally, heat and products travelling upwards from a fire (convection) can set alight anything combustible above the original outbreak.

Ever since people first learned to live with fire, it has been a potential threat to human life and property, for once flames take hold they can easily kill and wreak devastation. The fumes that fire creates can kill just as easily as the flames. Even small fires in their very early stages can produce large volumes of smoke, particularly when modern man-made materials are burning. In most fire situations, this smoke will be the killer, almost certainly quickly asphyxiating its victims long before the flames reach them. It also has a damaging material effect on personal possessions, the fabric of a home or workplace, and can be a potential threat to livelihood. Smoke levels can increase rapidly by the minute as a fire develops unchecked, as will temperatures and the rapid spread of the fire inside a building. In order for firefighters to successfully carry out rescues and tackle a spreading blaze, therefore, it is imperative that they get to the scene as quickly as possible.

■ ABOVE LEFT *Heat has travelled across the road by radiation to ignite the grass verge.*

■ ABOVE CENTRE *Metal-frame buildings aid the spread of fire.*

■ ABOVE RIGHT *Convection carries curling flames upwards to ignite combustible materials above the original fire.*

■ BELOW LEFT *Water thrown on a fat fire scatters the flames.*

■ BELOW RIGHT *A chip pan that has caught fire is the cause of many a kitchen conflagration.*

ACCIDENTAL OR MAN-MADE FIRE

In the past most fires were due to careless-ness. It is easy to imagine how sparks from a fire in a prehistoric camp might have floated up in the hot convection current to drop down and ignite a nearby patch of dry grass. Suddenly, flames spread rapidly and a bush or forest fire erupted, threatening everything in the area and causing panic. Today many devastating bush and forest fires are caused in the same way – by a poorly tended bonfire or a thoughtlessly discarded match or cigarette.

Fire has always been a major threat to dwellings constructed of timber and thatch. In medieval Europe, such dwellings were built in close proximity, so a fire in one soon moved along an entire street. Not only were candles

and waxed torches widely used to provide lighting, but it was then common practice to light fires indoors for cooking and heating. Even though some primitive chimney flues were provided, fires frequently broke out on the underside of roofs, often spreading with frightening speed to neighbouring roofs.

The Great Fire of London in 1666 is just one of many that have swept through bustling commercial cities. It started in a baker's shop in Pudding Lane and after just five hours had spread to engulf more than 300 houses and businesses. The flames raged in three directions, running from one building to its neighbour and leaping across the narrow streets. A total lack of any fire precautions meant that nothing whatsoever stood in the way of the flames, which continued to rage for four days and destroyed four-fifths of the old City of London. After the Great Fire, timber was banned as a construction material in London in favour of brick.

By the nineteenth century, many serious and often fatal fires repeatedly caused devastation in the growing urban areas around the developing world, where poor social housing conditions were widespread. Long after the arrival of electricity there was still much use of candles, gas lighting, open-hearth fires for cooking, and oil stoves for heating. Chimneys, too, often went unswept. All these conditions helped fuel rapid spread once an outbreak of fire occurred.

In spite of improved fire safety awareness and regulations, we are still vulnerable to accidental fire. High on the list of causes are faulty or misused electrical equipment, the careless disposal of cigarettes, a general lack of care and attention while using cooking stoves and equipment, and unsupervised children playing with matches. Another cause of fire, and one that is on the increase, is arson.

■ ABOVE *The fire that spread rapidly through this disused woollen mill forced the firefighting crews working inside the building to withdraw for their own safety.*

■ BELOW *Rural fires such as this grassland and forest fire can be protracted affairs when water supplies are scarce and the affected area is extensive.*

Compared to man-made fires, natural ones are relatively rare, but when they do occur they can be devastating. Spontaneous combustion triggered by prolonged intensely hot periods can lead to forest and bush fires that burn for weeks on end, destroying vast areas of natural habitat and sometimes engulfing towns and villages. The periodic eruption of volcanoes and the resultant red-hot lava flows can also ignite large tracts of adjacent vegetation.

THE FIRST FIREFIGHTERS

The earliest historical reference to firefighting indicates that first efforts are likely to have taken place in the second century BC, when an Alexandrian named Ctesibus invented a primitive hand-operated squirt that could throw a modest jet of water on to a fire. Resembling a large syringe, it was simply a narrow-bore parallel cylinder, about 1m/3ft in length, with a nozzle at one end and an internal piston connected to a handle at the other end. When in use, the nozzle was immersed in a bucket of water and the handle was slowly drawn out to its maximum travel. This sucked a charge of water into the squirt that was then discharged as a water jet on to the fire by pushing the handle back into the cylinder. However, such squirts would have had little impact on an outbreak of fire, and it can be assumed that in pre-Roman times fires were extinguished only when the burning material was completely consumed, a natural firebreak occurred, or when heavy rain fell.

In the early days of the Roman Empire, there are recorded examples of fire tragedies and destruction on a huge scale. For instance, during AD6 a single conflagration destroyed a quarter of all the buildings in central Rome, and it is probable that the origins of organized firefighting can be traced back to the aftermath of this particularly destructive outbreak. The steady growth of the Roman Empire saw increasing numbers of people living collectively in cities and towns, so it would have been in everyone's interest to minimize such devastating occurrences.

Emperor Augustus recognized immediately that more effective firefighting measures were needed, and undertook to provide the population of ancient Rome with a greater level of protection from the ravages of fire. He formed a dedicated firefighting corps of men, known as

■ LEFT *A contemporary print shows a typical early seventeenth-century fire squirt in action. To produce a firefighting water jet, the squirt had to be held by two men while being operated by a third. It would have been filled from the buckets lying in the foreground.*

■ BELOW LEFT *Chinese firemen work primitive manual pumps supplied by bucket chains as they fight a fire in old Peking. A team of firemen with pole-mounted hooks are standing by ready to pull burning material from the buildings.*

■ BELOW RIGHT *As this medieval manuscript illustrates, fire was used early on as a maritime weapon of war.*

vigiles, who underwent training before being formed into companies based at the fire stations that soon ringed the city. *Vigiles* wore a uniform of a toga and sandals and were under the command of a *siphonarias* (officer). Their duties were primarily to provide fire patrols throughout Rome, especially at night, and to deal immediately with small fires using bucket chains – lines of vigiles and helpers who passed buckets of water from person to person from a water source to the fire and back again. This system was a much more efficient way of delivering water to a fire than if each person walked or ran all the way carrying a bucket. Some companies of vigiles were given the job of pulling down burning buildings that stood in the path of a fire to create a firebreak, or to secure access into roof areas of buildings for other vigiles to direct their bucket chains and water squirts.

Vigiles also carried an assortment of other equipment, including ladders, axes, fire blankets, hammers, various iron tools, and primitive scaffolding to enable them to reach the upper levels of buildings. They were even supplied with sponges to clean up after a fire had been extinguished. Companies of *vigiles* subsequently appeared in many parts of the Roman Empire, where active fire prevention was constantly practised.

■ ABOVE LEFT ***Contemporary firefighters demonstrate a bucket chain in operation.***

■ ABOVE RIGHT ***As seen in this fifteenth-century print, late medieval firefighting methods were still basic.***

■ BELOW ***The Fire of Rome, July AD64, painted by Hubert Robert (1733–1808), raged for three days.***

Despite all this effort Rome and other parts of the empire were subjected to some huge fires. A major outbreak in Rome in AD64 blazed for three days and nights, while in AD120 a fire swept through much of Londinium's (Roman London) structure.

In truth, once a serious fire took hold, there was little anyone could do to stop it.

With the demise of the Roman Empire, it seems incredible that the basic fire-protection advances made during that period were lost, for after this time history does not record much

organized firefighting effort. The emphasis at this time was on salvage work and the recovery of personal possessions, letting fires go uncontrolled until they burned themselves out and died down after consuming everything in their path. In Britain, great fires destroyed large parts of Canterbury in AD619 and AD624. London experienced further huge conflagrations in AD798 and AD982.

■ ABOVE LEFT *A fire overwhelms a large building on the south side of the River Thames in eighteenth-century London.*

■ ABOVE RIGHT *A manual fire pump is put through its paces in this late seventeenth-century print.*

■ BELOW *Shouldering their manual pump, firemen dash to an urban fire in eighteenth-century Constantinople.*

HISTORICAL ACTION

In 1086, some basic attempts were made in Britain to create a general awareness of fire and its dangers. A nightly curfew was ordered requiring the covering of open fires and candles, but this rule proved unpopular and was often disregarded. In 1189 the first Lord Mayor of London, Henry Fitzalwin, issued a local law requiring new buildings to be better spaced and constructed of stone with slate or clay roofs rather than the usual combustible wood-and-straw structures of the time. However, none of these measures prevented fires from breaking out. The first Great Fire of London, in 1212, spread across the Thames and is estimated to have claimed a staggering 3,000 lives. Fire was a common hazard in other English cities of the time; Peterborough, York, Gloucester, Lincoln and Bath were all virtually completely destroyed at one time or another.

The situation was no different in the other great cities of Europe, where the risk of frequent fire also drove the quest for better firefighting equipment. In the early sixteenth century, the Portuguese introduced some very large metal fire squirts, far bigger than any in use up to that time. Each one required a number of men to hold it while it was filled with water and then discharged on to a fire. In 1518, Anthony Blattner, a goldsmith of Augsburg, Germany, attempted to provide some reasonable mobility for a firefighting response by mounting a large fire squirt on a wheeled carriage. Most major cities of this time had some system of fire

■ ABOVE LEFT *An old hand-pump and leather bucket once provided for the most effective firefighting effort.*

■ ABOVE RIGHT *A seventeenth-century German print of the Great Fire of London (1666) shows the enormous fire spread on the north bank of the Thames. By this time efforts were being made to create firebreaks at each end of the inferno.*

squirts and bucket chains in place, which at best relied upon individuals and a few engineers with an interest in the subject to organize a firefighting effort in the event of a large fire.

It was the second Great Fire of London, which started in a baker's shop on 2 September 1666, that acted as a turning point, galvanizing efforts to move the science and practice of firefighting into a new age. The fire burned for four days and nights spreading in three directions before many unaffected buildings were deliberately demolished in its path to form an enormous firebreak. By the time it had subsided in its intensity, an area of almost two square miles of the City had been razed to the ground. Thirteen thousand homes, 84 churches and 44 livery halls lay in a smouldering ruin. More than 100,000 Londoners were made homeless and the fiscal damage was breath-taking, but, remarkably, only six people lost their lives. The direct aftermath of the Great Fire led to the first serious measures to provide organized fire brigades equipped to tackle fire, and the next 50 years were to see some major developments in public fire protection.

■ RIGHT *The sheer extent of the Great Fire of London was captured in oil by Waggoner. The widespread devastation provided the impetus for further development of effective firefighting.*

Fire Companies and Brigades

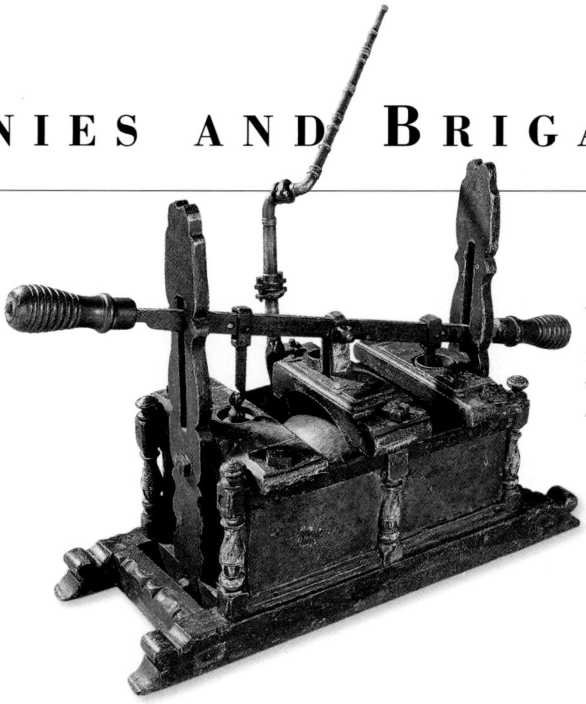

■ LEFT *Early pumps like this c.1680 manual fire engine could only provide an intermittent jet and were cumbersome and heavy. Water was poured into the central trough of the pump, and a pumping action on the two handles operated two plungers to produce a jet of water from the nozzle.*

As the aftermath of the Great Fire of London reverberated through Europe, everyone with an interest in fire extinction methods strove even harder to provide more effective means of tackling the threat of fire.

In 1673, a fire broke out in Amsterdam's Lijnbaan (Ropewalk). As in the Great Fire, the flames spread with incredible rapidity through the back streets and passageways, engulfing many buildings. Some success was achieved in controlling the fire using innovative firefighting equipment designed by the Dutch engineer Van der Heiden. Fortunately for the city's population, he had a few years earlier invented a portable manual pump, which he attached to specially constructed leather hoses.

By the time of the Amsterdam fire, action was being taken in England to try to ensure that the enormous damage and upset of the Great Fire of London would never happen again. In 1680, Dr Nicholas Barbon initiated the world's first Fire Office, where customers could buy insurance and restitution cover against potential damage caused by fire. Barbon's enterprise soon failed, as there were simply too many claims to be met. Five years later a different type of scheme was set up when an insurance company created its own fire brigade to actively minimize the extent of fire damage and thus the size of a subsequent overall claim. It did this by mobilizing a band of firefighters drawn from the ranks of River Thames watermen in the event of a fire.

When in 1711 a conflagration in Boston destroyed over 100 buildings, North America suffered one of its largest fires to date. It burned for eight hours before coming under some control, causing 12 fatalities. The aftermath of this huge fire spurred Americans on to be more reactive to the risks of fire by developing firefighting equipment that was on a par with what was becoming available elsewhere in the world.

Insurance fire brigade companies

In London good progress was being made, and by 1720, twelve different insurance fire brigade company schemes were in place. Each provided its firemen (watermen) with colourful uniforms to be worn when at a fire at an

■ BELOW *The workings of an eighteenth-century two-man manual fire pump are shown in this French watercolour of the time. Before the use of air vessels, the efficiency of manual pumps depended entirely upon the speed and physical stamina of the pumpers.*

■ RIGHT *A Hogarth cartoon of 1750 lampoons the typically chaotic firefighting efforts of early British insurance companies, when rival crews frequently impeded one another's operations.*

insured property. A company's firefighters relied on metal firemarks fixed in a prominent position to the front-facing wall of a building to identify the insuring company. Competition among the insurance companies in this growing business sector was keen and got increasingly fierce as the number of insurance brigades started to multiply around 1725. It became the practice that if the first insurance firemen on the scene found that the property was not insured with their company, they would simply stand by and make no attempt to tackle the outbreak. Worse still, when the appropriate insurance company fire crew did turn up, the first crew would actively harass and obstruct the newly arrived firemen. It was a sure recipe for chaos and inefficiency, but one that was to prevail for almost a century.

Alongside the development of equipment, firefighting practice was slowly becoming better structured and organized. By 1733, Boston had a functioning volunteer fire department, and four years later New York boasted no fewer than 35 firefighters. In 1774, George Washington himself was instrumental in setting up a fire department.

At the same time, Napoleon Bonaparte was addressing France's growing need for fire protection. He instructed that a division of the French army should provide the manpower for a regular fire brigade to protect Paris and its inhabitants. The division was known as the Brigade de Sapeurs-Pompiers. By 1800, the Paris firefighting force possessed 30 powerful

■ ABOVE *Metal firemarks were once fixed to the outside of insured properties. In the event of a fire, the appropriate fire brigade could clearly see that the property was entitled to benefit from its firefighting efforts.*

■ LEFT *Insurance company firemen were attired in resplendent livery. This fireman, standing by his manual fire pump, was employed by the Royal Exchange Fire Office c.1800.*

■ RIGHT *Two men could operate this early eighteenth-century Dutch four-man manual fire pump.*

■ ABOVE LEFT *In 1851, Frederick Hodges, the owner of a gin distillery, provided two horse-drawn manual fire engines to protect his company. Over the next decade, his company's firefighters attended hundreds of fires alongside London's regular brigade. This richly embellished Merryweather manual was presented to Hodges by grateful citizens in 1862.*

■ ABOVE RIGHT *James Braidwood, one of the fathers of modern firefighting, commanded the Edinburgh fire brigade from 1824 until he was invited, in 1832, to lead London's first professional fire brigade.*

hand pumps to assist them in their task.

Early on in the nineteenth century, Britain's fire brigades were still manned by generally poorly organized and trained volunteer or part-time personnel. In 1824, however, after a series of serious fires, the city of Edinburgh, Scotland, made a momentous decision that would revolutionize firefighting everywhere. They amalgamated the various insurance brigades operating independently in the city to create Great Britain's first municipal fire brigade and called it the Edinburgh Fire Engine Establishment.

JAMES BRAIDWOOD

The Edinburgh city fathers duly appointed James Braidwood, a 24-year-old surveyor, to lead the new 80-strong volunteer corps. Braidwood wasted no time in training and preparing his firemen for the tasks ahead. He drilled them relentlessly day and night, working off ladders and on roofs, and getting water to normally inaccessible areas. Before long Edinburgh had the most effective firefighters in the land.

News of Braidwood's success soon spread to London where the cramped social housing conditions and industrial processes of the time combined to create an enormous risk of fire and threat to life and property. By 1826, moves were afoot to merge London's principal insurance brigades into one effective force, and in 1832, Braidwood was invited to become Superintendent of the London Fire Engine Establishment (LFEE). Initially he had command of 80 full-time firefighters based at 19 stations across central London. Although Braidwood's new London brigade had to cover a population much larger than that of Edinburgh

■ RIGHT *Known as the Fire King, Eyre Massey Shaw led the London fire brigade for 25 years, from 1861, during which time he pioneered new firefighting techniques and equipment.*

■ RIGHT *A fireman of the London Fire Engine Establishment, c.1860, wears a recently issued uniform. Fire chief James Braidwood replaced the colourful, but impractical, insurance company uniforms with leather helmets, serge tunics and knee-length leather boots. The new style of fireman's uniform became the standard in Europe and elsewhere for the next hundred years or so.*

he was given the same number of firemen as the Edinburgh force. This number grew significantly, however, as the fire cover response was steadily increased to include the wider area of Greater London.

Braidwood had gained extensive organizational experience in Edinburgh and immediately set about putting it to good use. He replaced the diverse uniforms of the firemen's former employers, issuing his men with practical black tunics and leather helmets and boots. He introduced a proper rank structure and a pension scheme. He also instigated a new and strict training routine that encouraged close quarters firefighting. This involved crews trying, where possible, to get inside a building on fire in order to tackle the flames at their seat. Until then, most firefighting efforts had involved aiming water jets through windows in an attempt to contain a fire, rather than a strategy of extinguishing flames at close quarters. In practice, however, it was not possible for firemen to stay inside burning buildings for long before the smoke and heat forced them out into fresh air.

The new chief also drilled his men in the dark, setting them to deal with imaginary fires, often in awkward and difficult locations, such as in attics and on rooftops. They had to work at height, off ladders and with hoses, until they were completely proficient. To keep his firemen alert and to ensure a speedy response to a real call-out, Braidwood would also 'turn out' fire stations on test calls at odd hours.

James Braidwood reigned supreme for almost the next 30 years as a world-leading authority in his field, but his life came to a tragic and sudden end on 22 June 1861, when a small fire broke out in a riverside warehouse just below Tower Bridge. Flames quickly spread through the narrow alleyways to become a huge conflagration. Characteristically leading his men from the front, Braidwood was killed when tons of masonry in the gable end of a building crashed down. His funeral cortege stretched for 2.5 kilometres/1½ miles and brought much of London to a halt.

SIR EYRE MASSEY SHAW

Braidwood was succeeded as London's fire chief by Captain (later Sir) Eyre Massey Shaw, an

■ BELOW *When a major fire broke out in the City of London on 8 December 1886, a massed firefighting attack, using ladders and powerful water jets, was made as flames engulfed the Church of St Mary Magdalene on Knightrider Street.*

■ ABOVE *The Great Fire of New York broke out on 16 December 1835. Explosives had to be used to create a firebreak before the huge blaze could be brought under control.*

Irish army officer who had previously commanded the joint Belfast police and fire brigade. For almost the next three decades, Shaw became the Western world's driving force in firefighting and fire safety. When, in 1866, the British Parliament set up the Metropolitan Fire Brigade, the forerunner of today's London Fire Brigade, Shaw commanded the largest professional fire brigade in the world. The brigade had already been expanded in the early 1860s to 59 fire stations and included many manual escape ladder stations, and Shaw introduced more improvements. He brought in steam-powered pumps, installed a telegraphic communication system and set up an intensive training regime for his firemen. Such was Shaw's expertise that he was in great demand. He crossed the Atlantic to review several American fire brigades and also advised Queen Victoria, in England, on fire safety in the royal palaces. In the 1870s the Prince of Wales, a keen amateur fireman, regularly attended large London fires in his company.

American brigades

There was a similar steady expansion in the provision of effective fire brigades in America, although early in the nineteenth century these were still mostly manned by volunteers. Nonetheless, an increasing number of serious outbreaks of fire threatened the economic and social fabric of the emerging nation. One such fire broke out in the infant business district of New York during a spell of extremely cold weather in December 1835. It started in an area of warehouses and shops, and the savage flames rapidly engulfed everything in their path. The severity of the ice and frost meant ready access to water supplies was difficult, and it was not until several buildings had been blown up to create a firebreak that the spreading inferno was eventually checked and subdued.

The end of the American Civil War saw the establishment of America's first professional fire brigade, in New York, and in 1865 it included 33 horse-drawn manually pumped engines, 11 ladders and 600 paid firemen. Not long after that, steam pumps came into widespread use in America.

Chicago suffered a devastating fire in 1871. It started in a timber mill and spread to destroy four blocks of buildings. As soon as this outbreak was brought under control after several hours, another fire started nearby,

■ BELOW *This double-decker horse-drawn fire engine would have been developed for use by fire companies.*

■ RIGHT *The Great Fire of Chicago broke out on 1 October 1871. It raged for 24 hours and extended over an area of 13 square kilometres/ 5 square miles.*

possibly ignited by sparks from the original blaze. Fanned by a very strong wind, the second fire soon engulfed rows of timber properties and before long had become a conflagration. The strong wind rendered many firefighting jets useless, and the flames jumped across the river. Chicago fire crews, already weary from the first blaze, sent urgent telegraphic requests for help which brought crews from all around. The firefighting effort was also hampered by the thousands of Chicago's residents fleeing the advancing flames. The fire burned for 24 hours, before coming under control with the assistance of heavy rain. More than 300 residents died in this terrible fire, which made 100,000 people homeless and destroyed over 18,000 buildings.

As a consequence of the Great Fire of Chicago, the strength of the city's fire department was doubled, and by 1876 it could muster 390 officers and men, 34 steam pumps, 150 horses, 26 sets of wheeled rescue ladders and approximately 11,000m/35,000ft of hose. Like many other progressive city brigades, Chicago was also installing street alarm boxes to speed up the call-out process.

The provision and development of fire brigades in different parts of the world did not follow any pattern, except that, unsurprisingly, those cities and towns that had suffered a devastating fire seem to have been the keenest to provide a well organized and equipped fire brigade. Many countries were quick to take up British and American developments in equipment and training. For example, in 1875 Sydney, Australia, could boast the most up-to-date British Merryweather steam pumps, whereas in Yokohama, Japan, firefighters had only just phased out wooden hand squirts that were truly of seventeenth-century origin.

■ BELOW *In this 1861 print, American fire crews are seen tackling a major fire with an assortment of manual fire engines.*

■ LEFT *To compensate for the shortage of firefighting vehicles in London at the beginning of World War II, taxicabs were pressed into service. This Austin carries some hose and a short ladder and tows a trailer pump.*

The modern era

By the 20th century, most of the world's larger towns had made the provision of a regular municipal fire brigade. People understood that, apart from the constant threat to life, fire could have severe economic implications. In many areas, some of the financial cost of fire cover was beginning to be subsidized by both central and local government grants. In the smaller towns, however, volunteers continued to man the pumps and provide basic fire cover.

The major landmark in this period was the coming of the motorized fire engine, which enabled firefighters to respond more speedily to an incident and to carry with them an increasing amount of specialized firefighting and rescue equipment other than ladders and hose. The sheer power of firefighting water jets that came with motorized pumps was another improvement, and the first regular use of breathing sets and high aerial ladders meant that entire firefighting strategies could be more focused than in the past.

The changing world

During the early and middle stages of the twentieth century, international conflict and war presented fire brigades with their biggest

■ LEFT *Fire crews of the Vienna Fire Brigade proudly pose with three pumps and a turntable ladder, c.1920. A bugler stands on a running board to warn of the vehicle's approach.*

challenges to date. World War I saw a number of Zeppelin airship bombing raids upon several British cities and towns. In 1915 one particular raid caused 29 separate fires in London, which severely damaged the City financial district. For the first time in history, firefighters found themselves in action as bombs fell; a number of men were injured during such a raid.

This incident would seem like nothing compared to the aerial bombing raids experienced by both British and German cities during World War II. British firefighters were the first to suffer the terrible aftermath of incendiary and high explosive raids when, in 1940, Germany's Luftwaffe targeted London and provincial centres. From September onwards, London was raided on 57 consecutive nights. The service took a terrible pounding, even though by then a government scheme to reinforce the 1,600 separate and individual professional fire brigades across Great Britain with 23,000 volunteers was in place. On some nights more than 2,000 pumps were in use in London. The ports and other strategic targets were also badly hit, and a convoy reinforcement scheme sent pumps to support local crews.

Firefighters were literally in the front line of battle, and the fire services on both sides of the conflict suffered heavy casualties, with many regular and auxiliary firefighters being killed or injured. From the early part of 1942 it was the turn of German firefighters to feel the strain when the Royal Air Force and the US Air Force took their intensive bombing campaign to German cities and armaments factories. Entire urban areas were set ablaze with incendiary and high-explosive bombs, giving fire crews on the ground little opportunity to restrict the severity of the flames.

■ ABOVE *Continual German bombardment during the London Blitz put the capital's firefighters under severe pressure. This view from the dome of St Paul's Cathedral shows the fire devastation on 30 December 1940.*

The latter stages of the war saw the arrival of the German V-I Flying Bomb, followed by more devastating V-2 rockets. These fell in large numbers on London and south-east England in 1944–5, contributing to the tens of thousands of civilian casualties on both sides of the war. They also created new rescue challenges for firemen who had to assist in extricating people from beneath the debris of bombed buildings.

The British fire service was nationalized in order to standardize operational procedures and equipment during the war. Both sides pressed into service reserve government motor and trailer pumps and aerial ladders to supplement the normal firefighting strength. When peace came, it took the brigades almost a decade to recover. Under post-war economic conditions, fire engine and firefighting developments languished until the early 1950s, when a new generation of firefighting equipment began to emerge.

■ LEFT *In November 1943 a crew of Cologne firefighters tackle post air-strike flames with a meagre jet of water. Following intense attacks by Britain's RAF, German firefighters struggled with hundreds of fires.*

The Modern Fire Service

During the second half of the twentieth century the fire service developed at a steadily accelerating pace as it responded to a rapidly changing world. It embraced new technologies and materials as they were developed, while adapting to the continually evolving nature of firefighting and rescue work and an increasing incidence of emergencies.

The post-war age saw the introduction of better-quality domestic housing and a steady eradication of many traditional causes of fire in older dwellings, such as open fires, paraffin and oil stoves, and cramped cooking conditions. New properties incorporated fire protection within their structure and had better means of escape in case of fire. One innovation, for example, was the self-closing door designed to contain smoke within the affected part of the premises.

Yet, in spite of all these improvements, fire continued to be a threat. Modern homes contained a high level of flammable materials, including plastic and other man-made products such as foam fillings in furniture. When these were involved in fire they emitted considerable quantities of thick toxic smoke that could rapidly fill an entire dwelling with black, choking fumes. Furthermore, they could easily be set alight by a carelessly discarded cigarette. Additionally, the widespread use of electricity and a growing number of domestic electrical appliances in the home gave rise to increasing incidences of fire caused by either malfunction or misuse.

Another cause of fire in the resurgence of industry after World War II was the development of new manufacturing methods, which often involved high temperatures, and the widespread growth of chemical use in the production of new synthetic materials. At the same time, many industrial factories and

■ ABOVE *Many brigades make use of fully crewed rescue helicopters, like this highly trained Japanese team based at Osaka.*

■ LEFT *US navy firefighters deal effectively with a modern-day chemical fire.*

■ BELOW *Equipped with breathing sets and heat-resistant clothing, American firefighters prepare to enter a burning building in Boston.*

■ BELOW *The fire service uniform differs from country to country but is recognizable the world over.*

■ BOTTOM *Regular training sessions prepare modern firefighters for every eventuality. Here, a firefighter gets to work dealing with a burning fuel tanker.*

companies were located in old buildings, few of which were laid out with fire precautions and the safety of the workforce in mind.

In the wake of several major fatal fires in the 1950s, in industrial and other premises where fire precautions had been woefully inadequate, British authorities introduced fire-prevention legislation, and a number of the new laws were enacted. Higher levels of fire safety were required in petrol stations following a fire that caused 11 deaths in Bristol, in 1951; in factory premises after a fire in a West Yorkshire woollen mill in 1956, which directly caused eight deaths; in department stores after 11 shoppers died in Liverpool in 1960; and in licensed club premises following 19 fatalities in Lancashire in 1961. Similar legislation followed fatal fires in hotels, hostels and homes for the elderly. Other countries experiencing similar tragedies introduced fire legislation.

■ ABOVE *In some firefighting situations, aluminized heat-resistant suits and hoods are worn to protect against extreme heat exposure.*

Another increasing cause of fire in modern society is arson, whether motivated by criminal intent or insurance fraud purposes. To combat this trend, modern brigades employ trained anti-arson marshals and fire investigation teams. Working closely with law-enforcement agencies, they combine forensic skills with sophisticated equipment.

Current practice

Today, various local authorities provide a 24-hour firefighting service that can respond swiftly to an alarm call to any fire or emergency.

A critical part of modern fire brigade operation is the control or despatch centre, which handles all incoming fire and emergency calls and mobilizes response. These centres are staffed 24 hours a day by specialist uniformed personnel who, having despatched fire engines to the scene of an incident, will control all subsequent radio traffic, despatch reinforcements as necessary and generally monitor the progress of operations. In addition to attending emergencies, fire brigades contribute to general fire safety in other ways. They apply fire-prevention legislation and educate the public about general fire safety and awareness through visits to schools, youth groups, retirement homes and hospitals.

Modern firemen are trained to use a wide range of equipment and in the latest firefighting techniques, which involve tackling fires at close quarters inside a burning building. To cope with such adverse conditions as extreme heat, high levels of thick smoke and

■ LEFT *Thermal imaging cameras enable firefighters to see through smoke to locate casualties and the seat of a fire. This ISG Talisman Spirit was one of the first miniature infra-red firefighting cameras.*

■ RIGHT *A dramatic live fire test puts an aluminized firefighting suit through its paces.*

■ LEFT *Firefighters have removed part of a thatch in order to create a firebreak that will prevent flames spreading along the entire length of the roof.*

humidity, their equipment includes a personal breathing set and a flash-proof firefighting kit that enables them to get close to the seat of the fire. Technical aids such as thermal-imaging cameras, which see through smoke, and personal radios further allow modern firefighters to deal with fires and save lives more successfully than ever.

The whole basis of successful modern-day firefighting is to remove one or more of the three constituents of fire in order to extinguish a blaze. In ancient times, a water bucket chain probably only had a modest effect in cooling whatever small fire was burning. Early firefighting efforts also often attempted to remove the material source of the fire from the flames by creating a firebreak – perhaps pulling down a thatched roof in the direct path of the fire, or by the more drastic method of using gunpowder to demolish an entire building. Modern firefighting methods are, thankfully, more sophisticated although water is generally still the most commonly used extinguishing medium the world over. Water readily provides an immediate cooling effect, particularly when applied at high pressure and in fine atomized particles known as water fog. This lowers the ignition source below the temperature at which the combustion process can take place.

■ BELOW LEFT *Boston Fire Department crews enter the upper floors of a burning building from massed ladders.*

■ BELOW RIGHT *A prompt attack with an extinguisher prevents a small fire from escalating.*

■ TOP *A major fire at a plastics plant in Cleveland, England, produces a huge cloud of toxic smoke.*

■ ABOVE *This Sides 6x6 foam tender is in service at Charles de Gaulle Airport, Paris.*

■ ABOVE RIGHT *Firefighting in winter is hindered by freezing snow, fog and ice.*

Specialist incidents

Some types of fire, however, demand the use of special techniques. Large oil and petroleum fires require the oxygen supply to be cut off from the flames on the surface of the burning liquid. This is done by applying foam to the burning surface, so starving the fire of the oxygen it needs. A fire that involves chemicals also needs special attention, requiring the application of dry powder to exclude oxygen from the combustion process. Firefighters also need to take great care when tackling electrical fires. Water cannot be applied to such fires due to the risk of electrocution, via the conduction of the current through water. Instead dry powder or inert gas must be used to exclude the oxygen from the surface of burning electrical components such as cabling, switch gear, computers and televisions.

■ RIGHT *In an attempt to combat the rise in the number of arson fires during 2001, the London Fire Brigade introduced sniffer dogs as part of their fire investigation teams.*

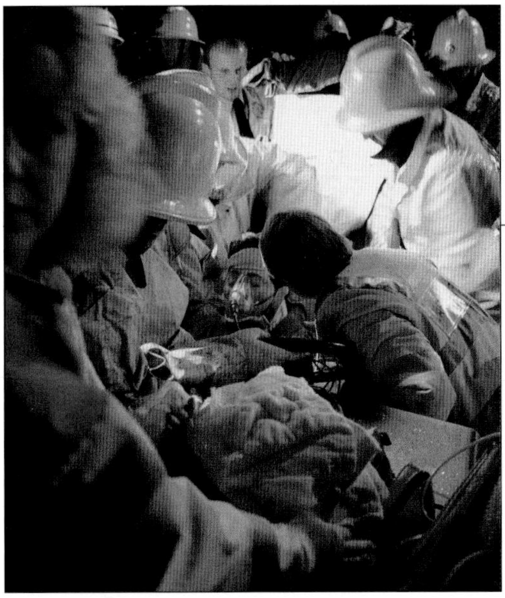

■ ABOVE LEFT *Fire brigades increasingly attend non-fire emergencies such as road crashes.*

■ ABOVE RIGHT *Firefighters work to release the driver of a car that has collided with a tram in central Manchester, England.*

■ BELOW *Fireboats are essential firefighting equipment for busy ports and harbours. They pump their jets directly from the water beneath them.*

In addition to the urban and rural fire brigades that cover the needs of the general population and most industry, specialist fire brigades now exist to serve particular fire and emergency risks. Large airports, for example, are required to provide their own professional fire and rescue service, which has to be equipped and trained to deal with a possible aircraft fire or crash where large quantities of burning fuel might be involved. Airport fire engines must therefore have a large foam capacity and a cross-country all-wheel drive, and also carry specialist cutting tools. Similarly, on-site industrial fire brigades that protect large petrochemical complexes also need sufficient quantities of water, foam and dry powder to deal with large-scale outbreaks of fire where flammable liquids or gases will be burning or pose an explosive threat.

Due to the nature of their high-level training and up-to-date equipment, firefighters are able to tackle a wide range of emergencies, and a significant number of emergency call-outs are of a non-fire nature, many involving life-or-death situations. Road traffic accidents, especially on motorways and other highway networks, have grown dramatically since the 1950s with our increased dependence on cars. As people are often trapped in their crushed vehicles, the fire service has progressively refined its expertise in dealing with such difficult situations. Other non-fire emergencies include gas explosions, leaking or spilled toxic and hazardous chemicals, machinery accidents, and people or animals trapped in various predicaments. The effects of a range of extreme weather conditions can also greatly increase firefighters' workloads. Incidents such as storm-force winds, lightning strikes and flooding after severe rain or thaw all place a huge demand on firefighters. In some countries they are also called on to deal with the effects of natural disasters, such as volcanic eruptions and earthquakes.

149
422

Fire Engine Development

Modern fire engines are some of the most high-profile vehicles on the road. They have come a long way since the first simple attempts in the seventeenth century to mount a manually pumped machine on wheels so that it could be pulled or pushed to the scene of a fire. The subsequent arrival of steam and then electric battery-powered fire pumps each heralded a new era for fire engine development as new engineering ideas and practice provided progressively more powerful vehicles for the world's fire brigades. With the coming of the motor age, fire engine design burgeoned as a prolific number of international manufacturers came on the scene. Today a wide range of pumps, aerial ladders, platforms and many other specialist fire engines are in use all around the world.

MANUAL PUMPS

The latter part of the seventeenth century was a landmark time for the development of the early manually pumped, wheeled fire engine. Prior to this time, pumps were carried to the scene of the fire by firemen, but the regular occurrence of serious fires at that time added purpose to the quest for more powerful and efficient fire engines as well as for ancillary equipment to assist in the battle against the flames.

■ LEFT ***Dating from around 1800, this manual fire engine saw service at the Woolwich Arsenal Ordnance Military Depot, in south-east London.***

EARLY DEVELOPMENTS

During this period various serious attempts were made to produce a reliable wheeled pump that could throw a powerful water jet on to a fire. The early pumps were basically glorified large squirts or syringes with a single-cylinder barrel that drew water in on the upward stroke of the plunger and discharged the contents on the downward stroke. A number of these manually pumped fire engines were described by the English author John Bate in his ***Treatise on Art and Nature*** (1634). In America, records of the time show that Joseph Jynkes, an ironworker, was commissioned to build manual pumps for several cities, including Boston and Philadelphia.

In 1655, a German named Hans Hautch was the first engineer to incorporate an air-vessel in a manual pump. This used air stored in a copper cylinder to ensure a steady and constant firefighting stream of water. Then in 1673, Dutchman Jan Van der Heiden, a pioneer of firefighting engineering, success-fully manufactured the first leather hose. It was constructed of 15m/50ft lengths of sewn leather fitted with brass screw couplings at each end. Once screwed together, this hose allowed water to be pumped over a short distance, dispensing with the need for labour-intensive bucket

■ BELOW LEFT ***Wheeled manual pumps like this one were developed in the late seventeenth century.***

■ BELOW RIGHT ***Pump pioneer Richard Newsham's first manual fire engine of 1734 used an air reservoir to produce a continuous water jet.***

chains and allowing firefighters to discharge water at close range on to a fire as it was being pumped manually. Van der Heiden also mounted his manual pumps on to sleds so that they could be transported down to the Amsterdam canal sides in order to maximize the available water supply. Van der Heiden's pumps and hose were successfully used in combination for the first time in 1673, to combat a serious fire that broke out in the Amsterdam Ropewalk.

Then, in 1721, Richard Newsham, a London button manufacturer with a keen interest in all things mechanical, turned his attention to improving the design of manual fire pumps. He produced a pump that depended on a clever system of levers, chain-operated pistons and air reservoirs, and outperformed everything else on the scene. The use of air resevoirs produced a constant firefighting water jet, providing that the water supply via a bucket chain or hose line did not fail.

By 1725, Newsham's largest manual pumps each required up to 14 volunteer 'pumpers' to work the long handles, one on each side of the pump. These large manual pumps were able to project a water jet as far as 50m/165ft and discharge about 727 litres/160 gallons per minute. Many were commissioned by the emerging insurance companies of that time, but there was as yet no apparent government support or encouragement. Newsham's successful engineering principles were soon being adapted and copied by fire engineers all over Europe and North America.

By the beginning of the nineteenth century, the development of manual fire engines in America started to match the pace in England. American manual fire-engine makers of the time included William Hunneman, James Smith, Patrick Lyon, John Rodgers, and Button and Company. Among their designs were powerful 'double-deckers', with one line of pumpers standing on the fire engine while a second line worked pump handles at street level.

Manual pump designs continued to be improved until well into the nineteenth century, but their output was directly proportional to the physical effort imparted at the pumping levers. In effect they were limited by the number of volunteer pumpers prepared to provide the sustained physical effort required to produce an effective and continuous jet of water. Pumping teams were proud of their strength and stamina and often took part in competitions. Such contests were held at London's Great Exhibition, in 1851, and at a similar event in Paris, in 1855.

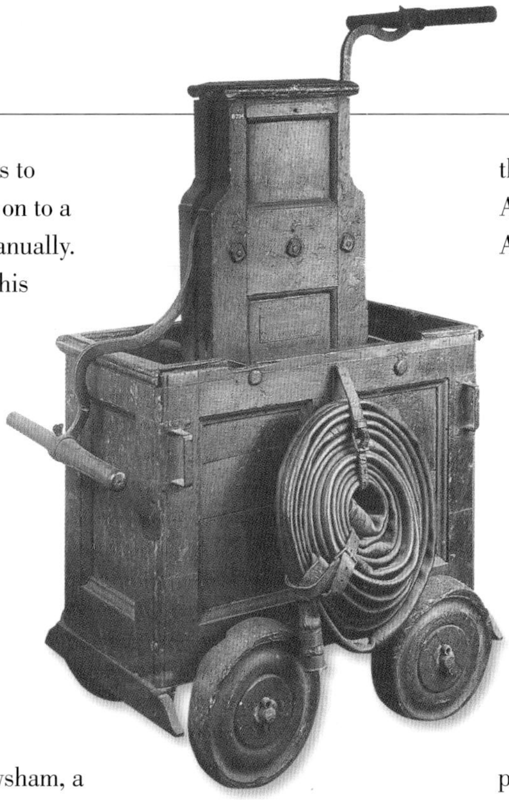

■ ABOVE *This c.1735 wheeled Merryweather compact manual pump carried leather hose. This pump was made almost 60 years after the leather hose was developed.*

■ BELOW *Richard Mason of Philadelphia built this wheeled manual pump c.1792.*

Horse Power

A further improvement in firefighting came when manual pumps were mounted on horse-drawn chassis. Apart from increased mobility and response speed, this development also meant that manufacturers could produce heavier and more powerful pumping units. Better design, stronger metal components and more robust pumping mechanisms combined to keep manual fire engine development moving forward at a steady pace.

■ ABOVE *Horse-drawn vehicles, carrying pumps and men, speeded up response to a fire.*

Horse power pioneers

In the United States, Patrick Lyon led the move towards horse power. In Britain, Richard Newsham had already mounted some of his heavier pumps on a horse-drawn chassis early in the eighteenth century, and by 1820 most effective manuals were horse drawn, with companies such as London-based Merryweather & Sons, and W. J. Tilley (subsequently Shand Mason & Co) leading the way.

Horse power meant that for the first time firemen could ride on the fire engine itself, and before long manufacturers provided footboards along each side of the manual pump's bodywork behind the driver, or coachman as he was often called. Handrails were also added so that the crew could hang on as the fire engine was galloped at some speed to the outbreak of fire. The crew member immediately behind the coachman remained standing in order to operate a long brake lever that stopped the rear wheels under the shouted direction of the coachman.

As adaptations were made to carry small ladders and secure a few lengths of leather hose and some brass nozzles, the horse-drawn manual pumps developed into the first self-contained fire engines. Travelling at speeds of up to 30 kilometres/20 miles per hour, horse power meant that firefighters arrived at a fire outbreak much more quickly than before, and without being exhausted from the physical effort of pulling a heavy pump.

In 1851, Merryweather produced a very successful standard horse-drawn vehicle, designed mostly around the

■ BELOW *This model 1881 Merryweather manual fire engine carried a toolbox on which the firemen sat as they were transported at speed to the fire.*

particular requirements of London's Fire Engine Establishment. The pump had two vertical single-acting cylinders driven by links from the outside pump handles, and a large in-built copper air vessel to ensure a constant discharge of water. The wooden body and frame was spring-mounted on large road wheels fitted with brakes and designed to be drawn by two horses. The bodywork incorporated several lockers for hose and other fittings. This model continued to be manufactured, both for use in Great Britain and for export, until steam power eventually supplanted the manually operated fire engine. In rural areas and on country estates, however, 'manuals' continued to be used for some years into the twentieth century.

The new vehicles depended on horses being available when a fire call came in. In rural areas, few brigades were busy enough to justify keeping horses, so arrangements would be made to use the nearest suitable horses to the fire station. In large cities, however, where call-outs were frequent, many brigades acquired their own horses to speed up turnout.

■ ABOVE *In the past, stately homes and country estates, like industry, might have owned their own fire engine, such as this c.1866 horse-drawn manual pump.*

■ BELOW LEFT *In the late nineteenth century, busy fire brigades bred and kept their own horses at brigade headquarters.*

■ BELOW RIGHT *A later innovation of the horse-drawn fire engine was to carry ladders and equipment, as well as men, to the scene of the fire.*

The best fire horses were bred to combine strength and speed. They were cared for at the fire station in purpose-built stalls close to the fire engine itself. All the fire horses of London's Metropolitan Fire Brigade were eventually descended from a single line of greys specially bred for stamina, controllability in the noise and bustle of a busy city throng, and their ability to remain calm.

Horse-drawn fire engines had no warning devices such as the penetrating bells, horns and electronic wailers we are accustomed to on modern vehicles. Instead, once they had turned out for a fire, the entire crew would continuously shout out 'Hi! Hi!' to alert road users and the general public of their impending high-speed approach.

The Age of Steam

Steam power was first successfully applied to a firefighting pump in 1829, thereby revolutionizing the service. Fire brigades no longer had to rely on a team of straining volunteers to get a decent firefighting jet of water. They simply let the steam drive the powerful jets of water for them.

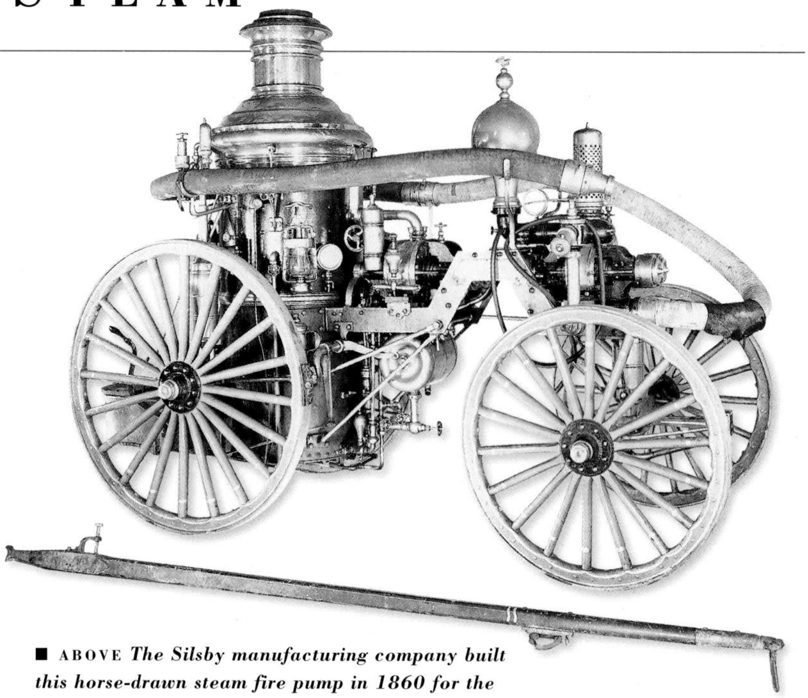

■ ABOVE *The Silsby manufacturing company built this horse-drawn steam fire pump in 1860 for the Philadelphia Fire Department, Pennsylvania, USA.*

■ BELOW *The first American steam-driven fire engine was constructed by Paul Hodge. It had to be jacked up to allow the rear wheels to rotate as flywheels.*

Braithwaite and Ericsson

The world's first steam-driven fire pump was the combined work of two London-based engineers, George Braithwaite and John Ericsson. Their 10hp, 2-cylinder steam engine drove a 2-cylinder fire pump that, like the later manual pumps, utilized a large-capacity air vessel to ensure a continuous firefighting flow of water through leather hoses to the nozzles.

The pump on Braithwaite and Ericsson's fire engine was mounted at the front of a horse-drawn chassis, behind the coachman's seat. The

pump's steam engine had an under-slung firebox fed with coke through a fire-hole door at the rear of the fire engine. The twin pistons of the steam pump were connected directly to the plungers of the fire pump. The boiler took about 13 minutes to reach full working steam pressure and once the fire engine had a full head of steam it could produce enough pressure to project a jet of water 27m/90ft high at approximately 680 litres/150 gallons per minute. The whole fire engine weighed 2¼ tons.

During the height of the cold winter of 1830, Braithwaite and Ericsson's revolutionary fire engine attended a serious fire in a theatre in the Soho district of London. It pumped water continuously into the building for five hours, long before which all the manual pumps of the London Fire Engine Establishment had frozen.

RESISTANCE TO CHANGE

Surprisingly perhaps, steam power was rather slow to catch on in London. For one thing, many of the volunteers who manned the pumps were reluctant to lose their 'pumping' payment as well as the generous provision of beer that was traditionally served to replace the sweat lost through their physical effort. There was also fear of using the new technology for pumping firefighting water. Even though steam engines had been safely used in British mines for some time, the power of steam was awesome and machines had been known to go wrong.

After the success of their first steam pump, Braithwaite and Ericsson constructed four similar fire engines. One of these was a 5hp single-cylinder model capable of throwing a jet of water over a distance of 30m/100ft that saw service in both Russia and France. The other three went to Liverpool and Berlin.

■ ABOVE LEFT *Torrent, built by Merryweather (1863), was one of the earliest horse-drawn steam fire engines.*

■ ABOVE RIGHT *With their steam pump at the ready, these c.1900 firemen are ready to confront a fire.*

■ BELOW *A Victorian steamer is connected to a water main.*

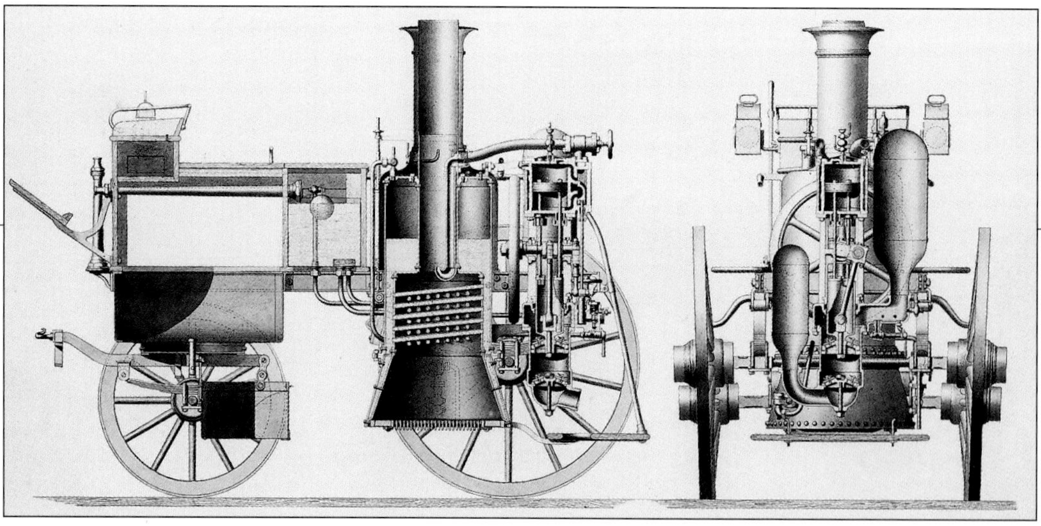

■ LEFT *These sectional drawings of an 1876 Shand Mason horse-drawn steam-powered fire pump show the engineering detail of the time. Shand Mason produced single and 2-cylinder pumps.*

Another factor in Britain's slow uptake of steam-powered fire pumps was concern that the sheer force of the water jets might cause additional damage to a building's structure. James Braidwood, the Superintendent of the London Fire Engine Establishment, personally resisted the introduction of steam power for over 25 years before he was killed at the huge 1861 Tooley Street conflagration. It was left to his successor, Captain Eyre Massey Shaw, to order the first 'steamers' for London's brigade, in 1863, and so begin the belated transition to steam power of one of the world's leading fire brigades.

Developments in steam power

There was no such reticence to adopt steam-powered fire pumps elsewhere. Paul Hodge, a New York engineer, constructed the first American-built steam-powered fire engine in 1840. Designed along the lines of an early railway locomotive, it was the world's first self-propelled fire engine, but it could also be hauled manually or by a pair of horses. When in use at a fire, the large rear wheels were jacked up off the ground so that they could act as large flywheels for the fire pump motion.

Other American steam pump designs soon followed. In 1851, William Lay of Philadelphia unveiled another self-propelled model. This was one of the first fire pumps to use a rotary pump able to throw 1800 litres/400 gallons of water per minute. Over the next ten years, American interest in steam-powered fire engines continued at a high level. Horse-drawn models were produced independently by Alexander Latta, Abel Shawk and Lee & Lanard, and soon companies such as Button, Silsby, Clapp & Jones, Gleason & Bailey, and Rumsey & Co became major manufacturers, producing new machines for many years.

By the early 1860s the two principal steam fire engine manufacturers for Britain and Europe were Shand Mason & Co and Merryweather & Sons, London-based firms who remained fierce competitors for over half a century. Shand Mason produced their first steamer, pulled by a team of three horses instead of the usual two, in 1858. Three years later Merryweather produced their first steamer, named the Deluge. With its 30-horsepower

■ BELOW *American LaFrance built this steam fire pump in 1896 for the Lynn, Massachusetts, Fire Department.*

■ ABOVE LEFT *The Amoskeag Company constructed this steam fire pump for the Lawrence, Massachusetts, Fire Department.*

■ ABOVE RIGHT *Many American steamers were heavier than British versions and needed to be drawn by three horses. This Amoskeag of New Haven, Connecticut, is a dramatic sight with smoke pouring from the boiler chimney.*

engine, it was probably the most powerful steam-powered fire pump built to date and was able to project a water jet to a height of 43m/140ft with a lateral throw of 65m/215ft. The two companies went on to produce both single and 2-cylinder models, Shand Mason preferring short-stroke high-revolution engines.

At fire stations, steam pumps were always kept ready for action, with the firebox carefully laid with kindling material and coal/coke so that it could be lit as the fire engine turned out. In later years, gas rings were lit under the boiler to warm the water inside. The air flow through the firebox during the dash to the fire would cause the fire to burn through so that on arrival at the incident, steam had usually been raised

■ RIGHT *One of Merryweather's first horse-drawn steam fire engines, this model was built in 1863 with the steam engine mounted midships horizontally. Later models produced by this engine manufacturer had the steam engine in a vertical position at the rear of the vehicle.*

■ ABOVE *The 'crew' of a preserved Shand Mason steamer take part in a display staged at a fire engine rally.*

ready to power the fire pump. The mechanical care of the engine was normally the responsibility of a fireman-engineer on the crew who, once at the fire, would tend the fire and boiler water levels, and lubricate the reciprocating parts of the steam engine. In practice, providing there was a good supply of boiler water, coal or coke, and lubricating oil, the engine would keep on pumping indefinitely.

Fire engine trials

As steam power became accepted, fire engine trials were regularly staged to give manufacturers the chance to show off the capabilities of their machines before large audiences of fire officers, government officials and the press. One of the largest such gatherings took place in London's Hyde Park as part of the 1861 International Exhibition. The event was so successful that another was staged in London two years later. There were ten entries for this second event, seven from Britain and three from America. Although all the steam pumps appeared to perform well and entertained the large crowds, the competition's outcome was difficult to gauge as complaints were made against the judges' lack of impartiality and their methods of assessment. Against all this publicity, steamer fire engines were coming into widespread use in the professional brigades around the world. In 1864, Shand Mason delivered steam pumps for brigades as far apart as London, Russia, Bombay, New Zealand, Poland, Denmark, Ireland and Lisbon. Manual pumps remained in cities as reserve fire engines for another 30 years and continued to operate in many rural areas well into the twentieth century.

Although the development in the United States of steam pumps had heralded the construction there of the first self-propelled steamer fire engine in 1840, horse-drawn steam pumps continued to be made. Indeed, for the next three decades the focus was on developing horse-drawn steam pumps, which performed reliably and for long duration at fires. By the 1870s several manufacturers had started to produce effective self-propelled steam pumps in which the boiler steam also powered a propulsion engine driving the rear wheels.

■ RIGHT *This scale model of a Shand Mason steamer, seen from the rear, gleams with beautiful engineering. The original c.1880 fire engine was used by the Metropolitan Fire Brigade.*

■ RIGHT *This powerful 2-cylinder Merryweather steam fire pump was delivered new to Southgate Fire Brigade, north London, in 1894. It represented the zenith of British steam fire-engine power and efficiency.*

■ BELOW *The self-propelled Merryweather Fire King steam fire engine was introduced in 1899. It was a powerful pumping unit and capable of good speed, but its braking system left something to be desired.*

MANUFACTURING RIVALS

The Amoskeag firm had, in fact, been producing some large self-propelled steam fire engines for US fire departments since 1867. One of the company's biggest models, claimed to be the largest fire engine in the world, was supplied to Hartford Fire Department, Connecticut, in 1894. Weighing over 7 tons, it could reach speeds of 48 kilometres/30 miles per hour and was reputed to have been capable of pumping a firefighting jet of water an incredible 107m/350ft into the air.

This American activity eventually spurred British manufacturer Merryweather, still the predominant European manufacturer of horse-drawn steam fire engines of the time, into action. In 1899, Merryweather produced a chain-driven self-propelled model called the Fire King. It weighed a hefty 5½ tons and was capable of a speed of 40 kilometres/25 miles per hour. It could also pump 1800 litres/ 400 gallons per minute, making it one of the most powerful fire engines of its time. This fire engine was subsequently exported worldwide.

The British Fire King and the American Amoskeag self-propelled steam fire engine suffered from their massive weight and were notoriously difficult to steer. Another problem was that the braking systems of both were incapable of efficiently halting such a mass. By the turn of the twentieth century, the era of the steam-powered fire engine, both horse-drawn and self-propelled, was coming to an end.

Motorized Power

The coming of the petrol-powered internal-combustion engine heralded a major step forward in the design and functional style of fire engines, and in the way firefighters tackled fires. More powerful fire engines were made possible, which could carry a growing variety of firefighting and rescue equipment. An innovative feature was a built-in water tank that fed powerful pumps driven directly from the road engine. This meant that for the first time in history fire crews had a firefighting water jet at their disposal on arrival at a fire, and gone were the days when crucial minutes were lost searching out a nearby water supply before anyone could tackle the flames. Motorized fire engines also gave fire brigades greater mobility, and faster response times.

■ ABOVE *The first self-propelled car used by the Metropolitan (London) Fire Brigade was a Stanley steamer acquired in 1903 for the chief fire officer.*

Electric fire engines

Before the widespread adoption of petrol-powered vehicles, a number of the larger professional fire brigades experimented with battery-powered electric fire engines. These were popular for a brief period from about 1905 but were extremely heavy due to the large number of lead-acid batteries needed to provide power to the electric motors. The other drawback was the fact that the batteries required frequent charging on mains electricity.

■ LEFT *Lisbon Fire Brigade bought some state-of-the-art equipment when it acquired this 1913 Delahaye pump.*

■ RIGHT *This well equipped 1913 pump belonging to Paris Fire Brigade had crew seats at the rear. It carried a hose reel drum behind the driver and a larger hose coiled on a removable drum behind the rear wheels.*

■ RIGHT *Battery-driven electric vehicles like this Cedes pump and escape carrier were short-lived novelties at the start of the twentieth century.*

■ BELOW *London-based Merryweather produced this electric fire engine around 1905. The limited power capacity of the vehicle's batteries, together with their heavy weight, rendered the production shortlived. This view shows the crew preparing a hose line to work up a ladder at first floor level.*

These appliances were pioneered by the French Cedes Company in conjunction with Daimler Motors of Austria, and a number went into service. Large batteries housed under the vehicle bonnet drove an electric motor mounted on the rear axle. At that time the heavy batteries lasted for a short time, sufficient for just one call-out of no more than 30 kilometres/ 20 miles. The London Fire Brigade also commissioned a number of Tilling Stevens battery-powered electric pumping engines, with batteries that weighed over 2,000 kilograms/2 tons, but these vehicles suffered from the same performance limitations as the earlier Cedes electric models.

Another disadvantage of electric engines was that their restricted battery power meant that the fire pump had to be driven by other means. Several designs soon appeared. One such, a cumbersome chemical apparatus resembling a large fire extinguisher, was carried on the rear of the electric vehicles. A chemical reaction expelled the contents of the water tank through hoses to the fire. Some engineers and fire brigades, such as in Hamburg in 1909, mounted an old steam plant on the battery-electric fire engine to provide the firefighting means. Even more adventurous was the action of the Hanover brigade, who in 1911 fitted an independent petrol-driven fire pump on the back of an electric road chassis.

THE DEVELOPMENT OF PETROL POWER

Several attempts were made to build an internal-combustion-engine fire vehicle at the turn of the twentieth century. They were virtually all based on an early car chassis and

■ LEFT *Merryweather c.1909 motor pumps were capable of 50 kilometres/30 miles per hour and delivered firefighting water at 2,250 litres/500 gallons per minute.*

■ BELOW *This 1920 America LaFrance model was in service in Vancouver.*

■ BOTTOM *A dozen brass-helmeted firemen pose proudly on a 1910 Merryweather motor pump for a photograph.*

often ended up as a run-around vehicle for the brigade's chief officer. In 1903, the Tottenham Brigade in north London took delivery of the world's first true petrol-engine fire engine – a new Merryweather model. Powered by a 24hp Aster petrol engine, it was designed to carry a 15m/50ft wheeled escape ladder. It also incorporated a small 'first-aid' water tank and hose reels actuated by chemical action. Tottenham's new Merryweather was located at Haringey, where a modern fire station had just been constructed.

THE FIRST PETROL FIRE ENGINES

One year later, in 1904, the first petrol fire engine to have an in-built fire pump driven off the road engine was manufactured for the Finchley Fire Brigade, in Middlesex, England. The decision to order the new petrol fire engine was largely due to the difficulty the Brigade was experiencing in obtaining suitable horses to pull its steamer. Many small brigades such as Finchley could not justify the cost of horses standing by in the station's stables, so had an informal arrangement with a local brewery or other business to borrow horses in the event of a call-out. During 1903 there had been several cases when Finchley Brigade had to wait up to 30 minutes for horses. In addition, poor mains water pressure in the area fuelled the fear that any major fire could not be adequately dealt with and would wreak havoc on life or property.

The Finchley Brigade's new vehicle was truly groundbreaking, partly due to its design, which had resulted from a careful collaboration between Chief Officer Sly and Merryweather's engineers. Powered initially by a 30hp Aster 4-cylinder engine driving twin rear wheels via a

■ BELOW *A chain-driven Delahaye pump and hook ladder tender of the Paris Fire Brigade, c.1920, transports a complete fire crew. The rolled hose drum mounted beneath the driving position is removable at the scene of a fire.*

chain drive, the engine was capable of a steady 30 kilometres/20 miles per hour on the road. It was later fitted with a 50hp motor to improve its road speed. The petrol engine also powered the 1136 litres/250 gallons per minute reciprocating fire pump that fed hoses from two delivery outlets at the sides of the fire engine.

The six-man crew had to stand on footboards on each side of the vehicle during transit.

Finchley's new fire engine was also radical in the equipment it carried – a three-section ladder, portable fire extinguishers and a 272 litre/60 gallon water tank that supplied the main fire pump. There was also a hose reel supplied by a chemical action apparatus. This fire engine was the forerunner of today's multi-purpose fire engines, which are able to pump water and carry a large range of firefighting and rescue tools and associated equipment. The historic Finchley fire engine is permanently on view in London's Science Museum.

At this time in both the United States and Europe, work was going on to produce a reliable petrol-engine fire vehicle that could provide power to both the engine and a built-in fire pump. In 1906, Waterous, an American manufacturer, went a step further when the company unveiled a two-engine fire truck – one

■ BELOW *A 1924 model Ahrens Fox heavy pumper with its characteristic front-mounted pump.*

■ ABOVE LEFT *London Fire Brigade introduced this Leyland foam tender, in 1910, for firefighting at petrol and oil installations.*

■ ABOVE RIGHT *In the 1920s the Paris Fire Brigade maintained a cine film unit to record its firefighting work in the French capital. The unit was mounted on a motor cycle and sidecar chassis.*

engine to drive the road wheels and another to power the fire pump. Everything was considered, and there were even instances during the early twentieth century when horses were being used to pull carriage-mounted petrol-engine fire pumps. Several American companies produced fire vehicles constructed with a petrol-engine tractor unit that pulled a steam-driven fire pump behind.

Across the United States, names that would grace the motor fire-apparatus field for many years were beginning to emerge, including Mack, American LaFrance, Pirsch, Seagrave, and Ahrens-Fox. By the outbreak of World War I, Dennis was beginning to dominate much of the fire engine market in the UK and around the British Empire, although Leyland, Bedford, Albion, Commer and Merryweather all produced fire engines of various types in significant numbers. Elsewhere, French car manufacturer Delahaye turned their hand to producing fire engines, and by the 1920s, Fiat (Italy and Austria), Isotta-Franchini (Italy), and Magirus and Metz (Germany) were among the growing number of international fire engine manufacturers.

■ BELOW *Early American Ford pumpers, like this 1927 model, had brakes on the rear wheels only.*

DESIGN IMPROVEMENTS

This was a time of growing technical improvement in fire engine design, with many manufacturers looking seriously at the precise needs of firefighting pumps rather than relying on adapting existing commercial vehicles in their range. Twin rear wheels, the use of pneumatic tyres, and power-assisted brakes on all axles are examples of this trend.

By the 1930s, fire engines fell into three broad types. The most numerous were the general workhorse vehicles that delivered firefighting water and carried a variety of general firefighting equipment in their lockers. Second, came aerial turntable ladders, by then reaching up to 30m/100ft. Third, was a steadily growing group of specialized fire engines, which included dedicated foam tenders and hose layers.

Until now fire engines had been open, and in most parts of the world were fitted with transverse seating for the crew. British fire engine design still saw firemen clinging to outside-facing seats while getting rigged in their firefighting uniforms. This particular British fire-engine body style was known as the 'Braidwood' (after James Braidwood, the

■ ABOVE LEFT *The Ford Model T British fire tender, c.1912, had a transverse-mounted fire pump beneath the driving position with two hose deliveries on each side of the vehicle.*

■ ABOVE RIGHT *This Dennis c.1933 G-type pump has a rear-mounted 1600 litres/350 gallons per minute pump.*

nineteenth-century reformer of fire brigades in Edinburgh and London). At this time several deaths and injuries resulted when crew were flung off a Braidwood-bodied fire engine on its way to a fire, often as it negotiated a sharp turn. As a direct result, several new models were introduced, notably that of Dennis, where the crew seating was provided in the vehicle's bodywork. Not to be outdone, in 1935 Leyland introduced the first totally enclosed limousine pumping fire engine, which set new standards of safety and comfort from the fire crew.

During the 1930s the diesel-powered engine started to appear in fire vehicles. Austrian manufacturer Perl AG installed a 50hp diesel unit in several pumping fire engines for the Vienna city brigade. In Germany, Mercedes Benz began to use powerful 4.8 litre diesel engine units for fire service applications. At the same time petrol-powered engines were developed to extract more power, particularly in America, to meet the pumping needs of firefighters faced with ever higher tower blocks. As early as 1931 American LaFrance had produced a 12-cylinder V12 petrol engine that produced 240hp, enough to power fire pumps to produce 6,810 litres/ 1,500 gallons of firefighting water per minute.

■ RIGHT *In 1935, the British company Dennis delivered a number of the new Big Six models to London Fire Brigade's own specification. They had a rear-mounted 2250 litres/500 gallons per minute pump and carried a 15m/50ft wooden-wheeled escape ladder. The bodywork incorporated two rows of transverse seats for the crew.*

MODERN FIRE ENGINES

With the storm clouds of war gathering over Europe, fire brigades on both sides of the conflict were faced with the enormous and protracted task of fighting fires that might result from relentless bombing raids. As more nations became embroiled in the war, fire engine development, along with most other engineering and economic activity, suffered dramatically. Even though the countries involved slowly emerged into the post-war period of recovery and rebuilding, it was not until the early 1950s that fire engine design picked up once again.

By the outbreak of war in September 1939, the British government had bolstered its regular firefighting force of 20,000 with some 23,000 volunteer auxiliaries up and down the country equipped with several types of utility fire engine for the perceived tasks ahead. Among these appliances were Austin and Fordson heavy pumping units and trailer pumps towed behind a variety of requisitioned vehicles, which in London included black taxicabs. Several 30m/100ft Leyland/ Merryweather turntable ladders were also used. The auxiliary fire crews used a number of extra fire boats to supplement the maritime and dockland firefighting resources of the professional crews. The German fire service tended to rely on its existing vehicles, which included Mercedes and Opel pumping engines, and Magirus and Metz turntable ladders.

■ ABOVE *This 1949 Kenworth HG721 heavy pumper with midships pump shows the developing style of post-war American fire engines.*

■ BELOW *This open cab-style fire engine is a 1958 Mack pumper.*

The 1950s saw a wider use of diesel engines, and by 1960 the first automatic gearbox systems for fire engines were in use in Europe. The increasing use of alloys and plastics in bodywork design greatly increased the store of firefighting and rescue equipment that fire engines could carry. Power steering and braking systems were also becoming standard, as were robust safety cabs to protect the crew in the event of a traffic accident.

TYPES OF FIRE ENGINE

While modern fire engines may vary in their outward styling and design, they can be grouped in three general types – those that pump water, high rise rigs and specialist vehicles. High rise rigs have extending ladders or booms that may reach up to 40m/130ft.

■ BELOW *This 1965 Ford/Crown fire hydraulic platform shows the move towards multi-use American fire engines.*

These may be turntable and tower ladders or aerial ladder platforms with fitted cages on the uppermost sections. The operational roles of the range of specialist vehicles included providing crews and equipment for rescue, breathing apparatus, foam units, protection against chemical and hazardous material, salvage, ventilation, lighting, command and crew refreshment functions.

Fire engines that pump water are known variously as pumps, pumpers or water tenders. Their primary function is to provide a firefighting water attack, and they are generally regarded as the fire service's workhorses. Every city and rural fire brigade is likely to have at least one pump, and it is this type of fire engine that will almost certainly attend every emergency fire call-out.

Pumping fire engines incorporate a water tank that feeds the fire pump to provide a firefighting stream as soon as the appliance arrives at a fire, and before an alternative source of water is located. These first firefighting water jets are fed through hose tubing coiled on a revolving reel, often one on each side of the fire engine, or through hose lines of various sizes, either flaked (folded in

■ BELOW *A 1972 PACO/Grumman heavy pumper.*

■ ABOVE *A 1989 Ford/S&S 6x4 tanker with midships mounted pump.*

■ OPPOSITE *A 2021 Pierce Rescue Pumper shows the lines of a modern-day American fire engine.*

lengths) ready for instant use or rolled-up in the fire engine lockers. Pumps usually carry about 0.8 kilometres/½ mile of hose, and shortly after getting to work at a fire one of the crew will connect the pump to a nearby street water main to maintain a supply of water.

FIREFIGHTING INNOVATIONS

On a modern fire engine, the pump is capable of providing water at high pressure through hose lines fitted with an adjustable nozzle. It can either produce a water jet that will directly knock down flames or a finely atomized spray to protect the crew from intense radiated heat. Pumps also carry a range of ladders, breathing sets, lighting and rescue equipment including cutting and lifting gear. In some rural areas, pumps have evolved into general-purpose fire engines that carry certain firefighting and rescue equipment that would normally be distributed over several fire engines in an inner city situation.

A wide range of chassis, engine power and transmission units can be found in fire engines across the world today, and most manufacturers provide a vehicle tailored to a fire brigade's precise needs. Many modern rural fire pumps are all-wheel drive with a high-ground clearance to allow for off-road operations, while a number of manufacturers have produced narrow-bodied compact fire engines to cope with narrow twisting roads. Many fire engines built for use in hot climates have air-conditioned crew cabs. In some cases the manufacturer designs and builds the complete

■ BELOW *A midships mounted Hush pumper of Fredericksburg Fire Department, USA.*

vehicle, while others construct the bodywork and various fire pump engineering installations and mount it on a suitable commercial chassis/cab of a fire brigade's choice.

Modern fire engines have plenty of shiny metal and colourful bodywork. Red, orange and white colour schemes are commonplace, often enhanced by fluorescent stripes or panels to maximize the fire engine's conspicuousness, both en route to and while working at an emergency incident. A particular feature of modern fire engines is their warning devices. Electronic directional wailers, sirens, hooters, and powerful blue and red rotating flashing beacons are there to warn other road users of a fire engine's approach, often at high speed. Importantly for anyone trapped in smoke or under debris, the sound of an approaching fire engine is reassurance that rescue is imminent.

■ RIGHT *This Mercedes-Benz Atego-based pump/ladder is one of a number in service with the London Fire Brigade.*

■ RIGHT *This 2019 Scania P320/Angloco pumping appliance for the UK's Lincolnshire Fire and Rescue Service features the latest-design Scania CP31L crew cab, best-in-class superstructure firefighting systems and controls, and a striking modern livery combining recognized emergency service 'battenburg' conspicuity markings together with community safety messages.*

EARLY LADDERS

■ ABOVE *Compressed air was used to extend this early German 18m/60ft ladder.*

Although the use of single-section ladders can be traced back to the Roman ***vigiles***, the real development in firefighting ladders came about during the early part of the nineteenth century, when multi-section ladders made it possible for firemen to reach upper floors.

MOBILE FIRE ESCAPES

In the early nineteenth century, London had a number of permanently manned 'street escape' stations sited on certain strategic street corners across the capital for rescuing people trapped in burning buildings. The first street corner stations were funded by voluntary contributions and were independent of London's fire brigade, but in 1866 the Metropolitan Fire Brigade took full responsibility for them.

Each station consisted of a cabin to house the watchman and a 15m/50ft wheeled wooden ladder made up of three extending sections that could reach the third floor windows of buildings. When a fire occurred, the ladder would be quickly pushed to the scene then wound up to the affected floor to enable trapped individuals to escape. A canvas chute was slung beneath the ladder down which trapped people and casualties could also descend. Weighing almost one ton, street escapes were cumbersome and required at least three men to safely manoeuvre them into a workable position.

■ BELOW *Firemen in 1910 Vienna use hook ladders to take a line of hose up to the upper floors of a building. The coiled hose drum has been detached from the nearby fire engine.*

Before long the escape ladders, together with their large carriage wheels, were mounted on specially designed horse-drawn fire engines. These mounted escape ladders had a quick release mechanism and were normally manned by four firemen and a coachman. The teams were able to respond to an alarm and effect rescues very quickly, and were closely followed by the horse-drawn pumps, which tackled the fire itself. Due to their speedy and effective response to fire calls, the horse-drawn escape ladder soon became a permanent part of the London brigade's first line response, leaving the city's street corner ladder fire stations to be gradually phased out.

In America the development of high-rise buildings led to the design of even longer mobile fire ladders for both rescue and firefighting access purposes. By the late 1890s the larger city fire departments were using

■ RIGHT *An 18.2m/60ft hand-operated turntable ladder c.1910. Hand winding provided the power for the various movements of the ladder.*

■ BELOW RIGHT *A 1921 Morris Magirus 22.8m/75ft turntable ladder. The ladder sections were powered by electric motors.*

hook and ladder trucks – horse-drawn fire engines with a main ladder comprised of several wooden sections mounted on a long two-axle wagon. At the scene of a high-rise fire such a ladder would be manually wound up to its maximum working height of 20m/65ft. Once extended, the entire ladder could be rotated through 360 degrees. Hook and ladder trucks also carried a number of smaller ladders for low-level use and long pole-mounted hooks. The latter were for pulling down ceilings and partitions to ventilate premises during firefighting operations, and to ensure that fires were properly extinguished and no smouldering remnants were overlooked.

As American buildings increased in height in the early twentieth century, hook and ladder trucks were eventually replaced by longer aerial ladders, especially when early motor vehicles became available for fire department use. Aerial ladders were able to reach up to 26m/85ft. The longest vehicles were fitted with a rear steering axle and needed a steersman at the back to negotiate tight turns en route to a call-out.

In Europe the arrival of the petrol engine heralded a new generation of high-rise fire service ladders of metal construction. Combined with new manufacturing and engineering techniques, including the use of gas and hydraulic power, these new ladder fire engines were soon to revolutionize aerial firefighting and rescue operations.

■ LEFT *A London Fire Brigade officer uses a megaphone to shout instructions to a fireman on a horse-drawn hand-operated 23m/75ft turntable ladder during a 1905 drill session.*

■ BELOW *A Paris Fire Brigade c.1920 hand-operated 18m/60ft wheeled escape ladder is mounted on a Delahaye chassis. At the fire it would be released from the chassis before being put to work.*

THE DEVELOPMENT OF LADDERS AND PLATFORMS

Wheeled wooden escape ladders, which were well established in Great Britain by the late nineteenth century, were the precursors of modern extending ladders. Usually constructed of three sections, they could be wound up to about 15m/50ft to allow people trapped by smoke in buildings above a fire to climb down to safety. They also allowed firemen some access into a burning building at upper levels, although it was not until the availability of the first self-contained breathing sets in the twentieth century that extensive firefighting inside buildings was possible.

In America, where the equivalent to the wheeled escape ladder was the hook and ladder truck, fire brigades started to look for better and longer mobile rescue ladders. In 1888, the E. B. Preston Company of Chicago, Illinois, constructed the first all-metal aerial ladder, although this still had to be extended manually.

The longer versions of these aerial ladder trucks were articulated and often needed a rear tillerman to steer the vehicle's back wheels round city street corners.

In Europe aerial ladder development was not far behind. In 1892 the German company Magirus constructed the first turntable ladder, where the extending section was mounted on a rotating turret able to turn through 360 degrees at various angles of depression. As with the first US aerial equivalent, this Magirus turntable ladder was built on a horse-drawn trailer and was extended manually. By the turn of the century, however, Magirus had perfected a powered elevation system using carbon dioxide gas. Other movements still relied upon hand-winding gear and the physical strength of firemen to winch the ladder sections up to the required working height.

■ TOP ***During a 1910 London Fire Brigade training session, the 15m/50ft wheeled escape ladder is about to be slipped off the Merryweather vehicle, and manually wound up to its working height.***

■ ABOVE ***Originally horse drawn, this American-built c.1920 26m/85ft rear-steer ladder of Lynn Fire Department, Massachusetts, has been converted to motor traction using a Knox Martin tractor.***

■ FAR LEFT ***A 1914 23m/75ft Merryweather turntable ladder is put through its paces.***

■ LEFT *In 1937 London Fire Brigade took delivery of a number of 30m/100ft all-steel Leyland/Metz turntable ladders. Here, a fireman surveys the London rooftops from the top of one of these new aerial fire engines.*

■ ABOVE RIGHT *This 1938 Leyland/Metz 30m/100ft turntable ladder served with the Lancashire County Fire Brigade, UK, until 1961. The rear nearside operating controls and gauges are clearly visible, together with the water pump mounted beneath the driving position.*

Daimler, another German manufacturer, produced several early turntable ladders, some of which were mounted on a battery-powered electric chassis. In 1906, Magirus introduced the first truly motorized petrol engine-driven turntable ladder vehicle, although it relied on hand-winding for its extension and other movements. Two years later, Merryweather constructed the first British 23m/75ft turntable ladder, the various movements of which were entirely powered by a gearbox driven directly by the vehicle's petrol engine. The combined achievements of Magirus and Merryweather meant that all the movements of the aerial ladder – extension, elevation and training through 360 degrees – could now be driven by a cable-and-gear mechanism. American aerial ladder makers soon followed suit, especially Pirsch who already was a pioneer in the development of all-metal ladders.

Another early twentieth-century development was the use of high-rise ladders as water towers for projecting a powerful jet into the upper floors of tall buildings. Increasingly, ladders had a hose line with a nozzle fitted to the uppermost extension and were able to reach 30m/100ft when extended.

Through the 1930s and 1940s the working heights of ladder fire engines continued to increase. In 1933 Merryweather delivered a

■ LEFT *A London Fire Brigade 1921 Morris Magirus 23m/75ft turntable ladder responds to a fire call.*

■ RIGHT *An American hand-operated water tower in action at a major tenement fire c.1930.*

30m/100ft turntable ladder vehicle to Hong Kong. Leyland/Metz supplied a 45m/150ft five-section turntable ladder to Hull Fire Brigade in the UK in 1936. In 1942, American LaFrance built a 38m/125ft aerial ladder for the Boston Fire Department.

By the 1930s the newer American aerials and water towers were using hydraulic power. In 1930 American LaFrance built a 20m/65ft water tower for New York that could deliver 38,590 litres/8,500 gallons per minute through multiple nozzles. One year later Pirsch produced the first fully hydraulic-powered aerial ladder truck. In Europe the primary manufacturers of turntable ladders continued to be the German companies Magirus and Metz, along with the British manufacturer Merryweather, based in London.

Hydraulics and turntables

Hydraulic power did not completely replace mechanical ladder drives on turntable ladders in Europe and elsewhere until the 1950s, however. By then the hydraulic platforms, a natural development of the turntable ladder concept, had made an appearance. These aerial fire engines consisted of several articulated booms with a fitted cage at the head, all mounted on a rotating turntable. For the first time a firefighter working in the cage at the top of a hydraulic platform had complete control over the fire engine's movements. A prominent

■ ABOVE LEFT *A Japanese 30m/100ft turntable ladder of Sunagawa Fire Brigade.*

■ ABOVE CENTRE *Osaka Fire Brigade crew work the cage of a modern aerial ladder.*

■ ABOVE RIGHT *During the early stages of a fire in residential flats, the operator of this aerial ladder platform edges the cage nearer to the smoke-filled building.*

■ LEFT *A Seagrave 30m/100ft ladder of the Yonkers Fire Department, New York, sets to work at a routine incident.*

■ ABOVE *This 45m (148ft) working-height Bronto Skylift aerial ladder platform, based on a Volvo chassis, was supplied to the UK's Royal Berkshire Fire and Rescue Service by Angloco Ltd in 2021.*

manufacturer of hydraulic platforms was the British firm Simon Engineering, whose Snorkel brand name became synonymous with hydraulic platforms in many countries.

In the latter half of the 20th century the design and functional style of turntable ladders and hydraulic platforms began to be merged. The Finnish company Bronto pioneered telescopic booms that carried a parallel-trussed steel ladder alongside. Some modern larger aerial ladder platform trucks have a height capability of up to 40m/130ft. Such large aerial fire engines require the weight stability of a four-axle chassis and have rigid jacks on each corner of the chassis base to help to counteract the forces at play when the heavy steel ladder or platform sections are extended. The cages of these vehicles are able to accommodate up to eight rescued people and are fitted with full operator controls. They also have connections for an air supply for breathing sets and are fitted with floodlighting. Other important features are water drencher sprays around and underneath the cage to provide a water curtain that protects the cage operator and occupants from convectional and radiated heat.

The speed of deployment of an aerial ladder or platform is always critical, and considerable training is required for its operation. The control systems are very sophisticated, with the latest models utilizing computer and advanced engineering technology. When an operator gets to work, the vertical stability of the ladder is paramount. All movements of the ladder, often with the upper sections operating at great height, are governed by safety and stability factors, which must take account of the condition and horizontal level of the road surface as well as weather conditions.

■ LEFT *A number of Austin K4 18m/60ft hand-operated Merryweather turntable ladders were provided by the British government during World War II to supplement the fire engines of civilian fire brigades.*

Specialized Fire Engines

Until the beginning of the twentieth century most fire engine development was concerned with pumps, which were moved to the scene of a fire and operated successively by hand, horse power, steam and then finally petrol and diesel, in order to provide a continuous and plentiful supply of firefighting water. The diversity of today's specialist appliances clearly underlines the wide range of technical and logistical support that modern firefighters need for complex modern situations.

Until 1900 virtually all fires were still being put out using water streams, but by the early part of the twentieth century, manufacturing processes had been developed which produced outbreaks of fire that could not be tackled using water alone. The increasing use of the motor car, for instance, led directly to the expansion of the petrochemical industry and fuel storage sites and therefore higher risk of fire involving burning liquids such as petrol, fuel oil and other refinery by-products. As water simply runs off such burning liquids, often actually spreading the fire to unaffected adjacent areas, other means of extinguishing fire had to be developed. After several attempts, particularly in the United States, a successful means of smothering petrol and oil fires was achieved using foam produced from bicarbonate of soda and other additives.

As soon as a successful foam concentrate was commercially available to fire brigades, special fire engines were commissioned to carry large quantities to tackle fires in fuel storage sites, refineries and the like. The London Fire Brigade introduced a foam tender, one of the

■ ABOVE *The role of the Paris Fire Brigade lighting unit, seen here at work in c.1910, was to illuminate the firefighting scene during night-time incidents.*

■ LEFT *The London Fire Brigade's 1929 Dennis emergency tender carried a range of rescue tools that included breathing sets, cutting and lifting gear and resuscitation and lighting equipment. This fire engine had a recently introduced enclosed body.*

■ ABOVE *4x4 all-terrain vehicles are used as first strike and mobile control units during rural firefighting.*

■ ABOVE RIGHT *The rear end of this modern American pumper is packed with trays of flaked, or folded, hose ready for instant action.*

■ BELOW *This 2019 Mercedes-Benz/Oberaigner 6x6/Angloco off-road fire response vehicle, for the UK's Essex County Fire and Rescue Service, was designed and configured as a versatile compact appliance, able to respond to hard-to-reach rescue incidents.*

world's first dedicated, or 'special', fire engines, in 1910. Mounted on a Leyland chassis, it carried a tank that could take 2,273 litres/500 gallons of foam compound and plenty of hose and special nozzles. As soon as it was fed with a water supply from a pumping fire engine, the foam tender could mount a concentrated attack.

Increasing mechanization and the growth of transport systems led to new types of accident from which victims occasionally had to be extricated using specialized equipment. As a direct result of these increasing non-fire emergency calls, fire brigades began to ask fire engine manufacturers to customize vehicles so they could carry all the equipment they needed for fighting particular types of fire and other emergencies.

Again, the London Fire Brigade was in the forefront of these new developments. In 1919 it introduced two emergency tenders, both on a Dennis chassis, equipped to deal solely with non-fire accidents and emergencies. The appliances carried lighting sets driven by a portable petrol-engine generator, lifting jacks, flame-cutting gear and a range of hand-operated cutting tools. Previously firefighting breathing sets had been fairly primitive, with a diving-style air supply line fed by bellows operated outside the building on fire. The emergency tenders carried innovative one-hour duration oxygen breathing sets and spare cylinders for use at deep-seated serious fires.

Fire service special vehicle applications soon grew to include hose-laying trucks. These were a radical development, even though many brigades had for some years provided manually drawn hose carts and, later, motor vans to convey additional rolled hose supplies to a fire. These hose-laying vehicles were designed to lay hose from the back of the van on the move at 30 kmh/19 mph. Sometimes up to 1.6km/1 mile long, the large-diameter hose relayed water from large trunk mains to the scene of a major outbreak.

By the 1950s most urban brigades ran one or more mobile command and control units, which were often based on a coach-type chassis. The unit would attend larger and more serious fires where strategic control and deployment of firefighters and resources was critical to the

■ LEFT *A mobile command unit, based on a Volvo coach chassis, provides a critical role at major incidents.*

success of the operation. Based at the unit, the fire commander would direct operations and receive reports on the progress of the firefighting effort. All reinforcements, radio communications, liaison with police, paramedics, traffic, and utility services would also be co-ordinated from the unit, as well as refreshments, relief crews and press contact.

Other modern day 'specials' include water tankers, or bowsers, for carrying large volumes of water to areas, usually rural, where existing water supplies are scarce. The largest of these water tankers are articulated, multi-axle vehicles capable of carrying up to 36,000 litres/7,920 gallons of water in one load.

Salvage tenders are usually mobilized to certain major or protracted fires to provide a concentrated effort to mitigate water and smoke damage to artefacts and business stock. They can also assist in the extraction of smoke from the affected premises using high-powered fans.

Lighting units provide crucial illumination across firefighting and rescue arenas, known in fire brigade parlance as the 'fire ground'. This can also include lighting the inside of fire-damaged buildings. Lighting units have a large electrical generating capacity, both on the fire engine and portables. They are also equipped with telescopic halogen lighting masts and a range of other lighting equipment.

Usually designed as a travelling self-contained kitchen, canteen vans provide meals for up to several hundred firefighters at a time. Dehydration, especially in hot weather, is a recognized hazard of firefighting, and these kitchen stations fulfil an important function.

Demountable equipment modules

Modern special appliances are increasingly based on self-contained demountable

■ BELOW *This is one of five 15,000-litre trailer tanker fire-fighting appliances specially designed by Angloco for use at the Tsing Ma Bridge, Hong Kong, which opened in 1997. For each unit to operate on the 5.5m-/18ft-wide lower-deck access road, it needed to be capable of being towed in either direction by a Unimog, which had a special lifting and rotating jacking system so that it could be pulled back without having to be turned around. This resulted in special towing arrangements, and two sets of lighting, brake systems and steerable turntables.*

■ LEFT *This airport foam tender shows the centre-mounted nozzle used to extinguish flames in the fire engine's path.*

■ BELOW *This is a 2009 Scania P310 prime mover with hook-lift and Angloco de-mountable foam pod. The pod carries six 1,000-litre foam containers and a removable foam proportioning module, plus a compact forklift to enable versatile deployment at incidents.*

equipment modules, so that functional units can be rapidly assigned to a prime mover for speedy transport to an emergency. At the scene the demountable unit can be dropped off to release the prime mover for other duties.

'Demountables' have grown to include the following specialist areas: chemical and hazardous material units (providing special protective suits, breathing sets, leakage containment equipment, decontamination facilities etc); breathing apparatus units (full servicing facilities for the breathing sets in use at a major incident); and heavy rescue units (very powerful heavy-duty specialized lifting, spreading and cutting equipment needed for rail and aircraft accidents).

■ LEFT *A remote-controlled tracked vehicle used for forcible entry.*

■ BELOW *A heavy rescue tender carries a greater range of more powerful tools and general rescue equipment.*

Airborne Fire Engines

The first flying fire engine was developed in America as early as 1918, when the San Diego Fire Department commissioned a Curtiss aircraft to provide a rapid firefighting response to outlying districts of its area. The aircraft was powered by a 110hp 6-cylinder engine and could reach a speed of 112 kilometres/70 miles per hour. Carrying a crew of two firemen, its firefighting equipment consisted of two 3-gallon water extinguishers, and four carbon tetrachloride chemical extinguishers.

While the success or otherwise of this pioneering effort is not readily recorded, it does illustrate that innovative fire chiefs were not slow in utilizing new and radical methods to speed up response time to outbreaks of fire. It was not until after World War II, however, that the use of aircraft for firefighting really came into its own, when development work by several Canadian fire departments led to the first use of 'water bombing' techniques from adapted aircraft to combat forest and grassland fires.

Before long the technique, which involves repeatedly dropping large quantities of water on to a country fire area, was commonplace, particularly in North America and Australia where forest and scrub fires often devastated vast areas. Modern firefighting aircraft are able to deliver up to 27,300 litres/6,000 gallons of water in a single drop. Fire-retardant chemicals are often added to the water to increase the effectiveness of each bombing run.

Helicopters fitted with large under-slung plastic and canvas buckets are also used during the forest-fire season. Although the water payload of a helicopter does not match that of a large fixed-wing aircraft, it has the advantage of being able to make repeated and

■ OPPOSITE *A Lockheed EC-130Q fire bomber drops its load of water during a run at Avalon, Australia.*

■ RIGHT *A Sikorsky S-64 'flying crane' helicopter adapted for use as a water bomber, and widely used in the US.*

■ BELOW RIGHT *A Canadair CL-215T turboprop amphibian takes part in trials on a burning building in Quebec.*

effective water drops. It can quickly refill its bucket by flying low with its scoop over a river, lake or pond that may lie close to the scene of the fire. Alternatively, a helicopter is able to hover above firefighters while they refill the reservoir using fire hoses.

Several fire departments, including that of Tokyo, have the dedicated operational use of their own helicopters and these can be invaluable for rapidly transporting firemen to tall buildings and rescuing people from them. Brigades that do not have the financial resources to purchase or lease their own helicopter usually have arrangements whereby the nearest civil or military helicopters can be made available at very short notice.

Helicopters are also invaluable for transporting equipment and fire crews to an emergency, such as a serious fire or a rail or road crash, that is not easily accessible. Modern twin-engine helicopters can carry up to nine firefighters or a payload of around 1000kg/ 2200lb. Using radio and thermal imaging links, a helicopter hovering above a major incident or large-scale forest or grassland fire that threatens to spread out of control can provide valuable aerial reconnaissance.

FIREBOATS

Modern fireboats are floating fire engines. Ship fires are often protracted affairs, so fireboats are designed to operate as self-contained maritime firefighting units. In addition to being able to produce a barrage of firefighting water jets through a powerful pumping capacity, modern fireboats are equipped with breathing apparatus servicing facilities, including air compressors for recharging cylinders.

Fireboats were first developed during the early nineteenth century to combat a number of serious ship fires and dockland area conflagrations. As manually pumped land fire engines were slowly developed and improved, several engineers saw the potential of mounting a fire pump on board a boat, with the fire pump suction hose dropped over the side to tap the unlimited water supplies all around. In 1840 the London-based fire engine manufacturer Merryweather supplied an 18m/60ft iron-hulled fireboat to St Petersburg. The on-board manual pump required 50 men to get it to optimum performance.

When steam power began to be widely used to power land fire engines, it was also applied to fireboat design. By 1860 the London Fire Engine Establishment had installed a number of steam pumps on board special floating platforms based at strategic points on the River Thames and within London's huge and complex dockland area. These platforms were towed to a fire by a steam tug, and were known as a 'fire float'. By the 1870s both Boston and New York harbours had their own steam fire floats.

The first self-propelled fireboat, the *Beta*, was commissioned by London in 1898 and stationed at one of the capital's four floating fire stations on the River Thames. *Beta*'s steam boiler and steam plant provided both propulsion and firefighting water. With a

■ ABOVE ***A fire at the Thameside warehouse at Albany Mill near Blackfriars Bridge, London, 1791. The firefighting attack is being mounted from manual fire engines on board river boats.***

■ BELOW LEFT ***This typical purpose-built firefighting tug has an inbuilt hydraulic platform to reach the upper deck of vessels.***

■ BELOW ***The London Fire Brigade fireboat, Beaver, seen here in about 1910, towed a fire float (right) that carried the steam-driven pumps for the water jets.***

■ ABOVE *Massed fireboats attack a fire on a North Sea oil rig.*

■ TOP LEFT *Firefighters protects the Boston waterfront.*

■ MIDDLE LEFT *New York Harbour has several fireboats.*

■ LEFT *Guyana Fire Service took delivery of this 14m-/46ft-long fire boat in 2019. The shallow-hulled vessel can pump 20,000 litres (4,400 gallons) per minute through its three monitors.*

■ BELOW LEFT *A London Fire Brigade fireboat lies off the Palace of Westminster.*

■ BELOW RIGHT *Two new London Fire Brigade fireboats patrol near the Millennium Dome in 1999.*

draught of only 48cm/19in, the new London fireboat could come alongside warehouses at very low states of tide as well as get close in to burning vessels.

Fireboat development continued apace into the twentieth century. In 1925, the Los Angeles fire department's newest vessel could pump up to 61,000 litres/13,500 gallons of water per minute from no fewer than 13 separate deck-mounted nozzles. Since World War II the steady development of ever-larger ships carrying huge tonnages, ranging from container cargo to petrochemical products, has ensured that the availability of fireboats capable of dealing with any maritime fire outbreak continues to be critical. Some of the most up-to-date fireboats can be found in the frenetically busy port of Hong Kong, where hundreds of huge container ships dock daily. The Hong Kong fire department provides a permanent presence of up to four powerful multi-decked craft that are manned around the clock and ready to respond to maritime fires the moment they break out. Ports in the United States also have fireboat cover, while oil terminals throughout the world provide some fireboat cover to ensure that any outbreak of fire while an oil tanker is discharging its flammable load is dealt with immediately.

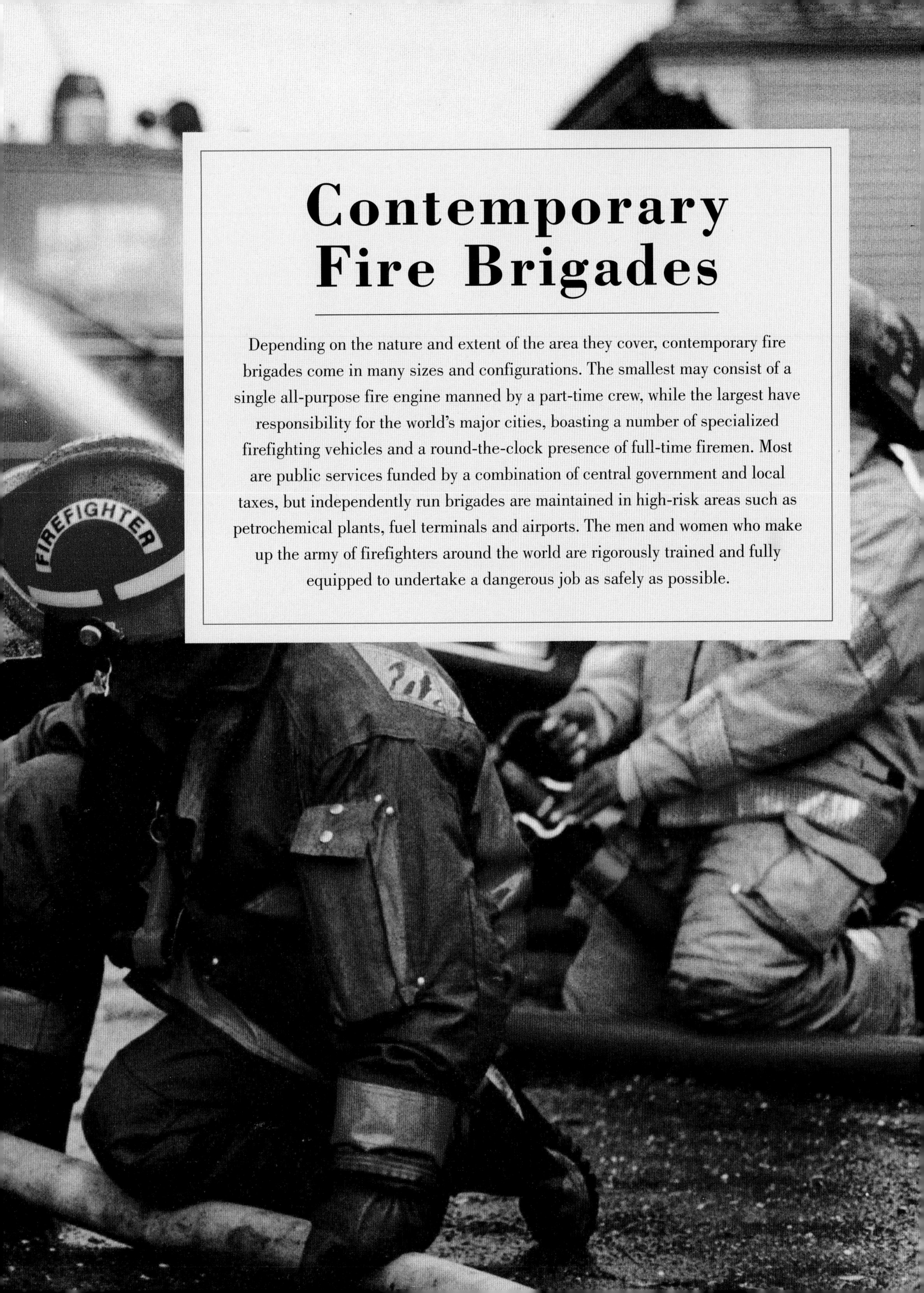

Contemporary Fire Brigades

Depending on the nature and extent of the area they cover, contemporary fire brigades come in many sizes and configurations. The smallest may consist of a single all-purpose fire engine manned by a part-time crew, while the largest have responsibility for the world's major cities, boasting a number of specialized firefighting vehicles and a round-the-clock presence of full-time firemen. Most are public services funded by a combination of central government and local taxes, but independently run brigades are maintained in high-risk areas such as petrochemical plants, fuel terminals and airports. The men and women who make up the army of firefighters around the world are rigorously trained and fully equipped to undertake a dangerous job as safely as possible.

Firefighting and Rescue Equipment

Modern fire engines carry a host of firefighting and rescue equipment, most of which would probably seem quite incomprehensible to nineteenth-century firemen, whose primary concern was to get a water stream on to a fire to restrict its spread to other buildings. In those days, they relied on lengths of leather hose joined together with screwed couplings and a nozzle (or branch in fire service parlance) at the end and a pump that, hopefully, would deliver a firefighting water jet. At worst the pump would be operated manually, but a progressive city brigade might own a powerful steam pump. The pump was on wheels and the hose was taken to fires on a handcart.

Water pumps and hose lines

It was not until the twentieth century, with the arrival of the motor pump and particularly the first specialized appliances, that fire engines had enough space to stow other firefighting gear such as hose, portable pumps, hand tools and basic lighting. When the first all-enclosed fire engines were produced in 1929, bodywork styles allowed for even more stowage to accommodate the steadily growing range of firefighting and rescue equipment. Modern fire engines need to carry a large amount of supplementary gear, so the ingenious design and use of locker space on a vehicle means that every available space can be utilized.

Water remains the predominant and universal extinguishing medium used by firefighters, with supplies usually available via a street hydrant or from a nearby natural source. Pumping fire engines carry varying quantities of water to enable an immediate firefighting attack on a fire for up to ten minutes, until an alternative source can be tapped. Depending upon the

■ ABOVE *From 1919 Dennis emergency tenders were used to provide pure oxygen breathing sets for deep penetration at serious fires. They also carried electric generators and floodlighting equipment.*

■ BELOW *Members of the Vienna Fire Brigade crew train with an early (c.1910) airline-fed smoke helmet and breathing set.*

■ RIGHT *Water has always been a firefighter's main weapon. Here, London Fire Brigade crews create a wall of water during a royal display in 1966.*

■ BELOW RIGHT *A Vienna Fire Brigade fireman tests an early 20th-century back-packed compressed air breathing set.*

scale of the blaze, the on-board water will be pumped through either a small-diameter high-pressure hose reel or a larger-diameter hose line.

The on-board tank will have to be refilled by hose from a local water supply as soon as is practical. Fire engines that operate in rural areas also carry portable pumps, which can be carried to a river, lake or pond to pump water from that point. Another way of getting water to a fire is to run a shuttle, using the on-board tanks of several pumps, to ferry water to the fire scene. This is then transferred to the tank of the pumping engine operating there.

Hose lines, which are either rolled or stowed folded ready for quick deployment, come in a variety of diameters, and most pumping engines carry about 600m/2,000ft altogether.
A range of hose connectors and adapters enable different combinations of hose to be used together to maximize water usage.

Other extinguishing equipment carried on pumping fire engines includes foam compound, which when mixed with water and aerated provides copious supplies of foam that may be needed to blanket the surface of burning liquids such as petrol or oil fuel. Smaller quantities of foam are provided from portable extinguishers carried on board. If a burning liquid fire involves very large quantities of flammable liquid, as might be found in a refinery or fuel storage depot, the use of a dedicated foam tender would be necessary. Such an appliance is capable of producing tens of thousands of litres of foam per minute. Dry powder and carbon dioxide extinguishers are also carried for use on fires involving electrical installations, which require smothering.

Pumping fire engines carry several ladders on the roof. Alloy ladders have replaced the traditional wooden versions, being more robust and requiring less maintenance. Various types of ladder are in use, but all have extending sections with the longest ladders reaching up to about 13m/45ft. Shorter versions are available for scaling fences, walls and other obstacles, and some of these come as combination ladders that meet a number of variable purposes. Some fire engines are specialized ladder vehicles, with aerial or turntable ladders, or platforms.

SAFETY AND CUTTING EQUIPMENT

Breathing sets are usually mounted behind the seats in the back of the pumping engine's crew cab, where they can be donned en route to a fire scene. A breathing set provides clean air for up to 50 minutes in the thickest toxic smoke, although this time will be significantly reduced if the firefighter is working hard and therefore consuming more air. At major fires, where large numbers of breathing sets will be in use, a mobile breathing set recharge-and-servicing unit will be set up to replace empty air cylinders. A safety control board is deployed whenever breathing sets are used at an incident. This monitors each firefighting team inside a smoke-filled building, how much air they have in their cylinders and the recorded time at which they should emerge.

Thermal imaging cameras allow fire crews to see through the thickest smoke to quickly locate casualties or the seat of a fire, and are now essential items of equipment.

■ LEFT *Two firefighters use powerful cutting tools to release a trapped driver. Road crashes present fire crews with difficult and challenging rescues.*

■ BELOW *Volvo pumps attend a serious crash on England's M62 motorway. Specialist rescue and cutting gear has been deployed to gain access to casualties.*

■ RIGHT *A fire crew works to free the trapped driver of a truck that has careered off the road and plummeted down an embankment in rural West Yorkshire, England. Access to such scenes can be challenging for firefighters and medical teams.*

■ ABOVE *After a two-hour struggle, a fire crew successfully haul a bull out of a pit into which it had fallen. Animal rescues are often problematic because of location, the size of the beast and the fact that it is frightened.*

Rescue equipment for dealing with non-fire emergencies such as road crashes and industrial machinery accidents increasingly forms an important part of a fire engine's inventory. High-powered hydraulic cutting and spreading tools enable firemen to take the roof off a car in seconds, while sophisticated lifting and jacking equipment, including inflatable air bags, provides a range of tools to effect rescues from the most difficult and challenging situations. When an accident or crash is very serious, perhaps involving a train or a number of road vehicles, or in the event of a gas explosion that has demolished part of a building, an emergency or heavy rescue tender will attend to provide the additional cutting and lifting gear required. These dedicated fire vehicles are self-contained travelling workshops, often crewed by firefighters experienced in rescue work at major accidents.

■ RIGHT *Following a train derailment in south London, which demolished part of a building and buried a number of vehicles, a firefighter uses a listening device to locate survivors.*

■ FAR RIGHT *An aerial ladder platform provides a working base from which firefighters can free the driver of an overturned lorry.*

Protective all-enclosing suits, usually two types, are carried to allow fire crews to safely work in an area deemed to be hazardous, such as at a fire or incident that involves a chemical substance, either at a plant or in transit. Chemical spill suits are worn over a regular firefighting uniform, together with gloves and a breathing set, to provide protection from the majority of chemical substances. Gas-tight suits provide a higher level of protection when dealing with certain highly hazardous materials that pose a serious threat if even a small amount comes into contact with skin or is ingested. A suit completely encloses a firefighter and his breathing set. Hazardous-material emergencies may also call for the use of a radiological measuring device.

■ ABOVE LEFT *A fire service line rescue team brings a casualty to safety after a pleasure park accident.*

■ ABOVE RIGHT *A Tokyo Fire Brigade robot rescue vehicle picks up a dummy casualty during a training exercise.*

■ BELOW *A fireman undergoes decontamination following an incident involving a hazardous and toxic material.*

SPECIALIZED RESCUE RESOURCES

In addition to a range of general purpose ropes and lines, a number of fire engines also carry line-rescue and abseiling gear, which is needed for rescuing people in precarious situations, such as halfway down a cliff face. Other specialist rescue gear includes mats for reaching people trapped in mud or quicksand, and even trailer-mounted inflatable boats. The rescue of pets and livestock may require specialist kit including slings and lifting apparatus such as sheerlegs and block and tackle.

Many firefighters are trained paramedics, and every fire engine carries a comprehensive first aid kit. A number also have defibrillation and resuscitation equipment, and the crew will be trained to deal with serious casualties with life-threatening injuries at the scene of an incident. Other on-board medical equipment can include specialist burn and wound dressings, a variety of splints, and neck and limb supports for people trapped in crash wreckage while extrication and rescue operations go ahead, sometimes before the arrival of a medical team.

Lighting at the scene of an emergency is also critical, and many modern fire engines have both built-in and portable generators capable of floodlighting a large area of operations. Some units have on-board telescopic masts to maximize lighting over a scene and portable clusters of lights to provide illumination at several points around an emergency site.

Other items of equipment likely to be found on fire engines are ventilation fans for drawing smoke out of an affected building, and various salvage items, such as waterproof sheets and dryers, to mitigate water damage caused by firefighting activities.

Communications are a vital part of firefighting and rescue operations. In addition to the personal radios that the crew deploy at the scene, the latest fire engines are equipped to act as a communication base, with a radio link to a control centre. There might also be a data link with a fast printer to provide the incident commander with vital hard copy information, for instance about the contents of a fire-affected building. Using further links into a dedicated chemical substance database, it is possible for the chemical properties of a particular hazardous material to be identified. Using the data link, the incident commander can receive precise instructions on how to deal with the substance, as the wrong treatment could worsen the situation.

Every item of firefighting and rescue equipment carried on board a modern fire engine is subject to a rigorous regular inspection and testing regime. This ensures that every piece of kit will be in reliable and sound working order when firefighters need it – in a life or death situation seconds really do count. Regular inspection and testing also helps fire crews maintain practical knowledge of the workings of all their equipment, some of which may only be occasionally used.

■ ABOVE ***Advanced carbon fibre air-cylinder technology has reduced the weight of modern breathing sets.***

■ BELOW LEFT ***This Japanese fire service Mercedes-Benz Unimog was specially designed for use in earthquake conditions.***

■ BELOW RIGHT ***A Kyoto Fire Brigade fireman, wearing a Japanese-designed protective uniform, gets a hose jet to work.***

FIREFIGHTING AND RESCUE OPERATIONS

When an emergency call comes into a fire station, the firefighters' objective is to get to the scene as quickly as possible, and in this the fire engine driver has a very critical task. Once in attendance at a fire, the driver operates the water pump and becomes responsible for supplying and maintaining both the immediate and long-term firefighting water needs of the crew.

The crew commander sizes up a fire situation within minutes of arrival, establishing first whether anyone is missing. The priority will be to locate and rescue anyone believed to be in an affected building. With the fire still spreading, a team in breathing sets will be ordered to penetrate and search the smoke-filled premises, taking a high-pressure hose line with them.

■ ABOVE *A massed rescue operation was put in place at Clapham Junction, South London, on the morning of 12 December 1988, following the collision of two commuter trains. Firefighters and medical teams extricated many passengers from the mangled wreckage; the crash left 35 dead and 46 seriously injured.*

■ LEFT *Firefighters of Detroit Fire Department get to work at a serious building fire.*

■ RIGHT *Tokyo Fire Brigade crews carry out the final stages of extinguishing a first floor fire above a shop. Several hose lines have been taken into the building off the ladders.*

■ BELOW LEFT *A fireboat crew help a distressed dolphin after it swam up the estuary of the River Thames.*

■ BELOW RIGHT *When the MV Sand Kite collided with the lock gates at the River Thames Barrier in 1997, the vessel's crew were safely taken off by a London fireboat.*

All rooms are searched methodically by the crew as quickly as possible and, hopefully, casualties are found and rapidly removed to fresh air where they can be given paramedic aid, if necessary. If an aerial ladder vehicle is at the scene early on, it will be deployed to give the rescue teams fast access to upper floors, where people may be trapped by smoke rising from a ground-floor or lower-level fire.

As soon as all rescues have been carried out and a building is confirmed as being clear of casualties, the firefighting effort swings into top gear. If the fire is in the upper floors of a building, smaller ladders will be pitched to enable additional hose lines to work alongside the main aerial ladder in the task of locating and attacking the seat of the fire.

Modern firefighting tactics usually involve getting as close to the seat of a fire as possible before unleashing a powerful cooling water jet. This can be difficult in a hot smoke-filled home of two floors, but in a multi-floor commercial building with a complex layout, locating the seat of the fire is never easy.

■ LEFT *A foam firefighting attack is launched on a 'crashed' light aircraft to prevent the ignition of spilt fuel during a training exercise.*

Control and safety procedures

Quite often, the incident commander will have to dispatch more reserve crews with breathing sets into the building. In this case the control and safety procedures of those teams working inside wearing breathing sets are even more paramount. Even with the aid of thermal imaging cameras, which see through smoke, firefighters can face a protracted physical struggle to find the flames. While they are searching the building the fire could be spreading unseen through service ducts and shafts, and there is a danger that their escape route may be cut off.

As a fire burns on, it gets hotter and the smoke more dense. At some stage in operations, the incident commander may have to decide whether or not a forcible ventilation would be a practical option. Using special extraction fans, this would remove some of the heavy smoke conditions from inside the affected building. Unless a fire is completely extinguished, however, ventilation must be undertaken with great care, as in certain circumstances the action can increase the severity of the fire.

A fire has to be monitored right from the beginning of any firefighting operations in order to watch for signs of an impending 'flashover'. This much-feared phenomenon occurs when unburnt products of combustion suddenly ignite into a rolling ball of fire, often with explosive force. The changing colour, pressure and speed of smoke emission from the fire, and any weaknesses in the building

■ BELOW *Modern road crashes create increasingly difficult situations for fire and paramedic crews to deal with. In 1993 this runaway lorry crashed into a shopfront, killing six people.*

■ RIGHT *A damaging fire swept through the iconic Notre-Dame Cathedral in Paris in April 2019, causing the spire to collapse. The first of 400 firefighters arrived on the scene within 10 minutes of the alarm being raised.*

■ BELOW *Following a devastating chemical explosion in Beirut Port in August 2020, fire crews had to deal with fire outbreaks in the local area for several weeks afterwards.*

structure are all indicators of a fire's behaviour, and at any point the incident commander may consider withdrawing all crews if their safety is under threat.

As a large-scale firefighting effort continues, reinforcing crews arrive continually and report to the control point that will be established at an early stage to co-ordinate the operation.

If the fire is a serious one, perhaps in large commercial premises with a complex multi-floor layout, the incident commander will have set up several firefighting command sectors. The commander of each sector will report regularly to the incident commander via their personal radio. Such contact is critical to enable the incident commander to continually assess and monitor aspects of the overall progress of the firefighting effort, such as

■ LEFT *Arsonists have set fire to a house in a residential area, leaving the fire service to bring the blaze under control and minimize danger to property and the public.*

making sure the risk of fire spreading into unaffected buildings is under control.

As the operation progresses, the incident commander also has to consider a variety of other factors. These could include any of the following: floodlighting an incident after dark, provision of water supplies, deployment of reinforcements, the communications network, overall safety supervision, salvage work to minimize and mitigate water damage; and liaison with police, medical services, local authorities and the press.

Arson is a growing problem for fire brigades in many parts of the world, so if there is any doubt about how a fire started, the likely cause may need to be forensically investigated once the fire has been brought under control. This work is done by a special fire investigation unit manned by experienced firefighters trained in forensic investigation. In conjunction with the police, they survey and photograph the post-fire scene, assess the pattern of burning and take samples of fire-damaged material to find out if any traces of accelerants are present.

NON-FIRE EMERGENCIES

As the number of non-fire emergencies tackled by firefighters has grown significantly in recent years, many brigades now rescue more people from non-fire emergencies than from fires. Operations at a non-fire situation can be just as challenging as for a fire, and follow the same general procedures. The sheer variety of call-outs at any time of the day and night can be staggering, ranging from freeing people trapped in lifts to locating survivors buried

■ BELOW *Erupting fireballs were a constant hazard to firefighting operations during this huge fire in a chemical factory and warehouse in Bradford, England. It was tackled by 200 firemen.*

■ LEFT *Major floods in the Welsh town of Crickhowell in early 2021 resulted in residents being evacuated by firefighters using boats.*

under rubble caused by bombs or earthquakes, or from rescuing a family from a smashed-up car to dealing with a large-scale hazardous chemical spill.

A fire crew may have to use specialized cutting equipment to extricate a trapped person from a dangerous situation, working speedily, yet carefully, often alongside a paramedic or medical team who will try to stabilize the casualty as the rescue work progresses. At a road crash where a driver and a number of passengers may be trapped and badly injured in a compacted car, roof, doors and floors may have to be cut away to gain access to the injured. A further potential hazard comes from air bags or seat belt pre-tensioners that have failed to activate in an accident. Air bags can suddenly explode and seat belts might suddenly snap tight.

When dealing with toxic chemical leaks, firefighters must don special all-enclosing protection suits before they begin work. Once they have made the situation safe, each crew member needs to be decontaminated under portable water-spray showers set up at the scene, and provided with clean clothing.

■ RIGHT *Rescue teams have had to cut through twisted and crumpled metal to extricate the drivers and passengers of three cars involved in this horrendous road traffic accident on a British motorway. The disaster was caused by a long steel beam load breaking away and swinging across the adjacent carriageway.*

URBAN BRIGADES

The history of organized fire brigades shows that the biggest and sometimes most challenging fires have occurred in heavily populated city areas, where the threat to life and property is never far away. As most fires are caused by human activity, such areas have an inherently high fire risk, and where a population lives and works in very crowded and cramped conditions with little or no provision of fire precautions, the risk is even higher.

Tall buildings, crowded shopping and business centres, older-style properties with few fire precautions or means of escape, coupled with traffic congestion, narrow, over-parked streets and blocked access for fire engines make life even more difficult for city fire crews when time is of the essence. To make matters worse, city centres often have to cope with large daily influxes of commuters on trains and roads and seasonal population fluctuations caused by large numbers of tourists.

To cope with the ever-present threat of fire, brigades in large cities and towns provide round-the-clock professional crews ready to

■ BELOW LEFT *A turntable ladder helps combat a major fire at night in a city centre.*

■ BELOW RIGHT *Urban terrorism, such as this bomb attack on a city tower, causes large-scale destruction that calls on the full resources of modern firefighters.*

■ RIGHT *The increasing incidence of arson, whether it involves torching a car or destroying a building, is a continual problem, especially for urban brigades.*

■ BELOW *Firemen outside a north London terraced dwelling give external support to colleagues working inside. These will be wearing breathing sets as they locate and extinguish the seat of the fire.*

turn out immediately after an alarm is raised. A three or four-hour shift system ensures that one group of the fire station's workforce is on duty at any time, day or night, with sufficient qualified firefighters to man all the station's fire engines. Shifts, or watches, can be up to nine hours during the day period and up to 15 hours at night.

In many countries, the response of the fire service to emergencies is governed by statutory regulations or codes of practice. These graduate the different areas served by each fire station into three or four fire risk categories, taking into account the potential fire threat to both life and property. In a city or large town, the highest categories are likely to be those buildings in streets and districts where the threat of fire is known to be considerable. Such premises might include high-rise and tenement flats with few alternative exit staircases, or industrial factories or workshops using processes that involve a significant risk of fire. When a fire call is received, the number of fire engines sent in response is directly linked to the known fire risk category, which also determines the precise time limits for the fire brigade's response.

In the highest fire risk category areas, a call-out to a fire in a high-rise tenement in the middle of the night will see at least three pumping engines, or pumps, responding along with at least one aerial ladder. In such a case, the first pumps are required to be at the scene within a few minutes of receipt of the original alarm call. Similarly, a fire call to a large urban factory known to have large quantities of flammable petrochemicals and other hazardous materials on site will, in addition to pumps, also bring the attendance of a foam tender and other specialist vehicles that might be needed.

■ ABOVE *New York firefighters contain a fire that has broken out in the engine compartment of a parked car.*

Conversely, only two pumps will be despatched to a detached dwelling house. This system means that in a city or large town, the overall fire service response to a call-out can come from a number of different fire stations. The priority of the brigade command centre, which receives all emergency calls for the area and alerts the appropriate fire stations, is simply to get sufficient fire engines, crewed by sufficient firefighters, to an emergency scene to immediately deal with the potential situation, whatever it may be. Once pumps and other fire engines have been despatched, the command centre must also monitor the overall fire cover for the city area to ensure there are enough fire engine resources to get to the extremes of the area within the required time limits. If the first crew commander at the scene requires immediate reinforcements, either for firefighting or rescue purposes, these will be rapidly mobilized from the nearest fire stations with available crews and equipment.

All city fire stations will almost certainly have several pumping engines attached, and many will have a high-rise aerial ladder together with other specialist vehicles according to the various fire risks in the station area and surrounding community.

Allocated fire station areas in cities tend to be fairly small and in the most heavily populated cities can embrace just a few blocks of streets. Fire crews know their individual station areas very extensively. Acquiring widespread local knowledge of fire risks plus a general familiarization with much of the locality and what goes on within the fire station area 24 hours a day is key to a firefighter's success. This knowledge will include the layout of the road network, street names, the location of street firefighting water hydrants and the access points leading into the larger building complexes, including high-rise structures and multi-basement layouts. It will also embrace the various entrances and exits of transport and subway systems in the fire station area. A sound understanding of the general layout of major industrial factories and manufacturing plants together with their fire alarm panels, sprinkler control points and the availability of water supplies is also crucial.

Even with round-the-clock firefighting provision, a number of serious inner city fires with high loss of life occurred during the latter half of the twentieth century, illustrating the difficulties involved in fighting urban fires.

High-rise firefighting problems

One such tragedy occurred in São Paulo, Brazil, on 1 February 1974, when a small fire broke out in the newly built 25-storey Joelma office block. Soon flames and smoke were pouring out of its windows, and several hundred office workers trapped above the flames found the inadequate staircase completely impassable in the thick, choking smoke.

The São Paulo Fire Brigade mounted a valiant rescue effort, but because the fire had spread upwards so rapidly, they could not reach the people trapped by the blaze. Furthermore, the inferno was fuelled by the plastic lining and panelling of the building. Because the

■ LEFT *The Grenfell Tower fire, London, which occurred in June 2017, pictured in the early morning after the fire started.*

■ BELOW *Fire rapidly engulfs an empty six-floor office block in east London despite the efforts of 100 firefighters at the scene.*

London's North Kensington district. The cause of the fire was reported to be a malfunctioning fridge-freezer in a flat on the fourth floor of the building, which caught fire at around 1.00 am. The owner of the flat immediately called the fire brigade, with the first appliance arriving on the scene just after 1.00 am.

The fire reached the ceiling of the flat, and burned around the window, reaching the exterior walls and setting light to the building's exterior cladding. The air gap between the walls and the cladding aided the fire's progress. The

firefighting effort could not easily be taken inside the building, external hose jets had to be used, but were largely ineffective.

Many of the workers trapped by the smoke and flames eventually managed to get on to the roof. Meanwhile, those ladders that could be used were brought into position; they virtually groaned under the sheer weight of the injured, shocked and distressed victims who were able to get on to them and be assisted down. A rescue attempt was even made by means of lines fired to the building from a harpoon gun. After two hours or so, the flames had died down sufficiently for helicopters to land on the roof and snatch 80 survivors to safety.

Sadly, when the fire crews finally forced their way into the office block to damp down the collapsed debris, they found more and more bodies on all floor levels. In all, 227 workers died in this awful tragedy; this death toll could most certainly have been reduced if properly designed structurally protected fire escape routes had been provided and other fire precaution measures had been in place.

Another major city fire occurred on 14 June 2017, when flames engulfed a 23-storey residential building, Grenfell Tower, in

fire spread rapidly, via the cladding, moving upwards to all the residential floors.

A major incident was declared at around 2.00 am, and at the height of the emergency, more than 250 firefighters and 70 appliances attended the scene, assisted by various other emergency services, including the Metropolitan Police, London Ambulance Service. Tragically, 72 people lost their lives as a result of the fire, and more than 70 others were injured. Over 60 hours after the fire started, it was finally extinguished.

The Grenfell Tower disaster was the worst residential fire in the UK since World War II, and following investigations into the cause of the fire, an enquiry began in the autumn of 2017. The early findings of the report were published in late 2019, and confirmed that the materials used for the exterior cladding of the building did not comply with regulations, and was the main reason why the fire spread with such devastating effect. The building also had 'stay put' fire policy, on the assumption that the design of the building would allow a fire in a single flat to be contained until firefighters could bring it under control, therefore residents were not immediately evacuated when the fire was reported.

■ RIGHT *Firefighters at work during the final stages of dealing with a serious fire.*

■ BELOW *Teams of firefighters working in the roof void of this office complex in the heart of the City of London are managing to bring the fire under control.*

FIRE CREW STRUCTURE WORLDWIDE

The structure of fire crews and the fire engines they man varies around the world. In the United States, city fire departments and fire stations, or 'firehouses' as they are known, are organized into specific 'companies' whose sole purpose is to man pumping trucks, aerial ladders or rescue fire engines. Elsewhere, fire engines attached to city fire stations are generally crewed by firefighters who have a wide mix of skills and qualifications across a range of disciplines. This can mean that the crew of a pumping fire engine for one tour of

■ ABOVE *Industrial fires bring their own problems. Here, a fire crew is soaking textile bales with water so they will not catch fire and so act to interrupt the fire spread.*

duty can man an aerial ladder the next. Each watch is under the command of an officer who is in charge of up to 30 or more firefighters, and each fire engine will have a crew commander, usually a junior.

In some countries, professional firefighters form part of a specific division of the military. French fire crews, known as Sapeurs-Pompiers, have been part of the army since Napoleonic days. Even though they operate as a self-contained fire brigade, they retain direct links with the armed services. Similarly, some firefighters in countries in Eastern Europe and the Middle East are also a uniformed part of the nation's civil defence organization.

Hong Kong has a very busy fire service whose risks vary from high-rise office and factory buildings, the densely populated Chinese quarters in the waterfront districts, through to one of the world's largest ports. It also has the fire and rescue responsibility for Chek Lap Kok International Airport.

In addition to their firefighting duties, specialized groups in the uniformed personnel of fire services also carry out various fire prevention and safety duties in the world of commerce and industry, and the community at large. This work includes inspections of sprinkler systems, hose reels, fire extinguishers and alarm systems; checks on fire precautions in sleeping areas such as homes for the elderly, hotels and hostels; and general fire safety lectures to schools and other institutions. New building design also comes under fire service scrutiny at an early stage to ensure compliance with the relevant fire safety codes, including means of escape in case of fire, emergency lighting and smoke detection systems.

Country Brigades

Unlike their city and urban counterparts who have to employ full-time firefighters, rural and country fire brigades are generally staffed by retained firemen drawn from the local community. This cost-effective method of providing fire cover does have its limitations so can only be used where there is a relatively low risk factor, such as a low incidence of high-rise buildings and low concentrations of people. Fires and other emergencies do occasionally occur, but the presence of professional fire crews on permanent standby is just not financially practical.

Although rural fire departments are often funded directly by the community they serve, their fire engines and equipment are every bit as modern and sparkling as those found in inner city brigades. Rural and country fire stations are usually smaller than their urban counterparts but nonetheless house a number of fire engines, mostly of a pumping and rescue variety. These will inevitably be of a compact design style, often with 4x4 drive and a narrow overall body width for negotiating narrow country lanes.

One particular difference between city and rural brigades is that the area of a rural fire station is often very large and diverse. Outside the township or village will be an expanse of open country, and one of the principal risks will be farmland, bush, grassland and forest fires, which regularly occur during the dry summer months. Such rural firefighting is usually long, arduous and physically exhausting, demanding great resilience and reserves of stamina.

Retained firefighters need to live close to the fire station they serve and be available to respond to fire calls around the clock. This means having an understanding employer, as

■ OPPOSITE *The 1994 bush and forest fires in Crystal Peak, Nevada, involved several hundred firefighters.*

■ RIGHT *San Francisco Earthquake: the engine that put the fire out in the Mission district.*

well as a sympathetic family. They are mobilized to fire and emergency calls by personal pager-style electronic devices that are carried at all times. In response to an alert the first fire engine will be on the road as soon as sufficient retained firefighters have arrived at the fire station to form a crew, usually of five or six. The turnout will be impressively quick and within minutes of the alarm being raised. In days gone by, rural crews would have been summoned by an electric siren, bell or even by a bugle or trumpet.

At the scene of most rural operations, firefighting water supplies are usually much less readily available than in a city or urban environment. Fire crews have to be adept at using any available natural water resource to be found in the vicinity – rivers, streams, lakes, ponds and sometimes swimming pools. Once located, this water is pumped through hoses to the scene of a fire, which may be a considerable distance away, using light portable pumps carried to the water source. The rigours and physical demands of rural firefighting can be likened to that of working amid a cross-country military commando course. On these occasions, personal radio contact links and co-ordination between crews is vital.

Laying out many lengths of hose to connect up to a remote water source is never a straightforward task and often is not practical

■ BELOW *Sri Lankan villagers work together to beat out an undergrowth fire at the jungle's edge.*

due to distance or difficult terrain. On such occasions many rural brigades operate a large water tanker to shuttle water from a remote source that is accessible from a road access point. The water tanker discharges its load, which can be up to 36,000 litres/8,000 gallons, into a temporary dam, or water tank, erected alongside the base pump. The pump draws its water from this supply to provide several constant firefighting jets while the tanker continues its ferrying operation. These water relays are not easy to regulate and call for plenty of physical effort and careful judgement to ensure that the water supply lasts.

The role of a firefighter in a rural area can be as demanding and dangerous as in an urban environment, because wild weather often strikes particularly hard. In many parts of the world, prolonged spells of dry weather bring the likelihood of fast-spreading grass, bush and forest fires, which threaten lives and property in the path of the rapidly advancing flames.

■ ABOVE *It took Swansea fire crews and local lifeboatmen several hours to rescue these two ponies from the deep mud of the Loughor Estuary, Wales.*

■ LEFT *A fireman has no option but to manually pull a heavy hose line along the edge of a forest fire area as he works on the fire. Firefighting in this type of rural situation can be physically arduous.*

■ RIGHT *A difficult rescue operation is in progress to release the driver of this car, which has careered off the road and overturned. A medical team is also in attendance.*

■ RIGHT *Life is full of variety in a rural firefighting force. This fireman has been asked to rescue a hedgehog that had found its way up onto the roof of a country house in Lincolnshire, England.*

■ BELOW *In recent years, wildfires in California have proved a major challenge for firefighters as wind-driven fires close on residential areas.*

A serious bush or forest fire requires a large-scale firefighting operation, often lasting for weeks. It will necessitate a huge logistical build-up to provide relief crews, feeding and refreshment facilities, water supplies and aerial support, both for reconnaissance and dropping water from the air (water bombing).

In recent years, parts of the United States and Australia have regularly suffered serious bush and forest fires, which have caused loss of life, both human and animal and immense destruction and disruption. In 2020, for example, by the end of the year over 9,500 fires had burned nearly 4.5 million acres of land in California. In August 2020, a massive fire burned over 1 million acres of land, destroying 10,000 structures. Many of the fires that contributed to this disaster were started by lightning strikes.

In 2019/20, the bushfire season in Australia was the worst for many years, burning 46 million acres of land in Queensland, and destroying nearly 6,000 buildings, including over 2,500 homes. The fires also had a huge

■ BELOW *Called out to deal with a simple hedgerow fire in Cornwall, England, a rural crew soon discovered that the fire was in fact large timber stacks burning out of control. With flames spreading in all directions, the crew had to quickly assess the situation, call for back-up and start containment.*

impact on air quality and wildlife. By late January, smoke from the fires had travelled almost 7,000 miles/11,000km across the South Pacific, reaching South America.

Outbreaks of fire involving farms and farm machinery can also spread quickly, especially during the dry months of harvest time. Burning machinery, perhaps an overheated combine harvester or baler, can set fire to adjacent standing cereal crops, a fire which can run away at an alarming rate to provide a further challenge when the first pump arrives.

Agrochemicals, often stored and used on farms in some quantity, can readily present rural fire crews with difficult situations. Chemicals and hazardous substances can intensify a fire. Even if they are not directly involved in a fire, crews tackling this type of rural blaze will need to be ready to adopt a high level of personal protection, using all-enclosing protective chemical suits together with breathing sets to safeguard them from exposure to or ingestion of toxic fumes. Once the chemicals have been dealt with in accordance with specialist advice, any of the crew who have had direct contact with the substances are likely to need full decontamination using portable water spray showers. Retained firefighters need to be particularly well trained and equipped to deal with this aspect of countryside operations.

Animal rescues are a common feature of rural non-fire emergency work. These literally come in all shapes and sizes when horses, cattle or sheep may get stuck fast in deep mud or bogged down in a slurry pit. The rescues can be difficult and of a protracted nature, often requiring plenty of equipment to be laid out before the rescue attempt begins. The weight of many farm animals will require the use of special animal slings, secured to cables and a powered winch mounted on a fire engine, or simply using a lifting block and

■ BELOW *Using a special tripod and sling, rural firefighters struggle to release a steer stuck fast in mud.*

■ RIGHT *The crew of a Dennis/Simon hydraulic platform remove part of a fire-damaged roof.*

■ BELOW *As this aerial ladder goes into action, its operator's task will be complicated by overhead power cables.*

tackle with ropes and lines via a sheerlegs tripod. The rescues usually have to be carried out under the supervision of a veterinary surgeon, as animals quickly become distressed and may need to be tranquillized before extrication and rescue is possible. Cleaning up after such incidents can be a pretty mucky and time-consuming affair, not just the various items of equipment but also the crews' uniforms.

Extremes of weather also provide for busy, sometimes chaotic, periods for rural fire brigades. The work can continue over a stretch of continuous day-and-night operations as the crews struggle to return a community back to normal. Storm force winds and rain can bring serious flooding, trapping people in their homes, and causing plenty of misery and suffering. Falling trees bring down power lines and often damage buildings. Vehicles can even be overturned and washed away.

Emergency call-outs occur at all times of the day and night throughout the year, and can impact on the working, social and personal life of retained firefighters. Inevitably, the families of retained firefighters are drawn into the work of the fire service, and often support all the effort that goes into making a rural fire station work effectively. Quite often, there is a tradition of family firefighting service that goes back over a number of generations. Unsurprisingly, country townships take great pride in the achievements and service provided by their firefighters. It is not unusual to find that they are at the centre of the township community and its various activities, often being the focus and driving force of many fundraising and charity events throughout the year.

INDUSTRIAL SITUATIONS

During the considerable commercial expansion of industry and commerce in the nineteenth century, it became both common and sensible practice for companies with significant fire risks on their own premises to employ an in-house fire brigade. This ensured that in the event of an outbreak of fire an immediate firefighting response was on hand to extinguish or at least contain flames, which could threaten an entire factory or production plant, before the arrival of the public fire brigade.

■ BELOW *Thick smoke turns day into night at this major fire in a chemical plant.*

WORKS FIRE BRIGADES

At first, works fire brigades were drawn from the company's ordinary workforce. In the event of a fire or other emergency, these men would quickly don their company fire uniforms and brass helmets then commence firefighting operations. The first works brigades relied on manual pumps, with the company name proudly emblazoned on the side. In larger factory and works complexes these were replaced by steam-powered pumps when they became available in the second half of the nineteenth century. Companies in the more profitable industries were quick to build proper fire stations within the factory complex, manned around the clock by a dedicated team of trained firemen.

One such early works fire brigade was that of the Hodges Gin Distillery in London's Lambeth district. Frederick Hodges, the distillery owner, took a personal interest in the whole business of firefighting, ensuring that his fire station was fully equipped and his firemen turned out in well-fitting smart uniforms and helmets that were also functional. He also built a 37m/120ft high observation tower so the firemen could keep a permanent watch for signs of fire outbreaks, both within the distillery and in the streets beyond.

Hodges' brigade became the first in London to replace their manual fire pumps with steam-powered pumps, taking delivery in 1862 of two Merryweather horse-drawn models, appropriately named Torrent and Deluge.

Hodges' new acquisitions could pump water jets 40m/130ft into the air at a rate of 636 litres/140 gallons per minute. His brigade's response to a call of "Fire!" was so fast that often they were the first to arrive at the scene, going on to play a significant firefighting role supporting the London Fire Engine Establishment's (LFEE) manual pumps at many large fires. At this time, the capital's public brigade, the LFEE, was vigorously resisting a move towards the introduction of steam-driven fire pumps. The effectiveness of Hodges's private fire brigade with its advanced equipment was undoubtedly one of the factors that led to the LFEE's eventual adoption of steam-powered pumps in 1863.

The development of works fire brigades continued unabated, and around 1905 some were beginning to introduce motorized fire engines every bit as grand and well equipped as those serving in the larger city brigades. By the early part of the twentieth century, many companies regarded on-site fire stations and dedicated firefighting crews as a positive step towards safeguarding their future prosperity, and the fire cover they gave was often more effective than that provided by the local municipal fire brigade. Many of the smaller works brigades, however, were staffed on a casual basis by workers who could only be expected to provide an immediate 'first-aid' response until the municipal fire crews arrived. Nonetheless, there are many recorded instances of a works fire brigade successfully bringing a fire under control.

Over the past few decades, the comparative cost benefits offered by modern fire detection technology over the spiralling costs of keeping a dedicated fire team on site has led to a steady decline in the number of large commercial

■ ABOVE *During a refinery fire training exercise in Cheshire, England, firefighters use one of the brigade's specialist ERF foam tenders to provide a powerful jet.*

■ BELOW *Working together as a team, a fire crew prepare to extinguish a leaking pipeline fire at a chemical plant in Cleveland, England.*

■ ABOVE *A London Fire Brigade crew prepares to undergo decontamination by water spray after dealing with the leakage of a toxic chemical.*

companies prepared to maintain an in-house fire brigade. Today the fire defence of much of commerce and industry relies upon the proven effectiveness of intelligent smoke-detection and alarms allied to automatic fire-control methods such as sprinklers, water-sprays, and inert gas systems. Such technological improvements combined with greater emphasis on the fire-awareness-training of employees and in-house procedures has inevitably led to higher levels of commercial fire safety.

High-risk industries necessarily continue to run their own firefighting units to ensure an immediate on-site response to any emergency incident. On-site works fire brigades are specially trained in dealing with the particular dangers of fires and other emergencies caused by the industry products and materials. An outbreak of fire or a leakage, for instance, in any high-risk premises such as nuclear power installations, petrochemical refineries, chemical plants and large gas storage installations could rapidly pose a serious toxic, explosive or pollution threat to surrounding communities. On a different level, the potential for huge financial losses through stoppages following a fire at any of the large new production plants, such as in car manufacturing, or in a mega-sized warehousing complex, is unacceptably high for the businesses concerned.

Works fire brigades carry out general duties such as constant fire patrols. They are also responsible for the ongoing training of other employees in general fire safety awareness and precautions, including the proper action to be taken in case of a fire being discovered and practising the techniques of using fire extinguishers on live fire simulators.

The crews perform regular firefighting drills, and often exercise on site with firemen from the nearest municipal or county brigades. When responding to a fire in one of these special industrial situations it is critical that the public fire crews have a sound understanding of the general layout of the plant or complex and its firefighting facilities and systems. When the

■ RIGHT *A fireman in the cage of a Dennis/Simon hydraulic platform directs a powerful water jet into burning industrial premises.*

plant and public crews practise together, the teams often simulate real fire and emergency situations that involve the use of a whole range of firefighting procedures and equipment.

A LARGE SCALE INDUSTRIAL FIRE

In spite of all these precautions, industrial fires do get out of control, and one such occasion was 21 July 1992, a day that many firefighters, and others, in West Yorkshire will never forget. Early in the afternoon, the works fire team were called to a report of smoke in a raw materials warehouse at the Bradford plant of Allied Colloids, manufacturers of a wide range of specialized chemicals. The plant covered a site of approximately 16 hectares/40 acres and employed 1,600 people.

The fire team found that two cardboard drums of organic compound had begun to decompose, but decided that no further assistance was required. Some 50 minutes later, there was a sudden explosion in the same warehouse, and when the first pumps of the West Yorkshire Fire Brigade arrived within six minutes, a severe fire was already engulfing the building. Extra pumps were immediately requested.

As the first fire crews got to work, both firefighting and supervising the evacuation of workers, further flashovers and explosions occurred. Burning liquid chemicals soon became rivers of flame, spreading fire through the plant and into high stacks of drums storing various chemical products. Fireballs shot across the storage area, sending liquid fire up into the sky like a grotesque firework display. The black smoke blotted out the summer sunshine and cast an eerie darkness over the district around the burning plant.

More pumps were ordered to the scene, and soon 30 pumps, three aerials and ten support tenders, with over 200 Yorkshire firefighters, were at work. A major problem was water. No fewer than 18 hydrants were in use at the height of the inferno, and a 1.6 kilometre/ 1 mile water relay was set up from a dam.

All residents downwind of the huge smoke plume were warned to keep their windows and doors shut. Later, the toxic chemical pollutants in the smoke led to fruit and vegetables being condemned, and for a while, even swimming in the local downwind rivers was banned.

The Allied Colloids fire was eventually brought under control by the early evening, after seven hours of intense firefighting efforts, often in the face of explosion and liquid fire. Fortunately no lives were lost, although 39 firefighters were injured and needed hospital treatment. The huge fire subsequently proved to be the largest blaze ever tackled by the brigade, and one that taxed the firefighting resources of the entire area.

■ ABOVE *This 2010 Mercedes-Benz Actros 3348/Angloco multi-media refinery tender was designed and manufactured for BP Trinidad and Tobago. It features a 4,500-litre water tank, 2,300-litre foam tank, balanced-pressure foam-proportioning system, and 500kg dry chemical powder unit.*

AIRPORTS

■ LEFT *Exercises at the Fire Service College, in England, include techniques for quelling, containing and preventing aircraft fire.*

From the earliest days of aviation, the risk of fire following a crash or spillage of fuel has been a major safety issue. However, it wasn't until the development of commercial aviation and the steady growth in the size of passenger-carrying aircraft that attention was focussed on the need for adequate aviation fire protection. This quickly became a priority as air travel distances increased across entire continents, necessitating the carriage of much greater fuel loads. From then on, airports had to train and maintain their own dedicated brigades to deal with all possible emergencies on their patch.

Several fire engine manufacturers had adapted existing water tender design for airfield firefighting early on, but real developments in aviation fire engines only began after World War II, when the Cardox Corporation in America designed a fire engine fitted with foam equipment that could blanket an aircraft fire. An integral foam compound tank linked to an in-built water tank produced an effective supply of firefighting foam that was then pressurized using carbon dioxide gas and discharged through a large rotating nozzle (also called a monitor) mounted on the roof of the fire engine.

Further developments followed and by the 1950s a range of airfield fire tenders became available, including some with all-wheel, cross-country rapid intervention capability. As the overall size and fuel capacity of passenger aircraft continued to grow so did the need for larger airport foam tenders that could carry

■ BELOW *Airfield foam and rescue tenders include a Simon Gloster Saro (foreground) and a Thornycroft Nubian model (background).*

■ RIGHT *An airport fire rescue unit equipped with a rooftop-mounted Snozzle. Mounted on a telescopic boom, this device is able to penetrate an aircraft fuselage and project a powerful water spray inside.*

■ RIGHT *US Air Force firefighters clad in close-proximity fire suits and breathing sets practise the rescue of a trapped pilot during a training exercise.*

■ BELOW *Norwegian airport firefighters train on a gas-fired simulator that can create a range of aircraft fire scenarios.*

more foam compound and water together with a wider range of powerful rescue tools. No sooner had the first 6x6 airport fire tender made an appearance, however, than the arrival of the first commercial Boeing 747 Jumbo Jet necessitated even bigger, faster and more powerful airport fire and crash tenders.

By this time, diesel engines were replacing petrol power in airport fire engines, and automatic gearboxes were coming into use.

Other new features included a hydraulic platform facility to raise firefighters to the height of the tail-mounted engines of some new aircraft types. Typical of the new breed of airport crash tender was the Thorneycroft/ Carmichael Nubian Major, a 6x6 vehicle powered by a 300bhp Cummins V8 diesel via semi-automatic gearbox that gave a speed of 64kmh/40mph in 41 seconds. The Nubian Major's 6,820 litre/1,500 gallon water capacity combined with a 700 litre/150 gallon foam compound tank produced a staggering 32,000 litres/7,000 gallons of foam per minute.

Over time, international agreements between the various aviation regulating authorities were refined. Now every airport handling revenue-earning aircraft is required to provide an efficient fire and rescue service that is adequate to cope with the size and consequent fuel load of aircraft using its facilities. This means that a small provincial airfield served by the smallest commercial aircraft needs only a modest all-purpose 4x4 fire pump manned by a four-man crew. At the other end of the scale, the largest and busiest international airports, such as Frankfurt, London Heathrow and JFK New York, are required to provide a range of permanently manned crash and rescue tenders that carry large quantities of firefighting foam and have fast all-terrain capability.

High-category airport fire engines, such as the Dutch Kronenberg tenders, are heavy three-axled vehicles, yet they perform impressively. Despite weighing in at approximately 30 tonnes, these vehicles can accelerate from 0 to 80kmh/50mph in just over 30 seconds. Each tender is capable of producing up to 9,000 litres/2,000 gallons of foam per minute through the roof-mounted guns or monitors.

Large airfield fire tenders have also been produced over the years for military use. The modern-day fire protection demands of some of the largest military aircraft, such as the Boeing B52, has led to the design of some very large fire engines, whose bulk is needed simply to carry a sufficient quantity of foam and water. At

■ ABOVE *Two Simon airfield fire engines – a Protector foam and rescue tender (far left) and a Pacer rapid intervention vehicle (centre) – stand alongside an ambulance of the Nepal Civil Aviation Fire Service.*

■ BELOW LEFT *This executive jet crashed through the perimeter fence at Northolt Airfield, west London, and slewed into a van on an adjacent main road. Fortunately, there was no fire or serious injury as a result.*

■ BELOW RIGHT *A rescue helicopter stands by on the runway at Osaka, Japan.*

■ RIGHT *This 2012 Scania/Angloco ARFFV is an example of an Airport Rescue and Fire Fighting Vehicle based on a high-performance commercial chassis, taking advantage of the benefits arising from their reduced costs and maintenance implications.*

its various bases around the world, the United States Air Force runs some monster fire engines, including the Oshkosh P-15 8x8 crash tender, whose twin 500hp diesel engines provide both drive and water-pumping power.

Time is unforgiving in any firefighting situation, but it is never more pressing than when an aircraft is on fire and large quantities of fuel are vulnerable and likely to intensify a fire. Airport fire stations are, therefore, usually located close to taxiways and runways so that the fire engines can get to a troubled aircraft as quickly as possible. Due to their sheer size, most large international airports have several fire stations located at strategic points. Foam tenders always form the first strike at any aircraft fire or accident, with the primary aim of rapidly knocking down or preventing a fire in order to allow other firefighters to get close into an aircraft to effect rescues.

On the training front, new levels of improved competency and skills are continually required of aviation firefighters to both match the increased fire risk of modern-day large aircraft and master the evolving operational capabilities of new airport fire engines. Alongside these developments have come improved training facilities, which recreate realistic live-fire training scenarios under safe and controlled conditions, and a better level of protection suits, breathing sets, hydraulic cutting and rescue gear, inflatable air bags and floodlighting.

With the prospect of a new generation of large twin-decked aircraft capable of carrying up to 600 passengers planned for the future, aviation firefighting and rescue arrangements will have to continue adapting as the twenty first century progresses.

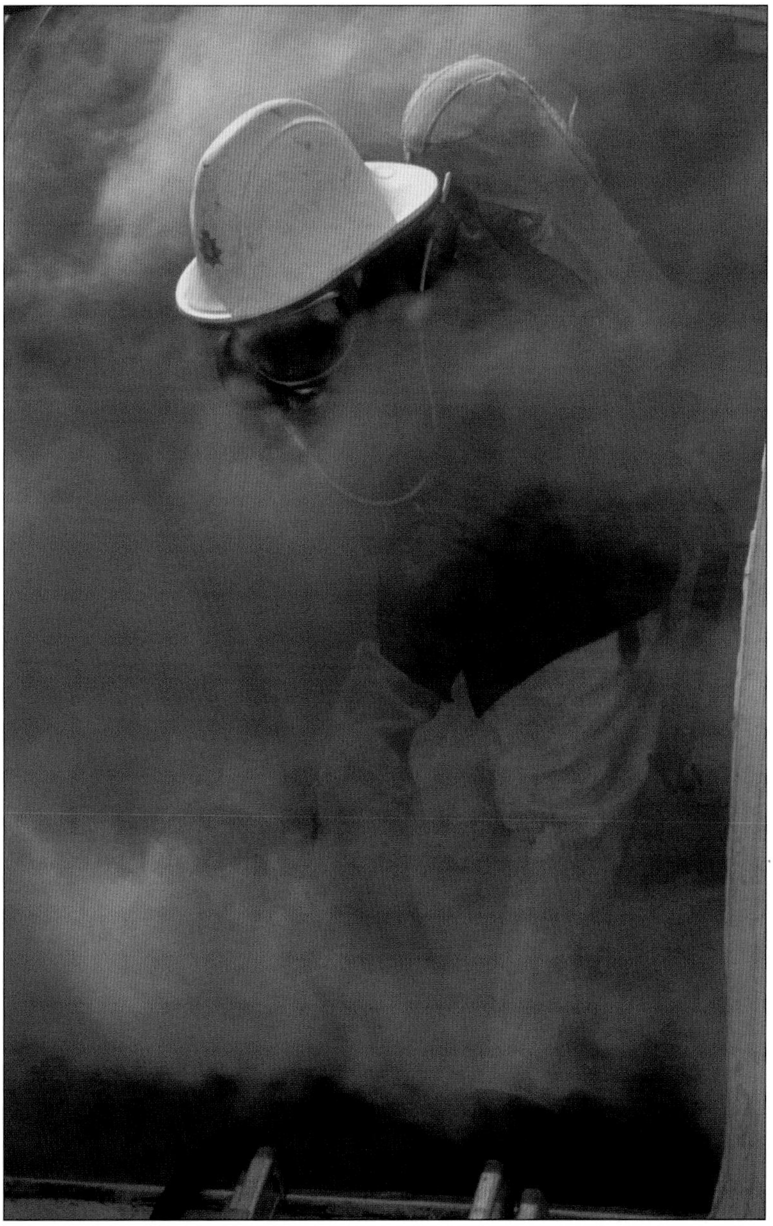

■ RIGHT *A firefighter wearing a breathing set emerges from a smoke-filled aircraft during a training exercise.*

TRANSPORTATION FIRES

An outbreak of fire involving any kind of transportation creates difficult and diverse operational problems for firefighters.

Most rail fires occur when a train is in service, usually through malfunction of equipment, perhaps in the restaurant galley, or from the careless disposal of a cigarette in a seat. The procedure for dealing with an on-train fire is pretty basic. The crew must stop the train and get everyone off as effectively as they can, and leave the firefighting to the experts whom they will have called out. If an emergency occurs in a remote spot, this can delay the fire brigades' response, as they will have to travel overland to reach the incident. This is where 4x4 fire engines are invaluable.

Trains are also at risk from fire following a derailment or collision involving diesel units or a tanker train containing flammable petro-chemical liquids.

Road vehicle fires can readily start when fuel or oil leaks or spills on to hot engine parts, such as an exhaust system or, in HGVs, buses and coaches, overheated brakes. They can also result from overheating then ignition of the wiring system due to an electrical fault. As elsewhere, the careless disposal of a cigarette is another cause of fire. Modern cars have a high content of plastic and foam seating materials, which burn fiercely once alight, as do some commercial loads. Following a crash, spilled fuel from the tank is likely to ignite in the presence of live electrical wires within the wreckage. Fire will almost certainly spread to other nearby vehicles.

Remote and inaccessible train and road crashes and fires are difficult enough to deal with, but when a fire occurs in a tunnel, the situation is even more hazardous. What makes tunnels so dangerous is that when heat and

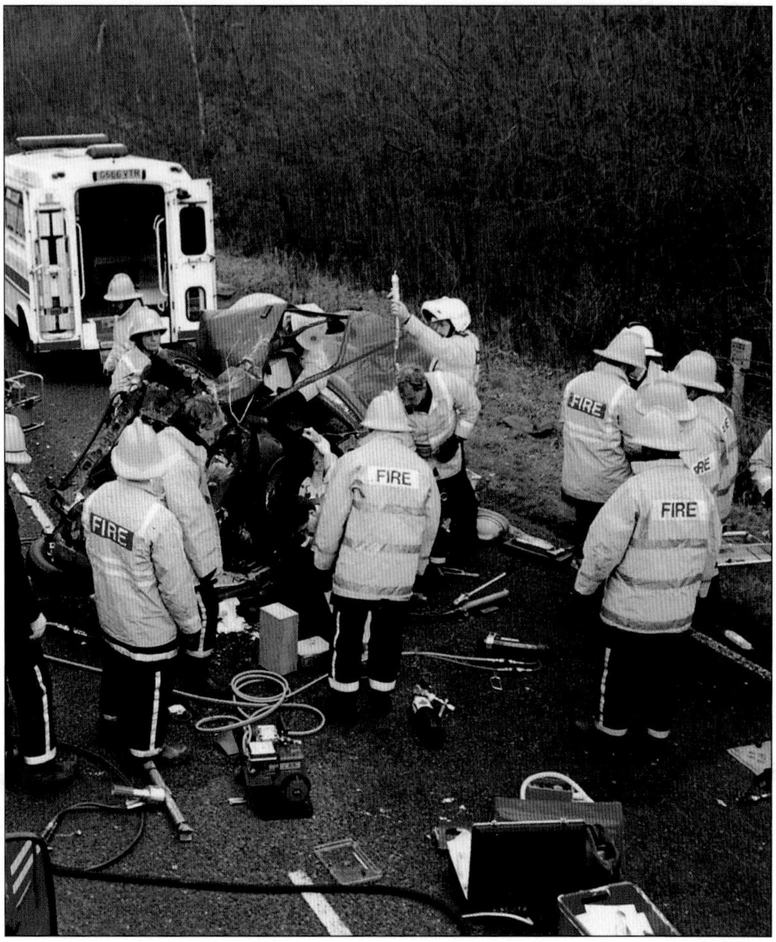

■ OPPOSITE ABOVE AND BELOW *Fire crews and medical teams work together to free car crash casualties.*

■ RIGHT *A London firefighter surveys the wreckage of the 1999 Ladbroke Grove collision and fire which involved two trains. Many fatalities and serious injuries were caused with a number of passengers requiring extrication from the wreckage.*

■ BELOW *Two specially designed double-ended Mercedes fire engines pictured deep inside the service tunnel of the 44km-/27 mile-long Channel Tunnel. Fire crews have ready access to the running railway lines linking England and France.*

smoke fail to find any other escape route, they are vented relentlessly along the tunnel, posing dangers to travellers and firefighters alike. A flashover, which is dependent upon the rate of fire spread and the potential fire loading of whatever is burning, is always likely given that there will be a flow of air through a tunnel.

Modern road tunnels have escape staircases or refuges at frequent intervals, but older tunnels do not. While there are codes of safety practice, these older tunnels do not meet modern fire safety standards, and the costs to update them are very often considered to be prohibitive. Failing to take sufficient precautions can have tragic results. On 24 March 1999, a lorry caught fire as it travelled through the 11 kilometre/7 mile Mont Blanc Tunnel, beneath Europe's highest mountain. In the ensuing chaos 39 travellers were simply unable to escape. The fire burned for two days before firefighters overcame the intense conditions to eventually extinguish the inferno. The subsequent inquiry made 41 safety recommendations, including a complete redesign of the tunnel's smoke and ventilation system. Two years later, a serious fire broke out in a vehicle in the St Gotthard Tunnel in Switzerland, causing the death of 40 people.

Another catastrophic tunnel fire occurred on 18 November 1996 in the 44 kilometre/27 mile Channel Tunnel that links the United Kingdom with France. Only recently constructed, the

■ ABOVE LEFT *The fire aboard the Ebn Majid in the English Channel in 1986 gave Dorset firefighters a hard time for several days and nights before they finally got the blaze under control.*

■ ABOVE RIGHT *The scale of this major rail accident is apparent from the widespread damage and wreckage involving two trains.*

tunnel incorporated the latest fire safety features, yet fire still broke out, creating horrendous physical conditions for firefighters. On this occasion, the fire started in a lorry that had been loaded on to the train, the smoke being noticed only as the train entered the tunnel. The train came to a standstill some 13 kilometres/8 miles into the tunnel, by which time the priority was to get everyone off the train and into the safety tunnel that lies between the two rail tunnels; this safety tunnel is pressurized to prevent the ingress of smoke.

Before long, the fire had spread into other carriages of the train, igniting more vehicles and their contents. This resulted in a huge volume of thick smoke and a rapid rise in temperature, despite the automatic emergency smoke extraction system coming on.

Once the alarm had been raised, French and British fire crews responded from opposite ends of the service tunnel, driving double-ended fire engines specially designed for use in the Channel Tunnel. Although there were no serious casualties among the train passengers, the fire reached intense proportions and the firefighting effort became a hazardous and physically demanding operation that lasted for many hours. As the firefighting effort continued and more and more crews entered the tunnel, they had to penetrate and endure a considerable heat barrier and high levels of toxic smoke. It was eight hours before the fire came under control.

At the height of the blaze, temperatures reached 1,000°C/1,830°F, which caused considerable collapse of some of the tunnel's structural sections. Such was the heat that some of the train's wagons became welded to the track. Kilometres of wiring and service ducting were destroyed, and it was many months before the Channel Tunnel was back in full operation, with improved fire and rescue procedures in place.

FIGHTING FIRES AT SEA

Fire on board ship can also turn into a nightmare scenario. The metal structure of the ship can quickly spread fire by conduction through bulkheads into unaffected areas. Ship fires usually start in the engine room, often with a broken fuel line spraying fuel on to hot machinery. All big ships now have a carbon dioxide or other inert gas flooding system, but this will only stifle a fire and prevent it spreading. Modern passenger ships also have sprinkler and automatic fire-detection systems installed, and the mega-cruise ships have fire-safety features on a par with those of new high-rise buildings. Some of a ship's crew will have basic firefighting training, but ship fires require plenty of experienced firefighters, who can take some time to get on board.

Some of the perils of a ship fire are illustrated by events that took place on 28 January 1986, on board the *Ebn Majid* as it steamed up the English Channel. When traces of smoke were noticed coming from the hold of the ship, the carbon dioxide fire system was activated, but as the smoke continued to thicken, the ship's master requested urgent assistance. The *Ebn Majid* was towed into Weymouth Bay by the Royal Navy where a firefighting team from Dorset Fire Brigade boarded the vessel to find it was carrying a mixture of cattle feed, rubber and a variety of flammable chemicals. A huge firefighting operation was mounted, which lasted for four days and nights during which 120 breathing sets were in use, all needing to be continuously recharged. By the time the fire deep in the lower hold of the ship came under control, more than 8,000 hours had been logged by crews using 41 pumping engines and special vehicles on the nearby quayside, together with a number of fleet naval tugs surrounding the *Ebn Majid*. The cause of this fire is believed to have been spontaneous combustion.

With cruise ships, sheer numbers of passengers can create logistical problems. Also, fire may travel along the narrow below-deck corridors to create conditions from which it can be difficult to escape. Typical was the fate of the Italian cruise liner *Achille Lauro*, off the North African coast. When a fire broke out in the engine room on 30 December 1994, the 1,000 passengers and crew had to abandon ship and take to lifeboats and rafts. Three passengers lost their lives during the dramatic rescue operation, and the *Achille Lauro* was left a blackened and smouldering ruin.

■ BELOW LEFT ***The aftermath of a helicopter crash showing a foam carpet surrounding the aircraft and fire engines still in attendance.***

■ BELOW RIGHT ***Against a background of thick smoke this modern fireboat blasts two powerful water jets on to a burning vessel.***

Fire Stations and Firehouses

Although many fire stations, or firehouses as they are known in the United States, are relatively modern structures, some have been in continuous service for a long time, adapting to changes in firefighting practice over the years. The 132-year-old Clerkenwell station, for example, is still a front line station of the London Fire Brigade. Here, as in a number of other older fire stations in Britain, the original Victorian layout is clearly visible, and a number of fittings are still in place on the walls and ceiling where formerly harnesses and other linkages used for the horse-drawn fire engines of earlier times were hung. In those far-off days, firemen worked incredible 24-hour shifts, living on the job with their families in two-room flats above the station itself. Whole families of firemen's children were brought up using the fire station drill

■ ABOVE *Crews of the Metropolitan (London) Fire Brigade on their horse-drawn fire engines line up on Southwark fire station's forecourt, in about 1895.*

■ FAR LEFT *A traditional American timber fire station (firehouse) incorporates a lookout and bell tower. This late nineteenth-century example is in Ridgeway, Colorado, USA.*

■ LEFT *This early nineteenth-century timber firehouse, in Nevada City, California, USA, has a lookout in the roof, with a bell on top.*

■ ABOVE *Seven London Fire Brigade motor fire engines and their brass-helmeted crews make a brave sight in front of the Southwark Headquarters c. 1923.*

yard as their playground, and the station commander had the regular duty of inspecting the family accommodation to ensure it was being kept in clean order.

Some old fire stations are housed within grand surroundings. When King George VI opened the London Fire Brigade's new five-storey headquarters at Lambeth in July 1937, the ground floor had seven bays along a 64m/210ft frontage. The entrance hall contained a bronze-and-marble memorial dedicated to all the brigade officers and men who had lost their lives in action. Ironically, the site headquarters was formerly a riverside wharf where a serious fire in 1918 killed seven brigade members.

Today, city-centre and urban fire stations tend to house a number of fire engines, which stand in bays ready for action. The central office, or watchroom, is situated close to the fire engine bays. It is called the watchroom because in pre-telephone days members of the public would run to the station's permanently manned office in order to raise the alarm. Nowadays, the watchroom houses a modern communication system with various links to the control and despatch centre, often situated many miles away, and generally serves as the nerve centre for the station. The station is mobilized to fire and emergency calls either by hard copy off the printer or by a broadcast radio message.

■ BELOW LEFT *Three modern American fire engines show off their colourful liveries.*

■ BELOW RIGHT *This three-bay firehouse in Alexandria, Virginia, USA, dates from the late nineteenth century.*

■ ABOVE *In Great Whale Town, Quebec, Canada, an unassuming two-bay fire station is part of a small hotel complex.*

Fire stations in large towns and cities are almost exclusively manned by full-time firefighters and so need to have sleeping and living accommodation for on-duty crews. Other facilities include lockers, showers, laundry, lecture room, equipment storage, breathing-set servicing, including an air compressor for recharging cylinders, a gymnasium or fitness training area and a muster bay.

Outside there is a fuelling point and covered wash-down area for cleaning the fire engines. Much of the routine inspection and maintenance work on the hundreds of items of equipment carried on the vehicles are conducted out here. Many larger urban stations also incorporate a training-drill tower structure that consists of several floors with windows at various levels for training sessions. Other training facilities are likely to include a building containing confined-space crawling galleries, with various obstacles, into which heat and cosmetic smoke can be introduced for breathing-set training. In some stations, firefighters with paramedic skills crew an

■ LEFT *An aerial ladder is being checked over in the fire-engine repair workshop of Boston Fire Department, USA.*

■ RIGHT *This architect-designed fire house at Uxbridge, Massachusetts, USA, was opened in 2017.*

emergency ambulance, which is stationed alongside the fire engines.

Fire stations in rural areas are generally much smaller than their urban counterparts, needing only to house one or two fire engines. Their structure tends to be simple, often single storey, and with very basic facilities. In addition to a watchroom, many rural fire stations have an external drill tower and yard area for ladder, hose and pump-training sessions, together with a building in which basic heat and breathing-set training can be carried out. Rural stations are normally manned by part-time retained crews or even volunteers who only attend the station for a call-out or a training session.

A feature of all modern fire stations is an area of the drill yard dedicated to road accident extrication practice. Here there will be several cars, usually in various stages of demolition following regular training sessions in the speedy use of powerful cutting and spreading equipment.

In addition to their primary function as integral parts of the fire emergency service, fire stations are increasingly used as a focus in the community for various fire safety education efforts. Displays of good fire safety practice set against examples of some of the preventable causes of fire are used to good effect by firefighters during visits by schools and various other local groups.

■ BELOW *Kent Fire Brigade's eight-bay fire station at Ashford, England, is close to the British terminal of the Channel Tunnel.*

FIREFIGHTING UNIFORMS

In the eighteenth and nineteenth centuries firemen's liveried uniforms were colourful but totally impractical, conceived more as ready identification of a particular insurance brigade than as effective protection against the physical dangers of firefighting. Even when more powerful pumps and water jets meant that firemen could work more closely to a fire and sometimes even inside burning buildings, they remained poorly protected against the dangers of scorching heat and falling masonry and timber as a burning building progressively weakened and fell apart.

Some of the first practical and radical improvements in firemen's uniforms came in 1824 when James Braidwood, the newly appointed Master of Fire Engines in Edinburgh, replaced the colourful frock coats of the recently amalgamated insurance companies with double-breasted wool tunics. He added leather helmets and knee-length boots to the new uniform. When Braidwood moved to London, in 1832, to take charge of the capital's fire brigade he continued making improvements to the style and effectiveness of his firefighters' uniforms and introduced silk neckerchiefs to prevent sparks from falling down their necks.

By the mid-nineteenth century, brass military-style helmets had become popular firefighting headgear in many parts of Europe. American firemen continued to use leather helmets along with longer-style bunker coats, which, with various improvements in fabric and design, have remained the preferred American pattern to the present day. In Europe and elsewhere, brass helmets were replaced in the 1930s by cork and plastic versions following several incidents where firefighters were killed after their helmet made contact with a live wire dangling from a fire-damaged ceiling. During World War II, firefighters on both sides of the conflict exchanged their peacetime helmets for steel military-style versions, but the rest of the standard firemen's wartime uniform was little changed from that of pre-war years.

■ LEFT *The early uniform worn by Paris firemen (sapeurs-pompiers), c.1860, indicates the force's military origins. Around this time, brass helmets became a commonplace part of firefighting uniforms.*

■ BELOW *Due to the increasing risk of electrocution, in 1934 brass helmets were replaced with a compressed-cork version, seen here on the left.*

■ OPPOSITE BOTTOM *London firefighters display various uniforms worn from 1866 (right) through to 'the Inferno' uniform, phased out in 2010 (left).*

Significant changes and improvements to firefighting uniforms began to be made during the 1980s following the introduction of technology that produced the first flame-retardant fabrics and fibres specially designed for firefighting use. This has led to great advances in the design style of firefighting uniforms, which now embraces head-to-toe clothing protection and is termed personal protective equipment (PPE).

■ ABOVE LEFT *This c.1936 London Fire Brigade uniform remained in operational use until the 1970s.*

■ ABOVE MIDDLE *A Japanese firefighter in military-style uniform.*

■ ABOVE RIGHT *The UK's latest firefighting suits provide maximum protection.*

One particularly serious British fire in November 1987 provided a springboard for uniform improvement. A sudden flashover up an escalator engulfed evening commuters at London's Kings Cross Underground station and 31 people died, including a fire officer. The subsequent inquiry made a number of recommendations, including the improvement of the level of personal protection for firemen facing such awful circumstances.

Protective clothing

Today's firefighting tunics and trousers incorporate a durable outer shell for physical protection, a moisture barrier that prevents hot water and hazardous liquid penetration, together with an in-built thermal barrier. With helmets and boots they achieve a blend of maximum protection against high temperatures and other dangers, while providing a maximum level of comfort when worn for lengthy periods in a hot and unpleasant environment.

Helmets have also been improved and are now constructed from toughened plastics, with the provision of a swing-down visor. Recently developed space-age materials have helped to reduce the overall weight of helmets while increasing facial and neck protection, and improving overall wearer comfort levels. Some helmet models have a wrap-around shape with a pull-down visor built into the structure. Fire-retardant material is also used in the manufacture of gloves and anti-flash hoods, which are particularly important when working with the risk of flashover and the resulting sudden high temperatures.

Modern boot design incorporates maximum foot-protection features, including reinforced toecaps, special soles and a sealing process that prevents the ingress of any liquids. The last feature is especially important in situations where these liquids could contain run-off from a hazardous chemical incident.

The conventional firefighting suit is not at all practical for protracted firefighting operations in bush and forest areas, which occur in summer months and can go on for weeks at a time. This work is physically demanding enough, without the extra burden of high ambient weather temperatures. The wild land firefighting coverall suit was designed to overcome all these problems. It reduces heat stress by providing a tough,

■ ABOVE LEFT *Japanese firefighters in breathing sets and lightweight protective suits await orders.*

■ ABOVE RIGHT *A Japanese firefighting team in full protective clothing and breathing masks hold a high-powered hose nozzle.*

■ BELOW *New York Fire Department officers in full uniform attend a colleague's funeral, Brooklyn, USA.*

■ RIGHT *Senior officers and firemen of the Vienna Fire Brigade in firefighting uniforms of 1920.*

yet comfortable, highly breathable suit that offers short-term protection against heat and flames.

Modern uniforms are increasingly subject to a range of stringent international testing standards across the various types of operational use, including those for general firefighting, wild land fires, hazardous materials and non-fire rescue. Modern fire suits are designed to be regularly laundered under strictly controlled procedures. In Europe, these standards have been set out in a recent EU directive. American standards have gone a little further and ensure that any build-up of dangerous hydrocarbons and other harmful toxins are removed during the PPE cleaning process.

Firefighting uniforms are one area where modern technology has been used to lighten the physical load upon firefighters, while providing the maximum level of personal protection as crews work in a hazardous and challenging environment. It is no surprise, however, to find that old-style fire helmets, including those made of polished brass, are still retained by many brigades for use during special ceremonial occasions.

■ BELOW LEFT *Modern uniforms protect firemen from the fierce heat of flames.*

■ BELOW RIGHT *A heavily protected Thai firefighter mounts a foam attack during a training exercise.*

FIREFIGHTER TRAINING

Firefighters undergo rigorous training to prepare them for the physical demands of the job and to use a range of tools and aids, as well as some high-tech equipment. They must be able to work quickly, efficiently and calmly in stressful conditions, as a part of a team or individually. They also have to work in all weather conditions, often in a dangerous environment. Working at height off ladders or in confined spaces in complete darkness must hold no fears, and a strong mental constitution is necessary as all firefighters witness tragedy and suffering during their front-line work.

TRAINING PROCEDURES

Usually brigades are staffed by full-time professional firemen and part-time retained firemen. Professional recruits attend an intensive basic course that includes theoretical work, study and plenty of practical drill. The latter involves learning how to handle virtually every item of firefighting and rescue equipment – fire pumps, hose, ladders, extinguishers, lighting, knots and lines, resuscitators, cutting

■ ABOVE *Firefighters practise their skills during a pump and ladder drill exercise.*

■ FAR LEFT *Fire crews work with two turntable ladders on a training tower in Zian Province, China.*

■ LEFT *Under the watchful eye of their instructor, recruit firefighters practise the carry-down of a rescued 'casualty' on an extension ladder.*

■ OPPOSITE *The New York Fire Training Centre, USA, has extensive fire-training buildings at its disposal.*

■ ABOVE LEFT *Paris firemen scale the outside face of a training drill tower, c.1920.*

■ ABOVE MIDDLE *A German fireman prepares to leap from the first floor in this jumping sheet drill, c.1910.*

■ ABOVE RIGHT *German firefighters' training sessions included a rescue chute drill, c.1910.*

and lifting gear and a range of other items. Recruits also have to qualify in advanced first aid and casualty-handling techniques.

Once recruits have satisfactorily completed the basic training they are ready to become part of an operational firefighting and rescue unit for a probationary period. They will ride a fire engine as crew members and gain experience from the wide range of incidents they attend. Ongoing training continues throughout a firefighter's career, and in order to maintain strength and stamina most have access to fitness-training equipment, which is often provided at their fire stations.

Breathing-set training is critical for all firemen, as there are few structural fire situations where sets are not worn. Personal breathing sets enable firefighters to survive and work in thick, choking smoke. Regular training in the use of this crucial piece of equipment is carried out inside a special building that is often attached to the fire station. Incorporating several floors, the building can be fitted with a number of different and varying obstacles and hazards. It can also be heated to create a humid atmosphere and filled with cosmetic smoke. Crews undergoing training are given objectives such as the location of a 'body' or

other simulated casualty, during which they must exercise all the safety and control features of breathing-set operation.

Specialist training

Firefighters must also learn how to deal with the nightmarish eventuality of a 'flashover', a situation where unburned gases suddenly ignite in a ball of fire. Two distinct forms of training have been developed for this. The first type burns carbonaceous materials (usually chip-board) in steel containers to create realistic fire, heat and smoke conditions that allow crews to both understand and experience real fire behaviour patterns. Unfortunately, these carbonaceous units take some time to set up and can only be used for one training burn at a time.

Gas-fired training simulator buildings have been introduced in recent years to provide readily repeatable 'hot-fire' training. These brick or steel structures incorporate a number of domestic scenarios designed to represent fires in a cooking pan, a settee, a television set and a bed, as well as a flashover facility. All the fires are controlled via a computer program linked to gas and temperature monitoring, and full ventilation in the event of an emergency shutdown. Such realistic but safe hot-fire training enables firefighters to learn how to recognize the early onset of a flashover and to perfect various water-cooling techniques to reduce their likelihood.

Another type of regular training is designed to hone extrication skills using heavy-duty cutting gear. Firefighters are often called to attend serious traffic and other types of accident to free trapped people speedily. Cars are often compacted in a crash, so releasing people involves cutting off car roofs, removing steering columns and taking apart sections of bodywork, often alongside a paramedic. The training involves working together as a team as quickly as possible and without causing the casualty any further distress.

Once qualified, a firefighter's career path can lead towards promotion via examinations in conjunction with suitable experience, making it possible for young professional recruits to aspire to the very highest ranks in the service. They can acquire further specialist skills such as driving, aerial ladder operation, fire safety, forensic fire investigation and line-rescue qualifications. Fire service drivers are trained to handle heavy vehicles while travelling at considerable speeds to an emergency. They need a high level of awareness and anticipation in all traffic and weather conditions on a variety

■ ABOVE LEFT *Line rescue training for urban firefighters includes rock climbing and abseiling sessions carried out on moorland cliffs and rock faces.*

■ ABOVE RIGHT *Shielded by the cooling protection of a water spray hose line, two recruit firefighters get close in to flames during a live fire training exercise in a gas-fired simulator.*

■ LEFT *Japanese firefighters undergo line rescue training involving traverses and descents from a variety of heights and positions.*

■ RIGHT *A USAF firefighter demonstrates the water flow through a hose line.*

of highways ranging from main network trunk routes through to the most narrow and twisting country lanes.

In rural and low-population areas, fire cover is provided mostly by part-time retained firefighters from the local community. These firemen live and work close to the fire station they serve. Recruits attend basic training, often spread over evenings and weekends. Working with hose lines, pumps and ladders they learn how to use the same equipment as that carried on professionally manned fire engines. On completion of their basic training, a recruit retainee officially joins the strength of the local fire station but continues to follow their normal occupation and lifestyle. When needed for a turnout, at any time of the day of night, they are called to the fire station by pager.

Firefighters attached to rural and country fire stations usually come together once a week for a continuation training session, which might involve a drill session using the pumps, ladders, breathing sets and other equipment carried on the fire engine. There is also the important task of equipment checks and routine maintenance. Every item of firefighting and rescue equipment must be in working order when it is taken from the fire engine locker at an incident – as someone's life may well depend upon it.

■ BELOW *New York recruit firefighters still have scaling/hook ladder training. Originally used to gain access into buildings from narrow alleyways, these ladders are rarely used operationally now, but the training helps to instil confidence in preparation for working at height.*

Fire brigades have a long and proud history of reliable service to the community at large, which, coupled with a high level of excitement, drama, action, and some excellent career prospects, contributes to making the work of a firefighter a very special calling. Full-time professionals and part-time firefighters throughout the world undoubtedly derive much job satisfaction from their work, a fact that is borne out by very low personnel wastage, with few firefighters leaving the service before their normal retirement date.

COMMUNICATIONS AND CALL-OUTS

■ ABOVE *London Fire Brigade switchboard and watchroom, c.1909, received all fire calls and despatched fire engines.*

Fire service control and communications centres are a vital, yet unseen, part of firefighting and rescue operations, for they handle every emergency call-out and the mobilization of each fire engine, and have the overall control of each incident, large or small. Taking advantage of the latest developments in new technology, they ensure a rapid response to any type of situation – a far cry from the early days of horse-drawn manual pumps when a fire engine's turnout speed was likely to be dictated by the availability of the nearest borrowed horse.

When fire brigades were first established in the eighteenth century, the only way to call out a fire engine was for a member of the public to run or ride to the fire station and alert the crew. Many brigades installed a large brass bell outside the station for raising the alarm. During the nineteenth century, a bugle call proved a popular method of calling nearby volunteer firefighters to the fire station to man the pump. The arrival of street fire alarms and the electric telegraph greatly speeded up call-out times.

In the mid-twentieth century the widespread use of radio for fire service operations was in its infancy. The state of fire service communications technology at that time can be illustrated by a brief historical reflection from the intense 1940–1 London Blitz of World War II. During this period of continual enemy air raids, all the mobilizing activity to send pumping fire engines to the thousands of separate fire incidents each day and night was done manually by the control centre's fire service operators, using written messages and tallies on boards to represent fire engines. Most of the urgent operational messages between the local commanders at major fires and the central control rooms were carried by teams of motorcycle despatch riders, who managed to keep going even while the bombs were falling.

In modern fire departments around the world the development of computers and communications technology in the late twentieth century led progressively to the centralization of emergency-call handling in control centres that were far removed from the noise and drama of front-line firefighting operations. When an

■ BELOW *In Japan motorcycles are used for communications duties at earthquake incidents.*

■ LEFT *Before sounding this street alarm, a woman uses her shoe to break the protective glass covering c.1920. The alarm triggered a panel in the nearest fire station giving the location of the alarm point.*

emergency incident occurs, the fire brigade is alerted after a member of the public calls the national emergency number using the public telephone network or a mobile phone. The call is quickly routed via the public telephone network to a fire brigade operator at the fire control centre for that particular area. The operator is trained to calm the caller, if necessary, and obtain a clear address or location for the incident, together with the caller's phone number. Meanwhile, the network operator monitors the conversation to check that a complete address is given. In the case of a distressed caller hanging up before giving complete details, the operator can trace the call and pinpoint the caller's address or location.

The control operator keys all the call information into the computer system as the caller is speaking. The system immediately identifies the nearest available fire engine to respond to the call and the precise fire-risk category of the address. When the location is a factory or large warehouse, the response will involve several fire engines, usually including an aerial ladder. A single pump would be despatched to a rural property. Within seconds, the call-out order is sent to the relevant fire station's printer giving the precise location of the incident and the type of premises believed to be involved. Some mobilizing systems also provide vital information such as basic details of a building's layout, the location of the nearest street hydrants and the presence of special risks, such as chemicals or hazardous materials. In some brigades, the address information is broadcast throughout the fire station as the crew turn out.

In a permanently manned station the crew can be on the way to the fire or emergency within a minute of a call being received at the control centre many miles away. When a call is to a rural or country fire station, central control activates the personal pagers, or alerters, of the retained firefighters, who live and work near the station. They will immediately dash to the fire station and be on their way within several minutes. As the crew turn out, the crew commander acknowledges acceptance of the

■ BELOW *An operator takes an emergency call, on an old-fashioned switchboard, at a centralized fire control centre.*

■ LEFT *The fire brigade mobilizing and control centre despatches and monitors all fire engines in a city. Such centres can co-ordinate their activities with other emergency services, such as police and ambulance.*

call, by either sending a radio message or using on-board push-button technology. Staff at the control centre continue to monitor an incident through to its conclusion. All radio traffic comes to control via a direct radio link with the mobile control centre at the scene of an incident. If upon arrival at a scene the first crew are confronted with a major fire or accident situation, they immediately request assistance and further fire engines will be despatched to the scene. At this point the control centre operators assess the reduced overall fire cover for the area and, if necessary, order distant unaffected crews to temporarily cover depleted fire stations. If the original incident continues to develop, control will mobilize any further urgent requests for equipment, such as extra breathing sets, floodlighting, foam, heavy lifting gear, refreshments and, once the incident is under control, relief crews. Control centre operators also liaise with their opposite numbers in the police and paramedic control centres, so that each service is aware of the various incidents occurring, and which might at any time need a tri-service response.

■ BELOW *All brigades in industrialized countries, including smaller regional ones, have computerized call-handling and mobilizing centres to guarantee a fast and efficient response to all emergencies.*

Revolutionary developments

Recent radio developments have revolutionized fire service operations. All crew members are equipped with a personal radio so they can stay in touch with each other at the scene. At a major incident, the multiple channels of these radios allow the mobile control unit to speak to the commanders of the various sectors of the fire and to other firefighters at work across the site. Radio links are also essential for relaying critical information at speed. When an emergency involves an identified hazardous chemical, for example, control immediately accesses a special database to obtain priority information on the substance. This data is then relayed via a radio link to the printer on board the mobile control centre at the scene, enabling the officer in charge to ensure the firefighters adopt correct and safe procedures for dealing with the chemical concerned.

Many large and busy fire brigades use a series of coded radio messages to cover a range of particular operational requests and situations. This shortens the transmission time and reduces the overall radio traffic, which can be critical when a number of fire engines are deployed at fires and emergencies at different locations at the same time.

■ BELOW *Officers inside a command support unit from the Northern Ireland Fire and Rescue Service use remote cameras and computers during a major incident to coordinate activities.*

HAMPSHIRE FIRE & RESCUE SERVICE
Hampshire County Council
VOLVO
Angloco
FL6
INTERCOOLER
L81 RTP

SECTION TWO

THE A–Z OF FIRE ENGINE MANUFACTURERS

The following section identifies most of the world's major fire engine manufacturers. It would be impossible to include every manufacturer that has ever existed, but here is a sample of those that have shaped the design and engineering of the modern fire engine, whether it is a pumper, aerial ladder or specialist rescue tender.

This section also illustrates something of the design development over the years. Today, few fire engine manufacturers produce a complete fire and rescue vehicle. Most brigades select a suitably modified commercial chassis/cab upon which a specialist bodybuilding company designs and fabricates the bodywork, together with fire engineering and other fittings necessary for a particular operational use.

■ OPPOSITE *This 1994 Volvo FL10/Angloco/Metz DLK 30m/98.4ft turntable ladder of Hampshire Fire and Rescue Service, England, negotiates a low arch leading into Winchester Cathedral.*

■ LEFT *A 2001 International/Australian Fire Company emergency response/pumper unit of the Australian Fire Service.*

AEC

A major British manufacturer of bus, coach and lorry chassis, the Associated Equipment Company (AEC) began to produce fire engine chassis before World War II, and its fire engines saw front-line service in commonwealth countries for almost 50 years. The AEC Regal, Regent and Mercury chassis were used extensively, in conjunction with several bodybuilders, to produce various fire engines, including pumping engines, or pumps, turntable ladders, hydraulic platforms and emergency tenders. During the later years of production, a range of specials were built, including foam tenders, control units, heavy rescue units and prime movers.

Some early AECs utilized a Meadows 9.5-litre petrol engine, although the heavy-duty Mercury chassis, which first appeared in 1953, was powered by the AEC AV 470 diesel engine. At that time AEC pumps were generally put on the Regent chassis, a popular bus and coach chassis. In the 1960s the TGM, a restyled chassis that incorporated a tilt cab, was introduced, making AEC fire engines among the first fire service vehicles to have this innovative facility.

AEC MERCURY TURNTABLE LADDER	
Year	1965
Engine	AEC AV 470 diesel
Power	9.6-litre
Transmission	5-speed manual
Features	Merryweather ladder

■ ABOVE *This 1952 AEC Regent/Merryweather pump escape served in Wales.*

■ ABOVE *A 1967 AEC Marquis Seven pump before delivery to Leicester City Fire Brigade, England.*

■ BELOW *A wooden extension ladder formed part of the equipment of this 1966 AEC Mercury/Merryweather foam tender.*

AEC is probably best remembered in the fire engine arena for being fitted with various turntable ladders and hydraulic platforms. Merryweather turntable ladders consisted of four steel sections with a maximum 30m/100ft extension. Early AEC/Merryweather turntable ladders utilized a power take-off to drive mechanically the various evolutions of the ladder, along with a manual jacking system. Merryweather introduced hydraulic power to its turntable ladders in 1957, enabling the operator to sit at a rear-mounted control console on the rotating turntable turret. The jacking system was also hydraulically powered. Later AEC turntable ladder vehicles incorporated a 1,600-litres/350-gallons-per-minute pump to supply an

■ RIGHT *A 1965 AEC Mercury/HCB Angus/Simon SS70 hydraulic platform belonging to Lincolnshire Fire Brigade, England, stands at the ready.*

independent firefighting water supply when the ladder was in use as a water tower.

The first hydraulic platform to be built on an AEC chassis arrived at Glasgow Fire Service, in Scotland, in 1960. It utilized a set of Simon SS model booms to provide a maximum working height of 20m/65ft and was one of a new breed of aerial fire engines that inspired the steady development and wider use of hydraulic platforms by the fire service.

Pumping fire engines using the AEC Regent chassis were used by a variety of bodybuilders to suit the needs of particular fire brigades. In 1961, for instance, London Fire Brigade introduced 11 dual-purpose Marquis pumps bodied by both Merryweather and Carmichael. In service these engines could be configured to run either as pump escapes (carrying a 15m/50ft wheeled escape ladder) or simply as pumps with a 10m/35ft extension ladder. Rear or transverse high-output pump options were available on AEC fire engines, usually with an integral 450-litre/100-gallon water tank.

AEC became part of the Leyland conglomerate in 1962 and by the early 1970s the AEC name had ceased to appear on fire engines.

AHRENS-FOX

■ RIGHT *A front-mounted pump and air vessel are typical features of the 1928 Ahrens-Fox NS4 pumper.*

Founded in 1908, in Cincinnati, USA, Ahrens-Fox was one of the earliest American manufacturers of motorized fire engines. It built a petrol-engine pumper in 1911 and devised its first aerial ladder in 1923.

Ahrens-Fox fire engines had a reputation for being extremely well engineered and they carried front-mounted pumps with prominent capacious air vessels. In the late 1930s the company produced some innovative, semi-streamlined enclosed-cab pumpers. Although it went into liquidation in 1936, it continued to build fire engines to special order into the 1970s during which several commercial rescue attempts were made.

In 2017, the Ahrens-Fox brand was licensed to HME, and appears on premium HME Ahrens-Fox fire-trucks, incorporating touch-screen control technology and other cutting-edge features.

■ LEFT *This 2020 HAF104P aerial is based on an HME Ahrens-Fox Spectre custom chassis and is fitted with a 32m/104ft four-section rear-mount steel ladder with smart platform.*

M-TYPE PUMPER

Year	1927
Engine	6-cylinder petrol
Power	55hp
Transmission	4-speed manual
Features	4-cylinder fire pump

ALBION

■ LEFT *An Albion pump, c.1935, built with an unusual forward control cab arrangement. Note the top-mounted hose reel drum.*

The Albion Motor Car Company first built fire engines at its factory in Glasgow, Scotland, in 1903. These early models, based on the Albion car chassis of that time, were designed as hose cars, sometimes with a chemical engine to provide a basic hose reel water supply. The company was one of the first manufacturers, in the 1920s, to use a shaft drive to the rear wheels. Over the next 50 years Albions went into service in several British fire brigades, mostly as pumps, and a number were supplied to countries as far away as Australia. Albion continued to build fire engines for use in Britain after World War II. Including water tenders or dual-purpose pumps, emergency tenders, foam tenders and salvage units, these engines utilized the Albion CX/Chieftain/ Claymore and Clydesdale chassis fitted mostly with 6.5-litre Leyland diesel engines, often with Carmichael bodywork.

By 1972, when Albion became part of the Leyland Motors Group, it had faded from the fire engine scene, although several of its fire engines remained in active service until 1988.

FT PUMP	
Year	1928
Engine	4-cylinder petrol
Power	70bhp
Transmission	4-speed manual
Features	Braidwood body

ALEXANDER PERRIE

Founded in 1946, and based in New South Wales, Australia, Alexander Perrie manufactured several hundred fire engines of various types for operational service in the New South Wales Brigade and the Northern Territory Fire Brigades, as well as for the Australian military services.

Typical of the Alexander Perrie pumpers of the 1970s and 1980s were the batch built on International 1810D chassis for New South Wales Fire Brigade. These were fitted with a Godiva 3,400 litres/750 gallons per minute rear-mounted pump and an 1,800-litre/400-gallon water tank. A number of this series of pumpers were configured to carry hydraulic rescue equipment.

Since 1984, the company has been the Australian distributor for Bronto Skylift aerial platforms, and the company later completed the fitting out of a specialized breathing apparatus and response semitrailer unit, again for New South Wales Fire Brigade. This fire engine is drawn by a Mercedes Actros 2643 6x4 with 430bhp engine and 15-speed transmission. The tractor has a sleeper cabin, and the trailer has a fully integrated and air-conditioned fibreglass body, a three-phase 240-volt power supply and cylinder-recharging equipment.

Today, the company specializes in the design and production of specialist vehicle bodies and the supply of fire-fighting equipment and spares, in addition to the ongoing distribution of Bronto vehicles.

■ ABOVE *Fitted with rear-mounted Godiva 3,400-litres/750-gallons-per-minute pump and 1,800-litre/400-gallon tank, this 1986 pumper also carries rescue equipment.*

ALFRED MILES

■ RIGHT *This 1950 Commer QX/Alfred Miles emergency tender once served in Bootle, England.*

This bodybuilding company was based in Cheltenham, England, and in the post-World War II period bodied a number of water tenders for rural fire brigades in the UK. Much of the work was based on Commer and Bedford chassis and adopted a style involving folding doors to the rear crew compartment, two transverse lockers and a low-level hose reel on each side of the fire engine. A rear-mounted 2,270-litres/500-gallons-per-minute pump was fed by an 1,800-litre/400-gallon water tank. Alfred Miles water tenders could be adapted for dual-purpose use, carrying either a 10m/35ft extension ladder or a 15m/50ft wheeled escape ladder.

■ LEFT *This Dennis F8/Alfred Miles water tender was produced in 1952.*

COMMER QX WATER TENDER	
Year	1954
Engine	3-cylinder 2-stroke diesel
Power	4.75-litre
Transmission	4-speed manual
Features	folding doors to rear cab

ALVIS

Having successfully produced a number of military vehicles and armoured cars through the 1920s and 1930s, Alvis Ltd of Coventry, England, developed this activity to embrace the manufacture of a number of airfield fire and rescue vehicles. These included powerful foam and crash tenders, all with 6x6 cross-country capability. A 1959 Alvis fire engine was built as an amphibious airfield fire tender for the Royal Ceylon Air Force. Like most of the Alvis range, it was powered by a Rolls-Royce B81 240bhp, 6-cylinder engine, with foam equipment supplied by the Pyrene company. Many Alvis 6x6 airfield foam tenders went into service with the Royal Air Force Fire Service in the 1950s.

ALVIS/PYRENE MK 6 CRASH TENDER	
Year	1954
Engine	R-R B81 8-cylinder petrol
Power	240bhp
Transmission	manual preselector
Features	Salamander chassis style

■ BELOW *Over 80 1954 model 6x6 Alvis/Pyrene military airfield crash tenders were delivered to Britain's Royal Air Force during the 1950s.*

AMERICAN LAFRANCE

American LaFrance was formed in 1903 out of various mergers of a number of earlier fire engine builders, one of which was the LaFrance Company, originally founded in 1873 as a steam engine manufacturer.

At first the company produced only horse-drawn steam pumps, but in 1910 it built its first petrol-powered fire vehicle in the form of a combination hose car. In addition to on-board seating for six firemen, the car carried lengths of ready-coupled hose, ready to run out at the scene of a fire. This Type 5, as the vehicle became known, had a Simplex 4-cylinder engine that drove the rear axle using a chain drive.

Before long American LaFrance virtually ceased building steam pumps in order to concentrate on motor-driven fire engines, and by 1916 had a catalogue of models, the most powerful of which was a pumper with an impressive firefighting water output of 4,500 litres/1,000 gallons per minute. The pumpers continued to be developed over the next two decades and the arrival of the V12 240bhp engine in 1931 allowed for even greater pumping capacity. With high-rise buildings getting taller in the USA, American LaFrance produced a super pumper in 1937 that could output 13,500 litres/3,000 gallons per minute through multiple hose manifolds.

■ LEFT *Gridley Fire Department in California, USA, formerly owned this preserved 1926 American LaFrance pumper.*

■ LEFT *Cranston Heights Fire Company, USA, owned this white 1931 pumper.*

■ BELOW LEFT *This 2002 FL80 pumper/aerial ladder was delivered to British Columbia, Canada.*

In 1929, American LaFrance was the first manufacturer to provide all-wheel braking on its fire engines. Towards the end of World War II, it introduced an innovative forward-control all-enclosed cab on its new 700 series model. Powered by an American LaFrance V12 petrol engine and with a 6,750litre/1,500-gallon fire pump, this highly successful vehicle soon set the post-war style in American pumping fire engines.

In 1973 American LaFrance introduced its first custom-built pumpers, entitled the Century series, a number of which went into service with the New York Fire Department. With an empty vehicle weight of 10.2 tons, the range came with a five-man cab and a Detroit Diesel V6 350bhp power unit

■ RIGHT *A full set of leather fire helmets sets off this well-preserved 1948 American LaFrance heavy pumper.*

■ ABOVE *Domestic pumps, such as this American LaFrance 1981 Century Model, are used to support airport foam tenders.*

driving through an Allison automatic transmission. All were available with pumping capacity options of 4,500–9,000 litres/1,000–2,000 gallons per minute. In order to provide a budget-price option, the company also built the Challenger and Conquest pumper models on other makes of commercial chassis.

From its earliest days American LaFrance was an innovative builder of aerial ladders, and by World War II had supplied well over 1,500 aerial fire engines. Since then, the Water Chief and Ladder Chief ranges, with 23m/75ft and 30m/100ft ladder options, have been very successful.

Over the years, American LaFrance went through several changes of ownership, including becoming a subsidiary of Freightliner from 1995 to 2005, before the company eventually hit financial problems and scaled back operations in the late 2000s. The company eventually ceased trading in early 2014.

■ ABOVE *This 1999 American LaFrance 148 RR/HUB pumper is currently in service with North Vancouver City Fire Department, in British Columbia, Canada.*

■ BELOW *The City of Seattle Fire Department, in Washington State, USA, runs this immaculate 1999 American LaFrance Becker mid-mount 32m/105ft rear-steer aerial ladder.*

ANDERSON'S ENGINEERING

Based at Langley, British Columbia, near Vancouver, Canada, Anderson's Engineering Ltd was formed in 1972 for the manufacture of custom-built fire engines. The company soon earned a reputation as a quality bodybuilder, able to supply a range of reliable pumpers, mini-pumpers, tankers, aerial ladders and platforms, rescue units, and various other tenders.

Anderson's early sales were to western Canadian fire brigades but their fire engines soon started to appear right across Canada and then overseas in countries such as Chile, Saudi Arabia, Guam and Indonesia. By the early 1980s Anderson's fire trucks were also being purchased by several American fire departments.

In 1986, Bronto Skylift entered into an agreement to allow Anderson to mount the Bronto aerial platform ladder range on various commercial chassis with Anderson bodywork. The first of these Anderson/Bronto aerials were mounted on International chassis. Later five Bronto 52m/170ft aerials mounted on Pacific 4-axle chassis were delivered to Montreal Fire Brigade. At the time, these were the tallest aerials anywhere in North America.

■ LEFT *Far from its Canadian place of manufacture, this 1995 Anderson Western Star 4x4 pumper provides firefighting and rescue cover at the Placer Dome Mine, in Zaldivar, Chile.*

■ BELOW LEFT *Sidney Fire Department, in British Columbia, Canada, run this 1994 FL80 Anderson long-wheelbase pumper. This fire engine carries a 2,270-litre/500-gallon water tank and has an output of 4,725 litres/1,045 gallons per minute.*

■ RIGHT *Designed for use in petrochemical installations, this 1982 Anderson foam tender is seen here in service at Shell Oil's Shellburn Refinery, Burnaby, British Columbia, Canada.*

■ BELOW *A 1994 Anderson/Duplex 6x4 33m/110ft rear-mount aerial ladder incorporates a considerable amount of equipment storage space.*

Following the acquisition of Bronto in 1995 by the group that owned Emergency One, Anderson's forged a new alliance with Smeal to mount and body its aerial ladders, subsequently delivering a number of these fire engines across Canada. However, despite a successful 28-year trading period, Anderson's suffered financially in early 2000, and they never recovered. The company finally closed its fire engine plant in November of the same year.

ANGLOCO

Originating in 1965, Angloco built its first fire appliance in 1974 and is the longest-established British company designing and manufacturing firefighting and rescue vehicles.

The independent company, headquartered in Yorkshire, England, produces an extensive range of specialist and conventional appliances for UK and international Fire and Rescue Services, supplying to over 70 countries including in the Caribbean, Middle East, Africa and Asia regions. Vehicles are based on commercial chassis from the likes of Scania, Volvo, MAN, Iveco, Toyota, and Mercedes-Benz. Customers include airports, oil refineries, municipal and civil defence services, industrial companies, and defence forces.

Export projects have included Scania-based vehicles for petrochemical sites in Qatar, a Mercedes-Benz based 4x4 Emergency Tender for Trinidad and Tobago, and a Toyota-based first response vehicle for Ghana. Recent significant production includes conventional pumping appliances, first response vehicles, and specialist Airport Rescue and Fire-Fighting Vehicles.

■ RIGHT *A 2012 Angloco Emergency Tender manufactured on a Mercedes-Benz Atego 4x4 for Trinidad & Tobago Fire Service.*

■ ABOVE *This 2020 ARFFV on a Scania 6x6 was part of a contract for over 80 new Angloco firefighting vehicles for the UK Ministry of Defence.*

AUSTIN

■ LEFT *This 1959 HCB/Angus bodied Austin FFK foam/salvage tender remained operational until 1974. It carried an aluminium extension ladder, roof-mounted searchlights and amber warning lights.*

Already well established as a major British car and commercial vehicle manufacturer in the 1930s, Austin entered the fire engine scene in a big way in 1939. With war clouds gathering over Europe, it produced large numbers of government utility fire engines for the wartime auxiliary fire service, subsequently known as the National Fire Service. The two chassis cab models involved were the K2 and K4. The 2 or 3-ton/2,036 or 3,054kg K2 version came as a towing vehicle designed to carry a five-man crew and pull a trailer pump. The larger 5-ton/5,090kg K4 model was built either as a five-man crew heavy pump capable of delivering 2,270 litres/ 500 gallons of water per minute, or as a hand-operated 18m/60ft turntable ladder. The steel K4 turntable ladder consisted of three extending sections made by Merryweather. These fire engines carried a crew of three and some were also fitted with front-mounted pumps. A number of all these wartime versions survived into post-war operational service with many being retired only in the 1960s, and a few have been preserved in working order in the UK. In 1959, Austin produced their 4x4 jeep-style Gipsy chassis, which a number of rural fire brigades used as a lightweight fire engine.

AUSTRAL

■ LEFT *The Caterpillar 3116 turbocharged diesel engine of this Firepac 3000 series fire engine is incorporated into the general Firepac features of automatic transmission, integral frame and air suspension. The vehicle's Rosenbauer NH30 pump can be either midship or rear-mounted.*

■ ABOVE *In 1996, New South Wales took delivery of four pumpless Firepacs, built on a slightly longer than standard wheelbase and with a powerful diesel engine. They were painted in experimental colours.*

While it was in existence, this Australian enterprise constructed a number of fire engines for the domestic market. These were built either on Austral's own chassis designs or those of various commercial manufacturers.

Austral's principal fire chassis was the Firepac, which came in two versions – the smaller 3000 and the heavier 4000. The pumper versions of these two models were constructed with Caterpillar turbocharged diesel engines, automatic transmission and Rosenbauer pumps. They also had air suspension as a standard feature. A number of Firepacs went into service in the states of Queensland and New South Wales. In the latter, they were also used operationally as hazardous material and rescue/salvage tenders.

In addition to pumpers, Austral manufactured a number of aerials for the Australian market. Among these were two Simon 40m/130ft aerial ladder platforms mounted on a Scania P113H-360, 8x4 chassis. This unique pair of vehicles was delivered to the fire department of Queensland.

When Austral was acquired by Varley in the late 1990s, the Firepac model was used as a basis for further development and it eventually reappeared as the 4-door Varley Commander.

■ BELOW *Some Austral fire appliances were built on proprietary chassis. This is one of two identical aerials, the only two of this type in Australia, built with a Simon ALP340 40m/130ft platform on a Scania P113H 8x4 chassis.*

AUSTRALIAN FIRE COMPANY

The origins of this Australian company go back to the dissolution of the Carey Gulley Engineering firm. The newly formed, privately owned Australian Fire Company initially took over the existing factory site before moving to its own headquarters base in Gepps Cross, South Australia.

The range of Australian Fire Company fire engines included small quick attack pumpers, heavy-duty pumpers, aerials and rescue tenders. Imported fire equipment included pumps from WS Darley, and aerial ladders from Metz, Snorkel and Bronto.

The company's fire engines are in service across Australia. The range includes the largest fleet of Freightliner fire engines, used by the Melbourne brigade. Other chassis used include the Scania G94 series, in various pumper guises in New South Wales and Canberra. In 1998 a Scania 113H with a Bronto F37HDT aerial ladder platform was delivered to Melbourne.

During 1998–99, the company fulfilled a contract for 26 crash tenders built on Emergency One HPR 4x4 chassis for the Australian military. Delivered in kit form, these were assembled with an Australian Fire Company aluminium body.

In 2000, the company, along with its designs and manufacturing styles, was acquired by the Skilled Equipment Manufacturing Company.

■ LEFT *Australian Fire Company's first 4-Series Scania fire appliance was delivered in 1998 to the Australian Capital Territory Fire Brigade.*

■ ABOVE *Victoria's Country Fire Authority has a trio of Telesquirt appliances in service. This Frankston-based 1998 example is typical, with a 5,000 litres/1,000 gallons per minute Darley pump and 1,800-litre/400-gallon water tank.*

■ RIGHT *Transfield Fire Service provides contracted fire protection to the Royal Australian Air Force. The Edinburgh base, in South Australia, has two of these Category 4 units in service to complement the Austral Crash Fire Rescue units also stationed there. Firefighting equipment consists of a Hatz/Darley pump, a 2,500-litre/550-gallon water tank, a 300-litre/66-gallon foam tank and a Feecon monitor.*

AVIA

After World War II, a number of Czechoslovakian pumping fire engines were built on the locally produced Avia chassis. Many of these were configured as light pumps, using the A30 2.68m/105in short wheelbase chassis powered by a 80bhp diesel engine. These were unusual in having an eight-man crew cab on a light fire engine, with a weight of a little over 5 tons. These lightweight fire engines carried a portable fire pump, a short extension ladder and a modest range of firefighting equipment.

■ RIGHT *This Deutz/Avia light pumping unit is pictured in service in the Spanish resort of Mallorca.*

LIGHT PUMP

Year	1965
Engine	4-cylinder petrol
Power	80bhp
Transmission	4-speed manual
Features	7-man crew cab

OTHER MAKES

■ 1ST ATTACK ENGINEERING INC
1st Attack Engineering Inc was formed in 1999 by Jeffrey Cook, who saw a requirement for high-mobility firefighting vehicles for use in off-road and brush locations He built his first fire-truck conversion in 1995, and since then the company has produced a range of custom vehicles for fire departments throughout the US, from the Fast Attack, based on a variety of pick-up chassis, to the M.E.R.V. (Mini Emergency Response Vehicle) based on a Kawasaki quad.

■ 4 GUYS
The 4-Guys business was started in Meyersdale, Pennsylvania, by four friends who began building stainless-steel milk tankers in 1974. They soon began building fire apparatus, initially elliptical tankers, followed by pumpers and rescue trucks for customers throughout the Eastern US. Pumpers (based on Spartan or HME chassis) and commercial pumpers (based on Freightliner, International and Kenworth chassis) made up over half of the company's output (around two vehicles per week) in 2019.

■ ALEXIS FIRE EQUIPMENT COMPANY
The Alexis Fire Equipment was founded by Gene Morris in 1947, in Alexis, Illinois. Serving the US Mid-West, the company expanded rapidly in the 1960s and '70s, before offering servicing support as well as manufacturing from the 1980s. Today, the company produces custom-build fire trucks, including tankers, pumpers, aerials, command units and rescue vehicles, based on a range of chassis with both aluminium and stainless-steel bodies. Alexis provides servicing, repair and refurbishment support for all types of fire trucks.

■ AMERICAN FIRE ENGINE COMPANY
The American Fire Engine Company had its origins in Seneca Falls, Elmira, New York State, in 1891, and in 1900 amalgamated with four other significant independent manufacturers of manual and steam pumping fire engines (Ahrens, Button, Clapp & Thomas, and Silsby) to form the International Fire Engine Company. In 1903 it changed its name to American LaFrance Fire Engine Company.

■ AMOSKEAG
The Amoskeag Manufacturing Company of Manchester, New Hampshire, USA, was one of the first American builders of steam-driven pumpers, and its fire engines were in service in New York as early as 1860.

It quickly became one of the more successful American manufacturers, supplying a large number of steam pumpers to some of the largest city fire departments from coast to coast. In 1863 Amoskeag took two of its latest models to the Crystal Palace Fire Engine Trials in London, England. American steamers tended to be more heavily engineered than British versions and both performed impressively.

In 1876, Amoskeag built the first successful self-propelled steam fire engine and thereafter continued to develop this type of vehicle, constructing a number of huge and technically advanced engines. The rear-driven axle of some later Amoskeag steamers incorporated a differential to help maneouvre the heavy vehicle round tight corners.

BARIBBI

Formed in 1929, Baribbi supplied most of the fire engines used in Italy until the early 1980s. The company had three factories, and at its peak was producing 300 vehicles per year, around half going to export customers. Baribbi built vehicles on OM/Fiat, and later IVECO chassis. The company built water tenders, tankers and airport foam/crash tenders. Some of their larger airport fire engines use a heavyweight 6x6 OM/Fiat chassis to carry an 11,000-litre/2,420-gallon water tank and 1,500 litres/330 gallons of foam concentrate. These Squalo (Shark) series vehicles had an all-up operational weight of just over 32 tons and were provided with a tilt cab. In 1992 Baribbi was acquired by Magirus.

AIRPORT FOAM TENDER

Year	1974
Engine	V8 diesel
Power	300bhp
Transmission	manual
Features	6x6

■ ABOVE *A c.1992 Scania/Baribbi emergency tender showing locker space and use of the roof for equipment storage.*

BEDFORD

By the early 1930s Bedford was producing several chassis suitable for fire brigade use at the Vauxhall Motors plant in Luton, England. A number of the smallest of these, a 2-ton/2,030kg truck chassis with a 3.2-litre, 6-cylinder petrol engine, had gone into service as pumping fire engines or hose carriers.

After World War II, Bedford chassis were used extensively for British fire engines as both pumps and turntable ladders, and a number were being exported to other countries. The 5- and 7-ton S and SB models were particularly popular during the early 1950s. Birmingham Fire & Ambulance Service set the standard when they commissioned 27 pump escapes built on the 3.2m/126in shortened SB coach chassis. This ran with a 15m/50ft wheeled escape ladder, a 450-litre/100-gallon water tank and a 2,270-litres/500-gallons-per-minute water pump.

■ BELOW *Horsham Fire Brigade, England, ran this c.1934 Bedford pump.*

BEDFORD (CONT)

■ BELOW *Peterborough Volunteer Fire Brigade, one of the oldest volunteer brigades in Britain, originally ran this late 1960s Bedford R series 4x4 pump.*

■ ABOVE *This 1951 Bedford pump escape was built on a shortened SB chassis.*

■ BELOW *1960s Bedford fire engines – a 1962 Magirus turntable ladder, a pump and a hose rescue tender – once served in New Zealand.*

■ BOTTOM *Bedford Green Goddess fire engines were commissioned by the British Government in 1953 as reserve pumps.*

BEDFORD TK/HCB ANGUS	
Year	1966
Engine	6-cylinder petrol
Power	176bhp
Transmission	4-speed automatic
Features	Rolls-Royce B61 engine

As part of an expanded civil defence programme, in 1953 the British government ordered hundreds of reserve fire engines for use by the Auxiliary Fire Service that then operated throughout the UK. These pumping and specialist fire engines were built on the Bedford S series chassis and finished in green livery. They used the Bedford 6-cylinder 4.9-litre petrol engine, and were fitted with an 1,800-litre/400-gallon water tank, a 4,500-litre/1,000-gallon pump and a 10m/35ft extension ladder. A significant number of these Green Goddesses, as they came to be known, have survived in an updated form into the twenty-first century for use as reserve fire engines.

During the 1960s and 1970s a wide range of Bedford chassis types, including the B, R, TJ, TK, TKL, TKEL and KGS series among a number of other Bedford models, were being used for hundreds of fire engine applications. These ranged from the 2-ton TJ to a 16-ton version of the TK. Later Bedford fire engines used Perkins and Cummins diesel engines. Although production ceased in 1988, many Bedford fire engines are still in service in various parts of the world.

■ BELOW *A Bedford TK pump escape stands at the ready at St Albans Fire Station, England, in the mid-1960s.*

■ BENEATH *Seen at a rally, this preserved 1968 TK Bedford water tender served in Hampshire Fire Brigade, England.*

■ BELOW *A number of 1972 Bedford/HCB Angus pumps were finished in yellow livery. This one was used in Coventry, England.*

■ BENEATH *This Bedford TK pump formed part of the fire engine fleet of the Malta Fire Service.*

■ ABOVE *This 1958 Bedford water tender is seen here shortly before it entered service with Fife Fire Brigade, Scotland.*

■ RIGHT *The New Zealand Fire Service took delivery of this new 30m/100ft Bedford/Magirus turntable ladder in 1962.*

Bickle Seagrave/King Seagrave

This Canadian company's involvement with fire engines dates back to 1906 when R S Bickle began to manufacture hand and horse-drawn chemical carts, before moving on to develop motor-powered fire engines around 1915. In that year, a move to Woodstock, Ontario, saw the founding of the Bickle Fire Engine Company.

In 1923, Bickle made an agreement with the Ahrens-Fox Fire Engine Company of Ohio, USA, to build their fire engines for the Canadian market. For almost ten years, Bickle used Ahrens-Fox chassis and some body parts for their fire engines and these bore the name *The Canadian Ahrens-Fox*. In 1924, the company moved to newer and larger premises in Woodstock and from 1928 began to build customized pumpers around a four-model range. The chassis choice for fire chiefs included Ford, Chevrolet, Packard, and American LaFrance.

Following enquiries from Montreal and Quebec City Fire Departments in the late 1920s for short-wheelbase aerial ladders, RS Bickle came to a commercial arrangement with the Magirus company of Ulm, Germany, a

■ TOP *A 1978 Scot 6x4 Fire King 16.7m/55ft Snorkel of Revelstoke Fire Department, British Columbia, with 4,767l/1,050gpm midships mounted pump.*

■ ABOVE *This 1966 GMC/King Seagrave pumper has a 2,837 litre/625gpm pump and 2,724-litre/600-gallon water tank.*

■ LEFT *Crowsnest Pass Fire Department, Blairmore. Alberta, run this 1974 Ford C900 6x4 Fire King 26m/85ft Snorkel. It has a 4,767l/1,050 gpm midships pump and 908-litre/200-gallon water tank.*

■ RIGHT *A 1982 International CO 1950B/King pumper of Esquimalt, British Columbia.*

■ BELOW RIGHT *A well preserved 1953 Bickle Seagrave light pump.*

prominent manufacturer of turntable ladders for European brigades. Under this agreement, Bickle imported the Magirus wooden ladder sections and built a number of Bickle/Magirus turntable ladders for Canadian fire brigades. These fire engines became the forerunners of rear-mount aerial ladders in North America. A further alliance in the early 1930s saw Bickle mounting new hydraulically operated wooden ladders built by Peter Pirsch & Sons of Kenosha, Wisconsin, USA.

However, in 1935 came a significant marriage between Bickle and the Seagrave Corporation of Columbus, Ohio, when Bickle took over the production of Seagrave fire engines for the whole of Canada. The name of the enlarged company was changed to Bickle Seagrave Ltd and before long it had become the largest fire engine builder in Canada, with a range that embraced most types of pumpers, rescue tenders and aerial ladders.

Following the death, in 1949, of the company founder, Robert Sydney Bickle the ownership of Bickle Seagrave passed through a number of hands. Following some difficult times, the company eventually ceased trading and closed down in 1956. At this stage, Vernon Bickle King, a nephew of the founder, stepped in. At that time, he had a successful truck and trailer business in Woodstock and purchased the manufacturing rights to the Bickle Seagrave company. Fire engine production resumed in May 1956 under the new name of King Seagrave. A new factory was opened nearby in 1962 and over the next few years, a steady flow of pumpers and hydraulic platforms were built. At the same time King Seagrave became the Canadian agent for American Snorkel aerials. By 1971, King Seagrave had a successful coast-to-coast operation with 475 employees.

However, with the acquisition of Seagrave by the FWD Corporation in the early 1970s, King Seagrave lost the exclusive right to market Seagrave fire engines in Canada. Recession in the early 1980s brought further difficulties. A change of ownership for the company preceded bankruptcy in 1984 and with it the end of two company names that between them had built fire engines for a large part of the Canadian fire service for almost 70 years. Mainly serving the domestic market, the company had also exported to several distant countries.

■ BELOW *This 1985 pumper has a 6,810 litres-/1,500 gallons-per- minute pump and 3,405-litre/750-gallon water tank.*

Brijbasi

With bases in New Delhi and Bombay, Brijbasi Hi-Tech Udyog Ltd manufactures a wide range of lightweight and heavy fire and rescue vehicles, based on a variety of chassis, including Tata, Mahindra and Leyland. The Brijbasi range includes first-strike units, water tenders, foam tenders and trailer-mounted, high-discharge foam and water monitors for use by various petro-chemical and industrial fire brigades.

WATER TENDER	
Year	1972
Engine	6-cylinder diesel
Power	180bhp
Transmission	manual
Features	2,270lpm/500gpm pump

■ RIGHT ***This Brijbasi Air Crash Fire Tender is based on a 6x6 Mercedes-Benz chassis and features a 10,000-litre/2,200-gallon water tank and 7,000-litre/1,550-gallon foam tank.***

Bronto

For over 40 years Bronto Skylift Oy Ab has been a leading manufacturer and innovator of high-rise firefighting vehicles, with both aerial ladder platforms and hydraulic platforms. The company, which has its headquarters in Tampere, Finland, was acquired in 1995 by the Federal Signal Corporation of America. Over 5,000 Bronto aerial fire engines can currently be found in operational service with fire brigades in more than 110 countries worldwide. Bronto firefighting aerial ladder platforms come in various height ranges from a basic F23 23m/75ft model to the staggering F88 at 88m/290ft, which has to be mounted on a heavy 5-axle chassis. A popular Bronto is the 28m/92ft aerial ladder platform (the 28-2TI model), which is in service in many city fire brigades and is often found mounted on the Volvo FL10 or the Scania G93M/P113H tandem-axle chassis. Bronto aerials also incorporate add-on features such as lighting, both at the ladder head and for the fireground, camera connections and rescue chutes.

■ LEFT ***A 1997 Emergency One Hurricane/Superior provides the 8x4 base for this 50m/165ft Bronto aerial platform. Belonging to Calgary Fire Department, Canada, it is one of the world's highest platforms.***

■ LEFT ***A Bronto Skylift F54HDT aerial platform fitted to a Scania chassis, used by the Corpo de Bombeiros do Paraná fire service in southern Brazil.***

BUFFALO

The Buffalo Fire Appliance Corporation was established in New York in 1895 to produce fire extinguishers and similar equipment. In 1922, the company built its first fire engine and from then on manufactured a range of pumpers, chemical trucks, and ladder trucks based on various commercial chassis types, even producing their own in 1928. Noted for its hand-forged metal bodywork, the Buffalo company had a reputation for stylish fire engines and produced some fine looking sedan-cab pumpers in the 1930s and 1940s. Factory output increased during World War II with up to 170 fire engines of various types being delivered. This was possible due to Buffalo's streamlined production facility which included two parallel lines – an innovation in fire engine production. Buffalo built their last fire engine in 1948 and from then on concentrated on manufacturing fire extinguishers.

■ ABOVE ***The straight bodyline of pre-war Buffalo fire engines is evident in this 1940 Buffalo Pathfinder pumper used by Winters Fire Department, California.***

TYPE III PUMPER

Year	1930
Engine	6-cylinder petrol
Power	70bhp
Transmission	4-speed manual
Features	Redesigned body

■ BELOW ***The deliveries of the midship-mounted pump of this restored 1931 Buffalo pumper protrude from beneath the front seats. The crew's uniforms and helmets await the call to action.***

■ RIGHT *A Boise rescue tender of Snohomish County Fire District, Arlington Heights, Washington, USA.*

OTHER MAKES

■ BAI

Founded in 1991, Italian company BAI (Brescia Antincendi International) has produced a range of firefighting and rescue vehicles based upon a number of commercial chassis such as Scania, Volvo and Mercedes. Constructed for municipal, airport, industrial and rural fire brigades, BAI fire engines include water tenders, foam tenders, aerial ladder platforms, airport fire tenders and forest-protection vehicles. For a brief period in the 2000s the company was owned by Oshkosh, but returned to Italian ownership in 2009. The company now has subsidiaries in Germany and China.

■ BELSIZE

A number of fire engines built during the early years of motorized fire engines used the chassis of the Belsize Motor Company of Manchester, England. These solidly constructed vehicles were capable of carrying 15m/50ft wooden wheeled escape ladders and had rear-mounted pumps. As early as 1912, the Belsize chassis was being used in conjunction with 18m/60ft wooden turntable ladders, some of which were operated using compressed carbon dioxide gas. By the early 1940s only a few Belsize fire engines remained.

■ BINZ

The Binz Coachworks company was formed by Michael Binz in 1936, in Lorch, Germany, and over the years has produced a wide range of specialist vehicles. More recently, the Binz vehicle list included fire service rescue and specialized fire engines, which were built both at Lorch and the company's second plant at Ilmenau.

Binz has sold fire vehicles on five continents, utilizing various short- to medium-wheelbase commercial chassis for their smaller fire service units, such as mobile command and control, and communication units. These included the Volkswagen T4 and LT, and the Mercedes Benz Sprinter series.

For the medium-size market, Binz has used commercial 7.5-tonne chassis, such as the Mercedes-Benz Atego or MAN, to produce mobile control units or respiratory/radiation protection tenders with plenty of working space capable of being either air-conditioned or heated, according to the season, at major and/or protracted operational incidents.

One of the largest of the Binz range of specialized fire engines was a tractor-drawn trailer, part of which incorporated a pushout extension when set up on site. This provided a 20sq m/22sq yd internal area from which strategy for major accidents and other serious incidents could be coordinated.

In 2012, the emergency-vehicle division of Binz was acquired by the RMA Group, and since then the company has concentrated on producing ambulances and small command and multi-use fire vehicles based on various van chassis.

■ BLANCHAT MANUFACTURING

Established in 1978 in Harper, Kansas, USA, Blanchat Manufacturing models include the Chaparral Brush Truck and Minuteman Rescue Truck series, plus the larger Patriot, all based on a variety of chassis.

■ BMC

The British Motor Corporation (BMC) was formed by the merger of the Austin and Morris motor companies in 1952. The new company produced a number of chassis types suitable for fire engine use. These included the LD 30cwt, which was used for vehicles like canteen vans and high expansion foam units, the 5-ton FG model, used as emergency tenders, through to the heavyweight 16-ton BMC Boxer. One of the latter went into operational use in 1970 for Staffordshire Fire Brigade, in the UK, as a 4x2 water carrier. It was capable of ferrying 4,500 litres/1,000 gallons of water to the scene of a rural fire where water resources were insufficient.

BMC became part of the Leyland Group in 1968 and within two years the BMC badge was no longer in use. The last operational BMC fire engine had been withdrawn from service by 1990.

■ BOISE MOBILE EQUIPMENT (BME)

Boise Mobile Equipment (BME) is an Idaho-based American build-to-order fire engine manufacturer. Its range of fire engines includes pumpers, rescue tenders, wildland fire trucks and a number of specialist fire and rescue vehicles for specific operational tasks.

BMEs truck designs are characterized by their tubular-frame body designs, produced in aluminium, galvanneal and stainless steel. The company has sold over 1,000 brush trucks specifically designed for fighting wildfires.

■ BRACO

Braco AS of Lierskogen, Norway, manufactures a range of fire and rescue tenders, providing a body structure and locker design to the precise specification of its customers, many of whom are Scandinavian fire brigades. With a choice of suitable commercial chassis, Braco's fire engine body superstructures are constructed of 100 per cent welded aluminium to withstand the extreme weather conditions of a northern climate.

Camiva

At one time amongst Europe's largest manufacturers of firefighting equipment, French manufacturer Camiva, was formed in 1971 by the merger of two vehicle-building concerns, Citroën-Berliet and Guinard. The company produced a wide range of fire engines, including various types of water tenders for urban and rural use, and airport and industrial foam tenders. It was one of the world's leading makers of turntable ladders, and Camiva's turntable ladders have been used by brigades requiring a compact high-rise vehicle for use in areas with restricted access. In 1997, Camiva became part of the IVECO-Magirus group.

■ ABOVE *This 1988 Camiva EPA 30m/100ft turntable ladder is mounted on a Dennis F127 chassis, with bodywork by John Dennis Coachbuilders.*

Carmichael

■ LEFT *A 1970 Carmichael-bodied Land Rover 4x4.*

■ BELOW *A 1987 Dennis RS135/ Carmichael breathing apparatus tender.*

Carmichael International was a British fire engine manufacturer and bodybuilder whose origins go back to the 1950s. The Carmichael works at Worcester, England, produced a very large number of fire vehicles, including water tenders, airport foam tenders, rescue tenders, turntable ladders and hydraulic platforms, for UK and overseas fire brigades. Carmichael proudly made the claim that it was the only UK company to produce a fully comprehensive range of firefighting vehicles. Seventy per cent of its production was exported to more than 80 countries around the world.

Over the years, Carmichael utilized a wide range of chassis types and makes in the construction of its fire engines. These included well established names such as AEC, Albion, Bedford, BMC, Commer, Dennis, Dodge, Ford, Land Rover and Leyland. In later years, in addition to Carmichael's own chassis, the list grew to include IVECO, Mercedes, Scania, Timoney and Volvo.

■ RIGHT *A Carmichael Cobra 2 airport fire tender in service with Cambridge City Airport in the UK.*

In 1972 Carmichael innovatively lengthened a Range Rover chassis at its factory by inserting an extra trailing axle to provide a 6x4 configuration. Powered by a 3.5-litre V8 petrol engine, this stretched Carmichael Range Rover proved especially suitable for road accident work on the UK's expanding motorway network. Over the next seven years 37 such vehicles, equipped with a front-mounted 900-litres/200-gallons-per-minute pump, went into service as fast-response emergency/rescue tenders. Carmichael produce an airport crash/foam tender – the Cougar – which was built on a Timoney 8x8 chassis for delivery to British Airports Authority Fire Service, London Stansted in 1993.

The 18-litre Detroit diesel engine with 825bhp gives an acceleration of 0 to 80kmh/50mph inside 32 seconds. Carrying 12,000 litres/2,666 gallons of water and 1,500 litres/330 gallons of foam concentrate, the Cougar can project up to 4,500 litres/1,000 gallons of foam per minute from its roof-mounted monitor.

The Carmichael International range of airport crash rescue tenders included the 6x6 Cobra 2,000 model, with a water capacity of 14,000 litres/3,000 gallons. With the largest crew cab and doors on the market, it accommodates five firefighters. Carmichael was the first UK fire engine manufacturer to use the clean-emission Euro 3 Caterpillar C18 4-stroke diesel engine in a number of its vehicles.

Carmichael's range of water tenders included the lightweight LPA model, based on a General Motors or a Land Rover chassis and fitted with a 1,135-litre/250-gallon water tank with a foam-making capability.

Carmichael ceased trading in 2018, and its assets were purchased by Terberg DTS UK to enable the continued support of the extensive Carmichael vehicle fleet.

CEDES

■ LEFT ***Batteries weighing 2 tons were stored beneath the bonnet of this 1905 Cedes electric pump escape, used by London Fire Brigade.***

Cedes Electric Traction, Austrian pioneers of electric vehicles including trolleybuses, produced its first battery-electric fire engines in the early 1900s for London Fire Brigade, who were looking for an alternative propulsion method for its fire engines. The drawback with self-propelled steamers was that precious time was lost whilst sufficient steam pressure was built up to move the engine. Although the Cedes battery-electric models were ready for instant turnout they were slow moving, especially on hills, and could not travel far without having to be recharged. In addition to the ten new Cedes pumping fire engines it commissioned, London Fire Brigade converted eight of its old horse-drawn wooden Magirus 30m/100ft-turntable ladders to work on the Cedes chassis. With the rapid development of the petrol engine, however, the move into electric traction was short-lived and by 1922 all London Fire Brigade's electric fire engines had been rebuilt on a motor chassis or withdrawn from service. Cedes itself went into liquidation in 1916.

22M/75FT TURNTABLE LADDER

Year	1908
Engine	two electric motors
Power	36hp
Transmission	direct chain driven
Features	two tons of batteries

CENTRAL STATES FIRE APPARATUS

■ RIGHT *A 1989 Mack MC/Central States pumper.*

In the 1970s, Lyons, South Dakota, USA, suffered a series of fires that prompted the start of the business known today as Central States Fire Apparatus. Harold and Helen Boer set up their welding and vehicle refurbishment enterprise in the mid-1970s, while Harold was the Chief of Lyons Volunteer Fire Department.

By the end of the decade, Central States was building fire engines, averaging 50 a year for various fire departments in America's mid west. The company grew rapidly and was soon employing 140 workers at its 8,900sq m/96,000sq ft manufacturing base. In the 1990s, it was one of several companies that came together to form Rosenbauer America, with the aim of providing a base for exporting American fire engine manufacturing expertise and design.

Central States' first custom-built pumper, constructed in 1983 on a Ford chassis for South Dakota Volunteer Fire Department, is still in general use. The current Central States range of fire engines includes pumpers, specialist tankers, aerials and rescue tenders.

■ LEFT *In service with Tuckwilla Fire Department, Washington, this Central States rescue/special operations unit is based on a 1996 International S4900.*

CHEVROLET

The American Chevrolet chassis was used for a number of fire engines during the 1920s and 1930s. Chevrolet trucks were built in the UK for several years from 1928 onwards, and a number of these were used as non-pumping fire engines before the Bedford company produced its own Chevrolet version for the British market. After World War II, Chevrolet pumpers could be found in service in several brigades in Europe as well as the United States. A typical American 1970s Chevrolet pumper would use the 3.7m/145in COE chassis with a V8 petrol engine and was fitted with a 3,400-litre/750-gallon water pump and a 1,600-litre/350-gallon water tank.

■ ABOVE *This preserved 1937 Chevrolet pumper once served with Kittanning Fire Company, Pennsylvania, USA.*

■ RIGHT *This Chevrolet/FMC mini pumper 4x4 has a mid-mounted pump and is powered by a 235bhp V8 petrol engine.*

■ RIGHT *This Chubb Pathfinder 6x6 foam tender is in service at Hong Kong Airport.*

CHUBB

Chubb Fire Security Ltd, the British fire protection company, was prominent in the early 1970s in designing a new generation of airport firefighting and rescue vehicles in response to the growing size of wide-bodied passenger aircraft such as the Boeing 747. The Chubb Pathfinder 6x6 airport crash tender, introduced in 1974, had a number of new features, such as a central driving position and a huge roof-mounted foam monitor capable of projecting 61,300 litres/13,500 gallons of foam per minute on to a burning aircraft or fuel fire. The Pathfinder was built on a Reynolds Boughton chassis and powered by a V6 Detroit diesel producing 635bhp.

During the 1970s Chubb built a number of high-output foam tenders for petrochemical fire brigades, but the company is particularly noted for the pump water tender it launched in 1975. The Pacesetter was the result of design collaboration between Merseyside Fire Brigade and a subsidiary of Loughborough University. Built on a Boughton high-performance chassis, it incorporated innovative fibreglass and alloy bodywork that included a six-man crew cab with easy-access power-operated doors and a low floor line. A 238bhp rear-mounted Detroit Diesel engine drove a 4-speed automatic gearbox capable of reaching 64kmh/40mph within an impressive 18 seconds. The 4,500-litres/1,000-gallons-per-minute fire pump was mounted on, and accessible from, the front of the fire engine.

■ LEFT *A 1991 Chubb National Foam 16m/53ft Telesquirt tender.*

■ BELOW *A Chubb Protector 6x6 foam tender with a high-output foam monitor.*

CITROËN

The chassis of this Paris-based truck and car manufacturer were used for many years to produce a range of fire engines that included water tenders, light pumps, forest-fire tenders, foam tenders and turntable ladders.

At the lightweight end of the range, the 1970 3m/117in-wheelbase, 350-chassis, with a 95bhp, 2.2-litre petrol engine, was available in a 4x4 option. Heavier Citroën models provided the base for the 30m/100ft Metz turntable ladders used by many French fire brigades, including the Paris brigade.

In the late 1960s Citroën took a major holding in the Berliet Automobiles Company, which itself had become a successful builder of fire engines destined for French brigades through its commercial and municipal truck division. In 1971 Berliet-Citroën combined with Guinard to form the new Camiva company, which produced a considerable number of fire engines.

COMMER

■ LEFT *Formerly used by London Fire Brigade, this 1913 Commer YC pump is still in working order.*

■ BELOW *A 1950 Commer FC water tender exemplifies the evolving style of post-war British fire engines.*

Commer chassis were built at the company's Dunstable plant in the UK, and in the years following World War II gained considerable popularity among fire brigades around the world as well as in the UK. One of the earliest post-war models was the QX chassis, which had a 6-cylinder under-floor petrol engine with 109bhp and was fitted with a 2,270-litre/500-gallon water pump. With a 3.6m/141in-wheelbase, this chassis was used extensively for rural fire brigade water tenders to provide a modestly priced, relatively compact, lightweight (6.5 tons) fire engine. From 1954 Commer utilized the new 3-cylinder 2-stroke Tillings Stevens 4.75-litre diesel engine and continued to provide water tender chassis into the 1970s. The 3-ton KC40 model, introduced in 1961, provided the chassis for a number of lightweight specialist fire engines. From 1960 the heavier Commer 86A 7-ton chassis was used for a number of 30m/100ft Magirus turntable ladders, with bodywork by David Haydon. In 1963 a Commer VAC was utilized for a Simon SS65 hydraulic platform for Monmouthshire Fire Brigade in Wales, the first of its type to go into operational service in the UK.

Commer ceased production of chassis suitable for fire engine use in 1975.

COMMER FC

Year	1950
Engine	6-cylinder petrol
Power	109 bhp
Transmission	4-speed manual
Features	under-floor engine

■ LEFT *A c.1950 Commer pump escape of Carmarthenshire Fire Brigade, Wales.*

■ BELOW LEFT *A c.1960 Commer pump escape carries a 13m/45ft wheeled ladder.*

■ BELOW RIGHT *A 1976 Commer Hi Line G-1211 water tender used by Harwell Fire Brigade, England.*

CROWN

■ LEFT *This 1976 Crown pumper is owned by Los Angeles County Fire Department, in California.*

Based in Los Angeles, California, USA, Crown Firecoach began building buses in 1904, with the first Crown fire engine appearing in 1951. The company's fire vehicles have seen extensive service in American fire departments, and several were exported to customers as far away as the Gulf States. From its early days, Crown focused on producing a single standard open cab, 3m/117in-wheelbase pumper that could be customized to any specification required. Crown also manufactured aerial ladders, both rigid and articulated 30m/100ft versions, drawn by tractor units.

From 1980 the company concentrated on providing pumpers with various specialist applications, such as a Snorkel platform. Noted for their chassis strength and longevity, one Crown safety feature was the suspension system that allows for the vehicle ride height to be varied according to its overall load.

Crown was acquired by GE Railcar in 1987, and the company ceased operations in 1991.

■ LEFT *This 1967 Crown pumper went into service at Second Street Station, Watsonville Fire Department, in California.*

■ BELOW *A 1981 Crown pumper of Marysville Fire Department, Washington, USA, is fitted with a 6,80- litres/1,500-gallons-per-minute midships pump and a 2,270-litre/500-gallon water tank.*

CUSTOM FIRE

■ BELOW *This 1992 Custom Fire 5,700-litres/1,250-gallons-per-minute pumper is built on a Ford L8000 chassis.*

Custom Fire began building its first fire engines at its base in Osceola, Wisconsin, USA, in the late 1970s and has grown steadily ever since. Today it delivers several new fire engines each month to many fire departments throughout the United States.

The range of fire engines produced includes mini and elaborate customized pumpers, heavy rescue tenders and command units, aerials and tankers. Custom Fire fire engines are unusual in that they feature a bolted body construction method instead of the more usual welding. This type of assembly ensures easier accident reparability, as well as allowing for vehicle modification at a later date should it be required. The company supplies fire departments throughout the USA.

■ RIGHT ***Decorated with a colourful livery, this 1989 Custom Fire incident command unit is run by Northfield Fire and Rescue Department, Minnesota, USA. It is built on a Ford L8000 chassis.***

OTHER MAKES

■ CRASH RESCUE

Formed in 1967, Dallas, Texas-based Crash Rescue Equipment Service, Inc, started life maintaining aircraft rescue and firefighting equipment (ARFF).

However, in 1978, Crash Rescue started to refurbish various types of ARFF for customers across the United States and in the 1990s came the company's Snozzle equipment designed for firefighting and rescue operations. In an aviation fire engine application, the Snozzle is mounted on an elevating extendable boom. Apart from allowing the firefighting nozzle to be placed through small openings in aircraft, such as windows and doors, the Snozzle can also carry an infrared camera.

The Snozzle is also particularly effective for getting a rapid firefighting attack under way in a building while other larger trucks are being deployed. The Snozzle is controlled by an operator joystick.

Fire Wagons, a division within Crash Rescue, manufactured a range of specially designed functional trailers. These included carriers for firefighting foam and equipment for dealing with hazardous materials and decontamination, triage stations for attendance at major accident sites, and mobile operational command and control centres.

In 2011, the Snozzle brand was sold to Oshkosh, and in the mid-2010s Crash Rescue was declared bankrupt.

■ CRIMSON FIRE

Created in early 2003, Crimson Fire was owned by Spartan Motors, Inc, and its headquarters were at Brandon, South Dakota. The company's origins actually go back to the 1990s, when Spartan Motors acquired three separate fire engine manufacturing concerns with a view to entering the fire engine market. Crimson Fire resulted from the amalgamation of two of these companies – Quality and Luverne.

Crimson Fire offered a range of fire engine types including pumpers, heavy and mini-rescue units, rapid intervention vehicles, and water tankers with a capacity up to 15,900 litres/3,500 gallons.

In 2012, Crimson Fire was rebranded as Spartan ERV, and then in 2018 the company became Spartan Emergency Response (ER).

■ CSI EMERGENCY APPARATUS

The CSI Fire & Truck company was originally formed in 1989 to provide vehicles and service facilities for the emergency services in Michigan, USA. By 1995, sales volume had increased to the point where the company moved into their own manufacturing facility at Grayling, Michigan. At the same time the company name was changed to CSI Emergency Apparatus.

CSI Emergency Apparatus manufactures and customizes a range of fire department water tankers, pumpers and other specialist emergency vehicles.

■ CUSTOM FAB & BODY (CFB)

Originally founded in 1994 in Tigerton, Wisconsin, Custom Fab and Body expanded to meet increased demand for fire and rescue vehicle production, and moved to new premises in Marion, Wisconsin, in early 2007. The company has built a range of pumpers, tankers and brush trucks to customers' specifications, based on a variety of chassis including Spartan, Freightliner, Kenworth, International and Ford F550.

DAF

A large number of the fire engines in use in the Netherlands after the early 1960s were built on a chassis produced by DAF, the Eindhoven-based truck manufacturer. When DAF acquired the British Leyland commercial truck company in 1987 the DAF name started to appear in fire brigades all over Europe. Since then, a number of DAF vehicles have also been built for UK use. These include water carriers (using the 16/17 and 20/210 chassis), breathing apparatus tenders (DAF Freighter), prime movers for demount - able units (DAF 60), and emergency tenders on the DAF T45, as well as the 1718 model used by the emergency support unit of Gloucestershire Fire & Rescue Service. This fire engine, following a trend in the equipment specification of other similar tenders, was equipped with a rear-mounted Hiab hydraulic crane for non-fire rescue work. One brigade in Lancashire, UK, commissioned over 80 DAF 60 model water tenders over a period of over ten years, the latest delivery of ten, fitted with Emergency One bodywork, taking place in 2016.

■ ABOVE *A Dutch fire service DAF 1100 water tender.*

■ ABOVE *A DAF LF 55 250 fire tender delivered to the Lancashire Fire and Rescue Service, UK, in 2011.*

LF 250 LA	
Year	2016
Engine	PACCAR Euro 6, 6.7-litre diesel
Body	PolyBilt copolymer plastic
Transmission	Allison 3000 fully automatic
Features	Emergency One copolymer body

DANKO EMERGENCY EQUIPMENT

Danko, a family-owned business, was formed in 1974 by Dan Kreikmeier, a former employee of the Smeal Fire Apparatus Company. After almost 30 years of growth, the company moved into new purpose-built 3,252 sq m/ 35,000sq ft premises in Snyder, Nebraska in 2002.

Danko manufacture a wide range of custom-bodied firefighting and emergency vehicles, including tankers, pumpers, airport units, wildland units and rescue vehicles. Rescue units are available with 3.7m/12ft and 6m/20ft bodies, pumpers with 3,800- or 6,000-litre/832- or 1,330-gallon tanks, and pump tankers with capacities from 4,500–16,000 litres/1,000–3,500 gallons. The vehicles are built predominantly on Freightliner and Ford chassis.

■ RIGHT *A Danko Pumper Tanker built in 2019 on a Freightliner chassis for the Pierce Fire Department in Nebraska.*

DARLEY

Based at Itasca, Illinois, USA, W S Darley & Co has been manufacturing fire engine water pumps since the early twentieth century. Today it combines contemporary technology with a long track record of engineering excellence. In addition to its fire pump range, Darley have built complete fire engines on various commercial chassis, such as Ford, International, Chevrolet and Duplex, for operational service in the USA and abroad. The Darley fire engine range includes custom-built pumpers, water tankers, rescue tenders, and airport foam tenders.

■ ABOVE RIGHT *A 2017 Darley Custom Curbside Single Axle CAFS Pumper Tanker built for the Orangeville Fire Protection District, Illinois.*

■ RIGHT *This 2000 Aerial Innovations 30m/100ft platform is mounted on a Spartan Gladiator 6x4 chassis.*

■ RIGHT *Sporting a green livery, this 1993 Spartan/Darley pumper is run by the Irishtown Fire Company, Pennsylvania.*

WASP QUICK ATTACK WILDLAND TRUCK

Year	2020
Engine	6.7-litre diesel 330bhp
Body	PolyBilt copolymer plastic
Transmission	automatic, all-wheel drive
Features	four-door crew cab

DENNIS

■ LEFT *The Dennis Big Four was very successful during the 1930s. This well-polished 1936 version has been lovingly preserved.*

Dennis first started manufacturing motorcars and tricycles in 1895 and produced its first fire engine in 1908 for Bradford Fire Brigade, Yorkshire, England. This was followed by an order from London Fire Brigade and from then on Dennis grew from its factory at Guildford, Surrey, to become the predominant British manufacturer for half a century or more.

By the early 1930s Dennis was supplying more than 100 pumping fire engines per year to brigades throughout the UK and overseas. The very popular pump-carrying 1934 model Big Four escape, a reliable and classic fire engine of its time, went into service as far away as Hong Kong Fire Brigade. In 1937, the 250th Dennis fire engine was delivered to the London Brigade, whose pumps were still of an open-air design.

After World War II Dennis introduced the F series, with coachbuilt wooden bodies and powered either by the Dennis 3.8-litre petrol engine with 70bhp or the Rolls-Royce B80, 8-cylinder petrol engine. The F-series continued to be built into the 1970s with versions for city brigades (the 1956 F101 with a 170bhp, 12.2-litre Rolls-Royce diesel engine) through to the best-selling narrow F8, with a width of 2m/6.5ft, designed specifically for rural firefighters.

By the 1960s, when Dennis claimed to have fire engines operating in 46 countries, more petrol-engine options were being offered to increase on-road performance of the F and the newer 2.1m/7ft-wide D series. These included the Rolls-Royce 195bhp version or the Jaguar 4.2-litre. Front disc brakes on Dennis fire engines also became an option for the first time in 1962.

F101 PUMP/PUMP ESCAPE

Year	1956
Engine	8-cylinder diesel
Power	170bhp
Transmission	5-speed manual
Features	Rolls-Royce 12-litre engine

■ ABOVE *The narrow-bodied F8 was designed for rural firefighting. The vehicle's 2m/6½ft width enabled it to speedily negotiate narrow country lanes. This fine example saw long service in Devon County Fire Service, England.*

■ LEFT *Powered by a 150bhp 5.7-litre Rolls-Royce petrol engine, the Dennis F7 set the post-World War II standard for years to come. This 1949 London Fire Brigade pump escape was just one example of the several hundred F7s that served in British fire brigades for some 20 years.*

■ RIGHT ***At the ready on the station yard, this 1985 Dennis RS pump is in service with the Port of Singapore Fire Brigade.***

In 1976 the R series was introduced; it incorporated a fibreglass cab on an air-braked chassis. It was available with the Perkins V8.640 diesel engine, which gave it an impressive all-round performance. In 1979 the R series was phased out in favour of the new RS model, along with the SS tilt-cab version. These two models had a new all-steel safety cab capable of accommodating a six-man crew with breathing sets inside the crew cab area. Over 1,750 of these very successful Dennis models were sold, mostly as pumps. However, in 1983 Dennis, then owned by the Hestair Group, took the decision to concentrate its fire engine production on chassis/cab manufacture, leaving the bodybuilding to various specialist companies.

In 1991 Dennis launched a new fire engine chassis/cab called the Rapier. This represented a complete break from the previous generation of Dennis fire vehicles, with a welded tubular space frame replacing the conventional chassis frame. The new concept gave a low overall frame height and allowed for the fitting of independent front suspension with disc brakes. The rear axle featured coil spring suspension. Other standard features included anti-lock brakes and traction control. All this meant that the Rapier was exceptionally stable due to its low centre of gravity. A Cummins C-series 8.3-litre engine with 250bhp driven through an Allison 5-speed automatic gearbox gave the Rapier a road performance unmatched by most of its rivals, with a 120kmh/75mph top speed allied to impressive cornering and braking ability.

■ ABOVE ***This preserved 1957 Dennis F21 38m/125ft Metz turntable ladder formerly served Rochdale Fire Brigade, England.***

■ ABOVE ***Now in preservation, this unusual Dennis F107 formerly served as a breakdown lorry for London Fire Brigade from 1964 until 1977. It was based at the brigade's Lambeth headquarters.***

■ RIGHT ***Pictured as it went into operational service in 1994, this Dennis Sabre water/rescue tender is one of Wiltshire (England) Fire Brigade's fleet.***

■ TOP *A 1988 Dennis RS water tender of Devon Fire and Rescue Service, England, stands in line with the RAF's Red Arrows.*

■ ABOVE *This 1980 Dennis F125 30m/100ft Magirus turntable ladder belongs to Kent Fire Brigade, England.*

In 1994, Dennis introduced the Sabre chassis/cab, which included a number of further technical refinements.

In 1998, Dennis was taken over by the Mayflower Corporation, but Mayflower collapsed in 2004, and Dennis passed into new ownership as Alexander Dennis Ltd (ADL). The production of Rapier and Sabre trucks continued, but due to changes in policy within the company, the final fire engine chassis – a Sabre – was produced in 2007. The body-building division of the Dennis business was separated from the main Dennis business in 1985, and continued under the John Dennis Coachworks (JDC) brand, however JDC finally closed its doors in 2019 to end the long history of Dennis fire vehicles.

■ LEFT *A 1992 Dennis Rapier water tender with a 14m/45ft alloy extension.*

■ BELOW *Humberside Fire Brigade, England, operate this 1984 Dennis F133/Carmichael/Magirus 30m/100ft turntable ladder.*

DODGE

■ ABOVE ***Whatcom County Fire District, Washington, ran this 1977 Dodge/LaFrance Custom 400 4x4, 1,135 litres/250 gallons per minute light pumper.***

■ LEFT ***A 1987 Dodge-Renault 100-Series Commando fire tender, as used by the Dumfries and Galloway Fire and Rescue Service, Scotland.***

Having begun fire engine manufacture during World War II, Dodge produced vehicles in the USA and UK. The American versions were from the parent Chrysler Motor Corporation range and included the 4x4, ¾-ton, T214 model, which had originally been used as a battlefield ambulance but converted readily into a pumper for use by country fire departments. From the late 1940s, the ⅝-ton, D500 chassis with a 5.2-litre, 6-cylinder petrol engine appeared in a number of pumper applications.

The later Power Wagon 4x4 chassis, an American Dodge that provided rugged cross-country performance, saw much operational service as a rural firefighting unit. Its chassis was also utilized for medium-sized airfield rapid intervention vehicles. With a Chrysler V8 230bhp petrol engine with automatic transmission, the Power Wagon was capable of an impressive 80kmh/50mph in 15 seconds and its monitor could deliver 12,000 litres/2,666 gallons of foam per minute.

In the UK, a large number of Dodge fire engines were built as pumps, aerial ladders and other special types, with bodies by a variety of bodybuilders. Early pumps were based on their 3-ton lorry chassis. In the 1970s, the K and G range provided a wider load span, from the K850 and the later 100 series G13 5-ton range for water tenders, through to the K2213, which was rated at 22 tons, and suitable for turntable ladders and hydraulic platform use. The K850 had a Perkins V8 diesel engine and a tilt cab, whilst the G13 had a more powerful Perkins V8.540 diesel engine allied to a 6-speed gearbox. The Dodge water tender's 1,800-litre/400-gallon water tank fed a Godiva pump.

From the early 1970s a large number of turntable ladders, including Magirus and Metz models, and Simon hydraulic platforms were built on Dodge heavy chassis, in particular the G1613 and G16C range. The company also built a number of specials, including foam tenders, emergency tenders and control units. In addition, several bodybuilders used the American Power Wagon Dodge chassis for their medium-sized airfield crash and foam tenders, whilst the 1979 Dodge 50 series was used by industrial fire brigades for light pumping/first strike fire engines. By the late 1970s, a number of Dodge G series chassis had started to appear as prime movers for various demountable equipment pods.

Dodge was acquired by Renault in the early 1980s and the old badge was soon replaced by that of the new logo. One of the last British Renault/Dodge engines went into service in 1995 with Avon Fire Brigade. As a custom-built road/rail support unit for emergency calls to the 5km/3-mile River Severn rail tunnel, its chassis incorporates a set of rail wheels to run on railway lines in the event of a railway emergency incident.

■ RIGHT ***This preserved 1949 Dodge/American pumper is fitted with a 2,270-litre/500-gallon tank and the same capacity per minute midships pump.***

DUPLEX

The American firm of Duplex is well known, particularly for the specialist combination fire engines it built for US fire departments. These R-300 series vehicles combined an aerial ladder with a pumper in order to perform a dual operational role. The midships-mounted aerial ladder reached up to 26m/85ft. A 2,270-litre/500-gallon water tank and a 5,700-litre/1,250-gallon, midships-mounted pump were also carried making this fire engine self-contained. In 1986, Duplex became part of the UK-based Simon Group, along with LTI. The new company continued to build pumpers and aerial apparatus using the LTI Olympian chassis, but the Duplex business was closed in 1998 after failure to find a buyer.

■ TOP *A 1973 Duplex/Van Pelt pumper.*

■ ABOVE RIGHT *Farmington Fire Co, Delaware, USA, run this gleaming 1994 Simon/Duplex 6x4 water tanker.*

■ RIGHT *The striking white livery makes this bodyline-styled, 1995 Simon/Duplex 6x4 rear-mount, 31m/102ft aerial ladder platform highly visible.*

OTHER MAKES

■ DAVID HAYDON

David Haydon Ltd, a specialist fire engine bodybuilding and engineering company based in the West Midlands, England, built a number of Magirus 30m/100ft hydraulically-powered turntable ladders under licence during the late 1950s. These ladders, together with the bodywork supplied by the company, were built on to various chassis, such as Bedford, Leyland and AEC. David Haydon also built the bodywork of a number of customized pumping and specialist fire engines, such as the Leyland Firemaster.

■ DELAHAYE

Like a number of other early car manufacturers, the French company Delahaye, which was founded in 1898 and is based at Tours and Paris, soon turned its skills to fire engine design. By 1907, when mechanized firefighting methods were first being developed, Delahaye had produced a pumping fire engine that, in addition to carrying hose reels and various hose connections and fittings, was capable of transporting 15 firemen to a fire.

Over subsequent years Delahaye fire engines were supplied to fire brigades throughout France and Europe. In 1926, a number of Delahaye pumping engines were built to the specific requirements of the Sapeurs Pompiers of Paris, the regimental fire brigade that safeguarded the nation's capital, setting the future standard for European fire engines. These rear-mounted pumps had a 1,800 litres/400 gallons per minute capacity, and provided detachable hose reels to provide firemen with maximum operational flexibility.

Delahaye merged with Hotchkiss in 1954 and within two years the Delahaye large vehicle operations came to an end.

Emergency One (UK) Ltd

■ BELOW *A 1995 Mercedes 1124F/ Emergency One (UK) water tender.*

Having delivered its first water tender to Strathclyde Fire Brigade in 1991, Emergency One (UK) Ltd is a relatively new fire engine producer. Over the past two decades, the company, which is based in Strathclyde, Scotland, has expanded considerably, moving into larger premises in 2012, and adding a second 14,864sq m/160,000sq ft facility in 2017 to allow additional storage and assembly.

The company has won orders for a considerable number of water tenders and other specialist firefighting and rescue tenders. These have come from every one of the eight Scottish fire brigades, as well as a number of English brigades. Emergency One (UK)'s fire engines are based on a range of chassis, including DAF, Mercedes-Benz, Scania or Volvo chassis. The company also supplies Magirus aerial equipment, and is currently developing the EVO – the world's first all-electric pumping appliance.

■ BELOW RIGHT *White-liveried fire engines are rare in the UK. This 2002 Scania G94 230/Emergency One (UK) water tender serves with Grampian Fire Brigade, Scotland.*

■ ABOVE *This 2002 Volvo FL6/Emergency One (UK) water tender of Hampshire Fire & Rescue Service, England, carries a 13.7m/45ft alloy extension ladder.*

■ RIGHT *The Emergency One E1 EVO is the world's first entirely electric fire appliance, launched in 2020.*

WATER TENDER	
Year	2002
Engine	6-cylinder diesel
Power	260bhp
Transmission	automatic
Features	range of rescue equipment

EMERGENCY ONE (E-ONE)

Having started life in 1974 at its Ocala headquarters in Florida, USA, Emergency One (known throughout the American fire service as E-One) is one of the newer American fire engine manufacturers. In a relatively short time it has rapidly built up an enviable reputation for its products, and delivered thousands of fire engines of all types to fire brigades in over 80 countries. Today, the company has around 900 staff located at four plants and has sold over 25,000 vehicles to customers around the world. In 2015, E-One became part of the REV Group which comprises a range of brands producing emergency and specialist vehicles, including fire-vehicle manufacturers KME, Ferrara, Spartan, Smeal and Ladder Tower.

From the start the company promoted a prefabricated modular style of bodybuilding that enabled its fire engines to be attractively priced and swiftly manufactured. The bodies are mounted on a variety of suitable chassis types, including Ford, Freightliner and General Motors.

■ LEFT *A 1994 KW/Emergency One 6x4 Rescue tender in service with Claymont Fire Department, Delaware, stands at the roadside.*

■ BELOW LEFT *Syncrude, Alta, Canada, operate this 1997 Emergency One HPR 8x8 with a 15m/50ft Snozzle. This specialist fire engine has a 7,360-litre/1,620-gallon tank and a 12,700-litres/2,800-gallons-per-minute pump capacity.*

Early Emergency One models included the Protector pumper range, which featured a midships-mounted pump, and had a water tank capacity of up to 3,400 litres/750 gallons. Later Protector versions came with a tilt-cab facility.

Another popular model was the Midi-Pumper, on a General Motors 4x4 chassis, designed for rural firefighting. With a 3,400 litres/750 gallons per minute midships-mounted pump and a 2,270-litre/500-gallon water tank, the

■ RIGHT *Built in 2000, this Emergency One Cyclone II 6x4 rear-mount 30m/100ft aerial ladder serves the City of Seattle Fire Department, Washington.*

vehicle provided a powerful firefighting attack that could be taken across most rural terrain. In 1980 Emergency One built a number of Snorkel telescopic booms on to a combination fire engine that was capable of operating as a pumper with an aerial firefighting arm. At the same time the company produced a number of successful compact 29m/95ft aerial ladders mounted on a 2-axle chassis. These innovative aerials were much shorter than the big and somewhat unwieldy rear-steer tiller fire engines then in use by a number of American urban fire departments.

Before long, E-One had developed its high-rise firefighting and rescue models to include the Strato Spear range. Embracing 33m/110ft aerial ladders, platforms and telescopic boom fire engines, these were at the time claimed to be among the highest aerials in the USA. The four-section ladders of the Strato Spear aerial ladder were constructed of welded aluminium, which, coupled to an underslung jacking system, made a stable working base. E-One has continued to develop the use of extruded rust-resistant aluminium in its construction methods, claiming that it is possible to mount the resultant lighter bodies on less costly chassis options. This in turn allows fire vehicles to carry more payload, with a less negative impact on braking systems, drivelines and axles. Virtually every type of firefighting and rescue vehicle is currently being built at the company's five manufacturing plants.

Recent models include the following: the Cyclone II Industrial pumper with remote-control roof-mounted dual foam monitors with flow rates up to 18,000 litres/4,000 gallons-per-minute; the Titan HPR foam tender range which comes in 4x4, 6x6 and 8x8 options; aerial ladders and platforms ranging from the Typhoon HP 75 23m/75ft and the CR 30m/100ft to the HP 32m/105ft. One of E-One's more recent models is the Titan 6x6 ARFF (Airport Rescue Fire Fighting) truck. The Titan is powered by a 770bhp Scania diesel engine paired to a six-speed transmission. Standard features include an extruded-aluminium roll-cage, a 12,000-litre/2,600-gallon polypropylene water tank and a 1,533-litre/337-gallon foam tank, and a Hale single-stage pump rated at 11,300 litres/2,500 gallons per minute.

Emergency One fire engines can be found in many guises right across the USA and around the world.

■ BELOW *The E-One Titan 4x4 AT (Air Transportable) aircraft crash tender is designed for on- and -off-road use to reach incidents inaccessible to conventional fire apparatus, and can be transported on C-5, C-17 and C-130 aircraft.*

■ RIGHT *A 2017 E-One Walk-In Rescue operated by the Lexington Fire Department, Kentucky, powered by a 550bhp Cummins diesel engine coupled to an Allison five-speed automatic transmission.*

■ OPPOSITE *This 1985 Emergency One Hurricane 6x4 rear-mount 33m/110ft aerial ladder now serves with Victoria Fire Department, British Columbia, Canada.*

ERF

■ LEFT *A preserved 1971 ERF F-series water tender attends a rally.*

Originally founded in 1933 by Edwin Richard Foden, ERF Ltd of Sandbach, UK, was an established manufacturer of heavy goods vehicles when in 1966 it launched two new chassis aimed at the fire brigade market. The lighter of the two, the F-series 84 RS model, was designed for water tender use, whilst the heavier F-series 84 PF was designated for mounting turntable ladders and hydraulic platforms. These ERFs were powered by either a Perkins V8 510 or 540 diesel engine with automatic transmission. Standard UK water tender specification included the choice of a 2,270-litres/500-gallons or a 4,500-litres/1,000-gallons-per-minute pump.

The interest in the new ERFs, both in the UK and abroad, was such that in 1972 a subsidiary section called the ERF Fire Division was established on a new factory site at Winsford, Cheshire, to build and assemble the ERF chassis and associated fire engineering elements. In 1977 a new company, entitled Cheshire Fire Engineering, took over the ERF fire engine business, although this remained wholly owned by ERF. Many ERF water tenders and hydraulic platforms built in the late 1960s and 1970s were bodied by Hampshire Car Bodies-Angus. The ERF hydraulic platforms, some of which were powered by Rolls-Royce 8-cylinder B81 engines, used the Simon SS range, giving working heights of 20–28.3m/65–93ft. A smaller number of ERF 30m/100ft turntable ladders were manufactured during this period using Metz and Magirus ladder sections.

ERF ceased manufacturing fire engines in 1982 and by the early 1990s few ERFs remained in operational service. However, ERF briefly re-emerged in 1996 when several new fire engines, all on the ERF heavy duty EC 8 series chassis, went into service in the UK. These included various vehicles for the Cheshire, West Midlands, Greater Manchester and Wiltshire fire services. In 2000, ERF was acquired by MAN, at which point production of the EC series ceased.

EXCALIBUR

Excalibur CBK Ltd, was based at Stoke-on-Trent in Staffordshire, England, and was a specialist fire engine body-building company. It produced its first two firefighting vehicles – a Bedford water tender and a Land Rover light pump – for Powys Fire Brigade, in Wales, in 1986. Excalibur CBK grew progressively to become a prominent manufacturer of a range of pumping fire engines, water tenders and emergency/rescue tenders, which it supplied to a significant number of brigades across the British fire service.

Excalibur used a number of chassis makes for its fire engines, including Renault-Dodge, Dennis, Mercedes and Volvo. The company ceased trading in the late 1990s.

■ BELOW *New to England's Lincolnshire Fire and Rescue Service in 1996 was this Volvo FL6 14/Excalibur rescue pump.*

OTHER MAKES

■ **EGI (KLUBB)**
EGI is based Les Ayvelles, France, and is a specialist manufacturer of aerial platforms. The company built its first hydraulic aerial platform in the late 1950s, and since then has sold more than 6,000 units in more than 50 countries. Today, EGI is part of the Klubb group, and produces platforms for mounting on a wide range of vehicles worldwide.

■ **EMERGENCY VEHICLES INC. (EVI)**
The origins of EVI go back to 1971 when Custom Ambulances of Florida was formed by Ernst R. Temme. In 1976, this company became EVF (Emergency Vehicles of Florida), and in 1988 this in turn became EVI. Today, the company operates from a 4,645sq m/50,000sq ft facility in Lake Park, Florida, producing a wide range of light units, dive units, light and heavy rescue vehicles, Haz-Mat vehicles and other specialist units for fire services throughout the USA.

FAUN

Faun-Werke GmbH, based in Nuremberg, Germany, has long been associated with firefighting equipment but is particularly noted for the large airfield crash and foam tenders it built during the 1970s. These vehicles were some of the first of the new generation fire engines developed to provide fire protection for the larger aircraft then coming into service, such as the Boeing 747. The Faun LF1410/52V, produced in 1970, was a massive 8x8 crash tender powered by a 1,000bhp Daimler/Benz V10 diesel engine with 4-speed automatic transmission, able to reach 100kmh/62mph in 65 seconds. Weighing 50 tons, it was at the time one of the world's biggest fire engines.

In 1990, Faun was acquired by Tadano Ltd, a Japanese crane manufacturer, at which point the manufacture of fire vehicles ceased.

■ ABOVE *This Faun/Sides 8x8 foam tender is in service at Palma Airport, Majorca, with its powerful roof-mounted foam monitor. The high ground clearance and all-wheel drive of these heavy specialist fire engines show how they are able to respond to an incident off the airport runways.*

FERRARA

■ BELOW *A 1999 Ferrara Fl-RK 33m/110ft 6x4 rear-mount aerial ladder.*

The origins of Ferrara Fire Apparatus go back to the late 1970s when Chris Ferrara, a volunteer firefighter with Central Volunteer Fire Department, together with several colleagues, began a quest to build a new tanker fire engine for their fire department. After many hours and much hard work, the new tanker was finally commissioned at a considerable saving to the department's funds. This success led, in 1979, to Ferrara founding a firefighting equipment company which enjoyed successive growth and steady expansion, including the refurbishment of a range of American fire engines. Then, in 1988, Ferrara Fire Apparatus built its

INFERNO PUMPER

Year	2003
Engine	6-cylinder diesel
Power	350–500hp
Transmission	automatic
Features	extensive locker space

■ LEFT *Shelby County Fire Department, Indiana uses a number of Ferrara vehicles, including this MVP Rescue Pumper delivered in 2016 and used for a variety of emergency duties.*

first own-brand fire engine. Today, the company is ranked amongst the top five fire engine builders in the USA. Ferrara Fire Apparatus Incorporated now constructs a wide range of pumpers, rescue tenders and aerial platforms. Ferrara fire engines are available on the company's own custom chassis range, which over the years has included the Interceptor, the Gladiator, the Penetrator, the Intruder and more recently the Cinder, Igniter, Inferno, Ultra and the Invader. The Igniter chassis is built for engines up to 450bhp, the Ultra up to 500bhp, and the Inferno up to 600bhp.

Ferrara's custom cabs and bodies are built from an extruded aluminium frame and marine-grade aluminium, providing strong and durable construction.

Today, Ferrara is part of the REV Group, though it retains its own unique identity.

■ ABOVE *A Ferrara Igniter Pumper delivered to Salem Fire Department, Massachusetts in 2016.*

■ BELOW *This 2014 Ferrara Igniter HD-100 aerial is in use with the Wayne Township Fire Department, Indiana.*

FIAT/OM

Based in Turin, Italy, Fiat has been manufacturing cars since 1899, but most of its chassis were produced by its commercial subsidiary, OM of Brescia. For many years OM chassis provided the base for a wide range of water tenders, airport crash tenders and foam tenders used for refineries.

The OM 150 series was used throughout Italy in the 1970s and 1980s. This 4-ton chassis boasted a 3,000-litre/660-gallon water tank and a high-pressure pump. The OM 260 series six-wheeled chassis was also used for larger foam tenders, where its 15-litre, V8 diesel engine with over 300bhp allowed significant water and foam payloads. OM chassis are also used for Italy's forest firefighting tankers, which carry 4,000 litres/880 gallons of water on the heavy-duty TLF chassis.

A number of light fire engines have also been produced using the Fiat 1,300 T2 van and the jeep-style Fiat Campagnola 4x4. Many of these vehicles carry modular units, including a 400-litre/88-gallon water tank and portable pumps, lighting units and other ancillary firefighting gear.

Today, Fiat's commercial arm is the IVECO group (Industrial Vehicle Corporation), which came into being in 1975. Under its own badge, it produces various chassis types for use by a large number of fire brigades around the world.

FIAT/OM 260

Year	1982
Engine	V8 diesel
Power	300bhp plus
Transmission	6-speed manual
Features	6x4 heavy foam tender

■ LEFT *Belonging to Vigili Del Fuoco, this c.1950 Fiat light 4x4 is in use as a general-purpose and support firefighting vehicle, particularly for rural incidents.*

■ LEFT *This c.1985 Fiat light 4x4 fire engine owned by Del Fuoco Fire Brigade, Italy provides general back-up duties in rural areas.*

■ BELOW *A 1992 Fiat 14 long-wheelbase general-purpose utility fire engine of Kellinghusen Fire Brigade, Germany.*

FORD

■ BELOW *An early Ford Model T pumper is seen here in 1924, while in service with Morristown Fire Department, New Jersey, USA.*

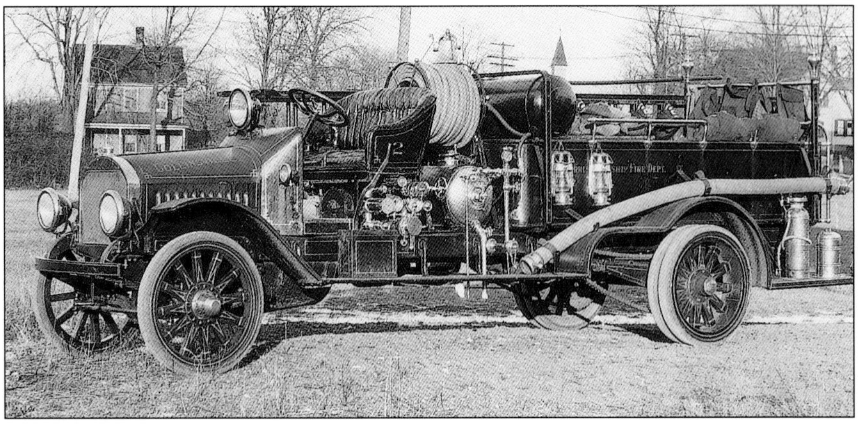

By 1915 Model T Fords were being used as cars by a number of US fire chiefs. At this time New York Fire Department modified a Model T for firefighting duties. Despite its short wheelbase, a number of other Model Ts soon went into service with fire departments across the USA, while in Britain the Ford A and BB series chassis were used for a number of compact open pumps during the 1930s.

The arrival of the Ford V8 engine in 1932 provided the type of performance that was especially suited to fire brigade use. The British government supplied the Auxiliary Fire Service with a large number of 8-cylinder V8 30hp Fordson 7V Thames series for use as wartime heavy pumping engines. But it was not until after World War II that Ford chassis saw increased use as fire engines – on both sides of the Atlantic and elsewhere in the world.

In the 1950s, Ford medium-size chassis, such as the F5 series, were particularly popular. In the Netherlands,

■ BELOW *The fine wooden bodywork and fittings of this preserved Dutch Fire Service 1938 Ford V8 light pump are a rare sight. This fire engine towed a dry powder unit, which in pre-war days was a relatively new firefighting feature.*

■ RIGHT *A Harrow Fire Brigade, England, crew aboard this c.1938 Ford lightweight pump. At that time, provision for crew in an American-style body was unusual for a British fire brigade.*

■ BELOW *A good example of early post-war fire engine development is this c.1950 Ford 30m/100ft Magirus turntable ladder, seen here in service at the Knokke-Heist Fire Brigade station, in Belgium.*

■ ABOVE *Operated by Falck Redningskorps, a private Danish fire service, this c.1980 Ford D1114/Magirus 30m/100ft-turntable ladder puts in an appearance at a German fire engine rally.*

■ RIGHT ***Fire crew of the Shropshire Fire Service, England, go through a drill with one of their new 1980 Ford 1317 water tenders. These vehicles had an 8.8-litre Perkins V8 diesel engine and carried 1,800 litres/400 gallons of water.***

the F5 model formed the basis of a water tender with a front-mounted 3,000-litres/660-gallons-per-minute pump feeding three hose reels from a 2,000-litre/440-gallon water tank. In Germany use was made in the mid-1950s of the Ford G398TA 4x4 chassis for water tenders.

In the 1970s American Ford lightweight pumpers included those on the short-wheelbase 4x4 Super Duty N1000 chassis and on the 4x4 F6000 series. These had a 4,500-litre/1,000-gallon water tank and a 3,400 litres/750 gallons per minute midships-mounted pump. Major American Ford pumpers used both the L series chassis of the 1970s and the 3.4m/135in C series. The latter came with a tilt cab, 276bhp engine and automatic transmission air brakes, a 4,500-litres/1,000-gallons-per-minute pump and a 2,270-litre/500-gallon water tank.

In the UK, during the 1950s and 1960s, the 4D Thames (3.6-litre diesel engine) and heavier Trader chassis (5.4-litre diesel) were popular for water tender or emergency/rescue tender use.

■ TOP LEFT ***This 1979 Ford Transit light pump served with Ford's own brigade at its plant at Southampton, England.***

■ ABOVE LEFT ***1940 Fordson 7V Thames heavy pumps carried a rear-mounted Sulzer 3,600-litres/800-gallons-per-minute pump.***

■ ABOVE RIGHT ***A middle range Ford, this 1980 A Series 0609 control unit is powered by a 2.4-litre diesel engine.***

■ RIGHT ***Based in Idaho, USA, this 1976 6x4 Ford C/Howe/LTI 20m/65ft aerial ladder is fitted with a 4,500-litres/1,000-gallons-per-minute pump.***

■ **RIGHT** ***This 1994 Ford L8000/New Lexington tanker has a water capacity of 8,200 litres/1,800 gallons.***

■ **BELOW RIGHT** ***A 5,700-litres/1,250-gallons-per-minute pump is carried by this 1985 Ford C8000/Van Pelt/FMC pumper.***

In 1965 Ford launched the improved D series 4 to 10-ton chassis with a 6-litre diesel engine. Over the next ten years, large numbers of water tenders were built on the Ford D1014 3.4m/134in chassis, especially for county fire brigades, together with emergency and foam tenders, hose layers, prime movers and other specials using the heavier D1317 and 1617 series Ford with the Perkins V8 540 engine.

A number of Ford A series 3.5–5.5-ton chassis with a 2.4-litre diesel engine also went into service in the UK, mostly as compact rescue tenders. For some years, the ubiquitous Ford Transit, particularly the 130 and 160 series, has been extensively modified for fire service use across Europe, usually as lightweight or first response fire tenders.

In 1986 the commercial trucks division of Ford was acquired by IVECO, however in recent years Ford's association with fire vehicles has continued, with Ford F-series pick-ups and chassis-cabs used as the basis for a wide variety of light-duty and fast-response vehicles around the world, powered by both petrol and diesel engines.

■ **LEFT** ***Kearsarge Fire Department, Pennsylvania, took delivery of this Ford F550-based 4x4 Pierce fire truck in 2021.***

■ **LEFT** ***A 1976 Ford C617/InterContinental tractor unit functions as a fire safety classroom.***

FORT GARRY INDUSTRIES (FGI)

The Canadian fire engine manufacturer Fort Garry Industries (FGI) began life in 1919 as an automotive repairer and distributor. In the early 1950s, the company built its first fire engine for a small-town fire department in Manitoba. However, it was not until 1979 that FGI took the decision to manufacture fire engines as a core part of its overall business activities.

FGI built its first modern fire engines, two pumpers for their local Winnipeg fire department, in 1986. These were built on a Kovatch chassis, believed to be the first in Canada. The following year it produced a number of pumpers for use in Winnipeg, based on a Spartan chassis. It built its first aerial ladder in 1989 and since then has used virtually every variety of North American aerial ladder for its high-rise fire engines.

One of the more unusual vehicles built by FGI is a tracked firefighting vehicle built for the Petawawa (Ontario) and

RESCUE TENDER

Year	1996
Engine	6-cylinder diesel
Power	350hp
Transmission	automatic
Features	front-mounted winch

■ ABOVE ***This 1996 Freightliner FL70/Fort Garry Industries rescue tender was built for service in the MOA Nickel Company, Cuba.***

■ BELOW ***A brand new 2003 Freightliner F61/KW T300 pumper is about to be delivered to Kapuskasing, Ontario, Canada.***

■ LEFT *In 2016, FGI delivered three of these tracked fire-fighting vehicles, based on a UTV International chassis, to the Canadian Armed Forces for use in Ontario and New Brunswick.*

Gagetown (New Brunswick) fire departments, and delivered in 2016. This vehicle is built on a UTV Achiever R-10 chassis and powered by an IVECO 6.7-litre diesel engine driving through a Brevini Hydrostatic Planetary Drive System. Over the past 30 years, FGI has delivered over 1,500 fire engines to fire depart-ments across Canada, and the United States. It has also exported its fire vehicles to over 15 countries, including China, Cuba, Pakistan and the United Arab Emirates.

In 2000, FGI moved into a larger modern plant in Winnipeg. It now produces a very wide range of fire engines, including pumpers, rescue units and aerial ladders, and is also the Canadian distributor for Sutphen, and a builder and distributor of Bronto Skylift products.

FRASER

Founded in 1953, the Fraser Engineering Group of Lower Hutt, New Zealand, incorporates a specialist fire vehicle section, which manufactures a range of fire engines for fire brigades of both New Zealand and Australia. The vehicles include heavy pumpers for urban use, foam tenders, industrial pumpers and airport crash tenders, built on a variety of chassis, including IVECO, Scania and Isuzu.

Altogether, Fraser has built more than 200 different fire engines. Recently, the company delivered a batch of heavy pumper units, all based on the Scania 94D-260 chassis, to the Metropolitan Fire Service of South Australia.

HEAVY PUMPER	
Year	2002
Engine	diesel
Power	260bhp
Transmission	manual
Features	high-output water pump

■ ABOVE *With Lowes Industries no longer in business, South Australia turned to another New Zealand manufacturer, Fraser Fire and Rescue Limited, to augment its pumper fleet. This Scania 94D-260 2002 example features a Waterous pump.*

FREIGHTLINER

■ BELOW *Henrico Fire Department, Virginia, took delivery of this Freightliner-based Pierce Tanker in 2021.*

Founded in 1939 and based in Portland, Oregon, Freightliner has become one of America's major heavy-duty truck manufacturers. When a fire department requires a bonnet-hood type configuration for a fire vehicle, several American fire engine manufacturers, including Emergency One, choose the heavy-duty Freightliner chassis.

Freightliners are also often used when an all-wheel drive is required. Freightliner tractor units are regularly utilized to draw various heavy articulated fire applications, such as trailer-borne command and control units.

FL80 PUMPER

Year	1996
Engine	6-cylinder diesel
Power	350hp
Transmission	automatic
Features	4,540 l/1,000 gpm pump

■ LEFT *A 1999 Freightliner/Hackney rescue and air tender sports an eye-catching livery.*

■ BELOW *This 1996 Freightliner/4-Guys tanker has a 13,600-litre/3,000-gallon tank.*

■ BELOW *Flaked hose is stowed above the pump bay in transverse lockers on this 1990 Freightliner/Anderson pumper, which belongs to the White Rock Fire Department, in British Columbia, Canada.*

■ LEFT *North Garden Fire Company, Albemarle County, Virginia, USA, run this 1996 Freightliner FL80/Smeal pumper.*

■ BELOW *This Freightliner-based Emergency Support Unit was in service with the Toronto Fire Department in 2014.*

OTHER MAKES

■ FAP

A manufacturer of industrial vehicles, FAP was based in Belgrade, Yugoslavia (now Serbia). It supplied the chassis base and bodies for various types of fire engine in use throughout Eastern Europe for some years. FAP originally used a French Saurer truck chassis, built locally under licence. These units had Renault engines, but in the 1970s FAP started to manufacture their own series. A typical FAP water/foam tender using a Saurer 4x4 chassis had a 6-cylinder, 8-litre, 130bhp diesel engine, a 3,500-litre/770-gallon water tank and a 1,600-litres/350-gallons-per-minute firefighting pump.

■ FOUTS BROS

Fouts Brothers was founded in Smyrna, Georgia, in 1952, and began producing fire trucks in 1990, initially concentrated on tanker production. In 2019, the company moved to larger premises to Milledgeville, still within Georgia. The company builds pumpers, tankers and rescue units on both custom and commercial chassis, still with tankers as the core products, producing around 7,500 trucks per year for fire departments across the USA.

■ FRONTLINE FIRE AND RESCUE

One of Australia's newest fire-vehicle manufacturers, Frontline Fire and Rescue, based in Malaga, WA, was formed in 2007 and produces a range of emergency vehicles, including pumpers, tankers and rescues on a range of chassis, such as Isuzu, Toyota and Scania.

General Motors

■ BELOW *This 1927 General Motors pumper shows the classic lines of post-World War I American fire engines.*

■ BENEATH *An immaculate 1956 General Motors pumper of Frankford Fire Company, Delaware.*

Since the 1950s the General Motors Corporation of America (GMC) has manufactured a number of special chassis that have been used by fire brigades as pumpers, rapid intervention vehicles and emergency tenders. By the 1960s, a number of GMC fire engines could be found in the Netherlands, including those providing a base for Magirus turntable ladders.

In America the GMC 7,500 series with a V6 engine was a popular choice for compact pumpers. Front-mounted

7500 SERIES LIGHT PUMPER	
Year	1972
Engine	V6 petrol
Power	6-litre
Transmission	5-speed manual
Features	front-mounted pump

■ BELOW *A long-wheelbase 1997 General Motors T8500/Hub pumper of Sasamat Fire Department, Belcarra, British Columbia.*

■ BELOW LEFT *This 1964 General Motors/LN Curtis pumper carries a 4,540-litre/1,000-gallon tank.*

■ BELOW RIGHT *A British long-wheelbase 1987 General Motors K30 fire engine runs as a rescue tender.*

■ BELOW MIDDLE *Wells Fire Department, Nevada, USA, own this 1985 General Motors 7000/Welch pumper.*

■ BOTTOM *This 1978 6x4 General Motors General/FTI heavy pumper is run by Kings County Fire Department, in California.*

pumps were available on this GMC chassis configuration giving outputs up to 5,700 litres/1,250 gallons per minute. A 4,500-litre/1,000-gallon water tank could be fitted to this model. From 1985 the later K3500 chassis with a Chevrolet engine was also popular with a number of UK bodybuilders, including Saxon Sanbec, American Vehicles and Angloco, for emergency/rescue tender use. Several of these GMC emergency/rescue tenders have been built with a stretched wheelbase to improve their overall equipment carrying capacity.

General Safety

■ BELOW *Grand Forks Fire Department, North Dakota, USA, run this 1987 Spartan/General Safety pumper.*

■ BOTTOM LEFT *This 1975 Ford C8000/General Safety pumper carries a 3,400-litre/750-gallon water tank and pumps 4,500 litres/1,000 gallons a minute.*

Correctly known as General Safety Equipment, this company was founded in 1929 in Wyoming, Minnesota, by the grandfather of the current president, Kevin Kirvida. The continuing family involvement over the years has helped General Safety establish a proud tradition of quality and innovation.

The company's achievements were marked in 1950, when its production work for military bases received the US Army/Navy E Award, the highest recognition given to civilian companies.

Today, General Safety manufactures a range of finely crafted pumpers, aerials, airport crash tenders and industrial fire engines.

Together with Rosenbauer International, Central States and RK Aerials, General Safety is a partner in Rosenbauer America. This joint enterprise was formed in the 1990s to use the partner companies' combined expertise in technology, design, manufacturing and other resources to provide an American base for the export of US-designed fire engines.

■ LEFT *A spacious rear crew cab is a feature of this 1993 Kenworth/General Safety heavy pumper.*

■ BELOW *A 1992 Freightliner/General Safety pumper carries a 20m/65ft Snorkel boom.*

PUMPER

Year	1992
Engine	6-cylinder diesel
Power	350hp
Transmission	automatic
Features	19m/65ft snorkel boom

GLOSTER SARO

■ BELOW ***In service with Gatwick Airport Fire Service, London, in the mid-1980s, this Gloster Saro Meteor 4x4 foam tender features front-end ground clearance and bumper-mounted auxiliary monitor.***

Gloster Saro, a member of the British aircraft manufacturer Hawker Siddeley Group, built a number of specialist airport foam and crash tenders, in particular for the Royal Air Force. Earlier models used the Thornycroft 6x6 Nubian chassis with a Rolls-Royce B81 engine, together with 4,500-litre/1,000-gallon water tank and 225-litre/50-gallon foam concentrate tank.

In 1979 Gloster Saro introduced the Javelin 6x6 model, which was capable of a foam discharge rate from the large roof-mounted monitor of 45,500 litres/10,000 gallons per minute. The lighter Meteor 4x4 model also became available at around the same time. Other Gloster Saro airfield foam and crash tenders designed for military use were based on the Scammell low-line chassis.

JAVELIN FOAM TENDER

Year	1979
Engine	V16 diesel
Power	600bhp
Transmission	automatic
Features	45,400lpm/10,000gpm output

■ RIGHT ***The central driving position is a feature of this 6x4 Simon/Gloster Saro Protector heavy foam tender.***

GRUMMAN/HOWE/OREN

This American fire engine manufacturer, which had its headquarters at Roanoke, Virginia, is also well known for military and business aircraft. The direct involvement of Grumman Allied Industries, Inc, in fire engines, dates from 1968 when it acquired the Howe-Oren Company, a long-established joint manufacturer of American fire engines.

The Howe element of this company had built horse-drawn pumps as far back as the 1880s and delivered its first motorized pumper in 1908 before going on to construct hundreds more over the following years. In 1965, Howe bought the Oren Company, which at the time was a much smaller manufacturer of traditional pumpers. Grumman soon

■ ABOVE ***In service with Whatcom County Fire District, Evershon, Washington, this 1984 Chevrolet Kodiak Grumman pumper incorporates a 4,500-litres/1,000-gallons-per-minute pump and a 4,500-litre/1000-gallon water tank.***

■ RIGHT *Jamestown Fire Department, North Dakota, runs this 1983 6x4 Grumman 29m/95ft aerial ladder. It is fitted with a 6,800-litres/1,500-gallons-per-minute fire pump.*

brought a new and modern styling to the Howe-Oren range of fire engines, at the same time introducing a new series of its own custom-built pumpers.

These vehicles went under the name of the Firecat, Minicat and Wildcat series, depending, among other things, on their pumping and water tank capacity. The Grumman Firecat was available on various commercial chassis, such as Ford, International Harvester and GMC. The aluminium-bodied Minicat series came on a Ford or Chevrolet chassis and was designed primarily for a fast, all-terrain cross-country ability, where its 1,350-litres/300-gallons-per-minute pump could be used to good advantage.

Grumman closed its fire-apparatus operation in 1992, and today the Roanoke plant is used by KME.

OTHER MAKES

■ GFT INTERNATIONAL
GFT International GmbH manufactured a prolific number of fire engines at its factory in Munich, Germany, and delivered an impressive 2,000 fire engines during its period of operations. The wide range of firefighting and rescue vehicles, which included water tenders, turntable ladders, aerial platforms, airfield crash tenders and hose layers was based on various commercial chassis, including Mercedes and MAN. The company went into liquidation in 2014.

■ GRÄF & STIFT
In addition to trucks, Gräf & Stift of Vienna, Austria, produced a range of fire engines. After World War II, heavier Gräf & Stift fire engines such as turntable ladders were mounted on the 120KN chassis fitted with a 120bhp diesel engine. This chassis was robust enough to accommodate a 30m/100ft-turntable ladder. The company's range of lightweight fire tenders was expanded in the 1950s by their merger with the Vienna-based truck manufacturer OAF. Many OAF light fire tenders were built on the A90, 1.5-ton, 4x4 chassis, which carried a portable 750-litres/165-gallons-per-minute pump.

■ RIGHT *Tacoma Fire Department, Washington, run this 1989 Spartan Gladiator/ Grumman pumper.*

■ BELOW *This white-liveried 1988 6x4 Grumman tanker is in service with Rohoboth Beach, Delaware.*

■ BELOW *A 1991 Isuzu/Hackney hazardous materials unit in service with Kent Fire Department, Washington.*

■ BOTTOM *A 1999 Hackney Heavy Rescue Tender showing the wide range of rescue tools carried on board.*

HACKNEY

Soon after it was founded in 1946, the American company Hackney began specializing in truck bodies for the delivery of consumer beverages. The introduction of the all-aluminium sideload, roll-up door body occurred in the 1960s and demand for this developing technology led Hackney to open a second, more modern manufacturing plant in 1972 at Independence, Kansas. Today, the company is the world's largest producer of side-loader, overhead door truck bodies and trailers.

Hackney built its first purpose-built fire engine in 1984 for the fire department in Salem, Oregon. This was termed an emergency support vehicle and soon a number of other American

fire departments had convinced Hackney of the growing need for a new generation of rescue and support tenders to carry the ever-increasing amount of specialist equipment used in fire and rescue operations.

Today, the dedicated fire engine division known as Hackney EV is a leader in the design and build of rescue fire engines and emergency support units. These include heavy, medium and light rescue units, rescue/pumpers, mobile air units (for replenishing and servicing breathing sets at the scene of major incidents), hazardous material trailers, and incident command units.

Hackney's Classic heavy rescue

DF0976 HEAVY RESCUE

Engine	380bhp Paccar PX-9
Features	NightScan 6m/20ft light tower mounted between cab and body with six 1500-watt flood lamps

■ BELOW *This Hackney-bodied Freightliner emergency response unit operates at Dover, Delaware.*

■ MIDDLE *A mobile air-support vehicle built by Hackney in partnership with Darley for the Illinois MABAS organisation. The vehicle has a system capable of filling 80 air bottles per hour.*

vehicles incorporate the company's drop/pinch frame technology which makes use of the space below the chassis frame, which is typically wasted on many vehicle designs. This allows heavy and bulky components to be wheeled in and out of low compartments to avoid unnecessary lifting, and also maximises storage space.

■ BOTTOM *This 2014 Hackney heavy-duty rescue based on a Kenworth T370 chassis, serves with the Pumpkin Center Fire Department, Jacksonville, North Carolina.*

HAHN

■ BELOW *Rebuilt in 1992, this Hahn HCP12 pumper serves with North Providence Fire Department, Rhode Island, USA.*

Hahn Motors Incorporated had their manufacturing base in Hamburg, Pennsylvania, USA. Founded in 1923, the company built a significant number of durable and reliable fire engines, including pumpers, tractor-drawn, rear-mounted aerial ladders, and rescue/salvage tenders for fire departments across the USA. Unusually for a medium-sized manufacturer, Hahn built their own custom fire engine chassis, which for some time was also used by other smaller fire engine manufacturers. Hahn also utilized a number of commercial chassis, such as those of fire engine manufacturer International, for its vehicles, depending on a fire department's particular technical specification.

After World War II, Hahn's forward control fire engines were designed with an identifiable rounded frontal shape to their crew cabs. During the 1970s a typical Hahn tractor-drawn aerial ladder unit was powered by a General Motors V8 Detroit diesel delivering 350bhp through an Allison automatic transmission. Such an aerial fire engine would be fitted with a Grove 30m/100ft centre-mounted ladder, which, due to its considerable length was provided with a

CUSTOM	
Year	1973
Engine	V8 diesel
Power	350hp
Transmission	automatic
Features	tractor for aerial ladders

■ BELOW *Lime Rock Fire District, Rhode Island, operates this powerful 1988 Hahn HCP12 pumper.*

■ RIGHT *Blades Fire Company, Delaware, owns this 1970 International/ Hahn pumper.*

■ BELOW RIGHT *This 1984 Hahn rescue and salvage tender is operated by Milford Fire Company, Delaware.*

■ BOTTOM *A 1930 Hahn pumper of t he Brandywine Hundred Fire Company, Bellafonte, Delaware.*

rear-steer tiller cab. A 908-litres/200-gallons-per-minute inbuilt pump was fitted to provide an independent basic firefighting attack. In the 1980s, the Hahn HCP 12 pumper was a popular choice with many East Coast fire departments and a number of these were built with pumping capacities up to 6,810 litres/1,500 gallons per minute.

Hahn ceased production in 1990, although a number of the company's fire vehicles, including some that have been refurbished, remain in active service with American fire departments.

HME

Now known as HME Ahrens-Fox after merging with Ahrens-Fox, Hendrickson Mobile Equipment, Inc (HME) was already the largest independent builder of custom fire engine chassis in North America. Founded in 1913, HME is widely recognized for a tradition of technological innovation. From its manufacturing headquarters at Wyoming, Michigan, HME builds fire engines not just for American fire departments but also for diverse customers around the world. The company utilizes the latest computer technology for its customized fire engine design in order to accommodate every conceivable special feature that a fire department may require.

Today, HME Ahrens-Fox products display an integrated HME-Ahrens-Fox badge, and the two companies have combined in an innovative process of vertical integration to provide world-leading fire-fighting technology.

■ ABOVE *This 1984 Hendrickson/Van Pelt pumper can deliver 4,500 litres/1,000 gallons per minute.*

■ LEFT *A 1979 Hendrickson/Van Pelt pumper of Anderson Fire Department, California.*

In 1992, HME introduced the 1871 series of pumper chassis, aerial ladders and platforms. The numbering of the 1871 chassis range was a deliberate recognition of the year of the Great Fire of Chicago as well as the company's own historical origins close to the city. The cost-effective HME Silverfox was introduced in 2002, and remains an industry standard for high-performance custom pumper capability and functionality.

From 2014, the integration of HME and Ahrens-Fox began, and the companies' combined technologies led to the launch of a new range of aerial products under the HME-Ahrens banner. A further raft of technology updates was introduced from 2017, with glass-screen technology, touch-screen controls and a stainless-steel centrifugal pump launched alongside a new range of vehicles including the Model 18 Type 1 Interface and RAT (Rapid Attack Truck) pumpers.

■ LEFT *The Ahrens-Fox WUI (Wildland Urban Interface), built on a high-ground-clearance 4x4 chassis, is highly manoeuvrable and can cope with demanding terrain to deal with wildland fires.*

■ RIGHT *This International/HME/Boise Mobile Equipment heavy rescue tender was delivered in 2000 to Barrington Fire Department, Arlington Heights.*

■ BELOW LEFT *HME MiniEvo mini-pumpers are based on Ford F-series or RAM chassis – RAM 5500, powered by 6.7-litre Cummins diesel engine shown here – and feature a 416-gallon/1,800-litre water tank.*

■ ABOVE *The Detroit Fire Department took delivery of the first of several HME Heavy Rescues, powered by 370bhp Cummins diesel engines and Allison 3000EVS transmissions, in 2017.*

HINO

Tokyo-based Hino began building trucks in 1917 and has since expanded to become a global company. In 2001 Hino became a subsidiary of the Toyota Motor Corporation.

The first Japanese firefighting and rescue hydraulic platform, used by Tokyo Fire Brigade, was built on an open-cab Hino chassis. In the 1970s the Hino 6x2 twin-steer heavy COE chassis was used to mount a 32.6m/107ft turntable ladder powered by a Hino DK10 200bhp diesel engine. It had air brakes, a water tank and an integral fire pump as well as a search light and a spray system at its top to protect the firefighter from radiated heat.

Hino also built a range of water tenders on the Ranger chassis, as used by Tokyo Fire Brigade. These had a midships-mounted 2,200 litres/484 gallons per minute water pump and a 2,500-litre/550-gallon water tank. Other Hino chassis, such as the FH22 range, have been used outside Japan as water tenders for both city and rural firefighting use. Some of the most recent Hino chassis, particularly the low-profile 6x4 configurations, are utilized for aerial ladder platforms, and the Hino Ranger has been widely used as the basis for rescue units and pumpers.

■ ABOVE *A Hino FH22 OKD 4x4 water tender in operational service with the Cyprus Fire Service stands at the ready.*

■ RIGHT *A Hino 6x4/Morita Super Gyro 30m/100ft aerial ladder platform serves in Japan's Miyazaki Fire Department.*

HONDA

■ LEFT *This Honda Sunward mini 4x4 is used by the Hong Kong Fire Service on offshore islands.*

Many fire brigades with serious access problems in parts of their territory have made use of the range of lightweight and mini-pumping fire engines produced by Tokyo-based car manufacturer Honda. Hong Kong Fire Service, for example, ran nine Honda Sunward mini-pumps (among the world's smallest fire engines) in the late 1980s, to negotiate narrow thoroughfares and lanes on the offshore islands. The Honda mini-pump was crewed by a single firefighter and comes in two versions, one equipped with a portable pump and hose to serve as a firefighting unit, the other carrying breathing sets. The Honda Acty has also been used as the basis for mini-pumpers.

MINI PUMP	
Year	1988
Engine	twin-cylinder petrol
Power	250cc
Transmission	manual
Features	4x4

HOWE

For almost 80 years, the Howe Fire Apparatus Co of Anderson, Indiana was a name to be reckoned with in fire apparatus construction. Founded in 1872 by J C Howe, the company waited more than 30 years before it built its first pumper. Within ten years productivity had increased dramatically with a US army order for 100 fire trucks to be built on Ford T chassis. Howe also utilized chassis built by Chevrolet, International, Diamond, Oshkosh, Dodge, and Duplex among others.

The company headquarters burnt down in the late 1930s but the incident did not stop productivity and the corporation continued to go from strength to strength. In 1965 Howe acquired Coast Fire Apparatus, a rival manufacturer, but was itself bought out by the Grumman Corporation in 1976. Fire engines continued to be manufactured under the Howe logo for several years, but in 1983 productivity ceased and the Howe name disappeared from the market.

■ ABOVE: *A 1971 Ford L900/Howe pumper, Lake Samish Fire Department, WA.*

■ BELOW *This 6x4 Howe/LTI 26m/85ft rear-mount aerial ladder dates from 1976.*

HUB

Founded in 1959, in Matsqui, British Columbia, Canada, HUB built its first fire engine, an F-series Ford pumper, in the same year. The company grew steadily and by the 1960s was constructing a range of fire engines on various commercial chassis, including International, Ford and GMC, for fire departments across Canada. By 1979, HUB was also using Mack chassis for its pumper range.

In 1986, HUB entered the aerial fire engine market through an agreement with British manufacturer Simon Snorkel. At that time Simon hydraulic platforms were rare in Canada. Several HUB/Simon aerials were manufactured over the next few years, including a 31.4m/103ft Simon model mounted on a Mack series R chassis destined for North Vancouver Fire Department.

■ ABOVE *A 1986 6x4 Peterbilt/HUB/Simon 23.5m/77ft hydraulic platform.*

■ LEFT *Built on a raised-roof Spartan MetroStar chassis, this 2019 HUB Pumper is powered by a 450bhp Cummins diesel.*

From 1988 to 1991, HUB was the Emergency-One dealer in Canada, and in 1998, a further partnership with LaFrance was struck. This collaboration saw the first of a range of HUB fire engines being built on the Eagle chassis for Canadian fire departments. The company continues to expand its output, with pumpers, rescues and tankers built predominantly on Freightliner and Spartan chassis.

MISSION FIRE RESCUE

Year	2018
Engine	Cummins L9 diesel
Power	450bhp
Transmission	Allison EVS 3000 automatic
Features	2,500-litre/555-gallon tank

■ ABOVE LEFT *A Freightliner-based HUB Pumper.*

■ LEFT *An early example of a North American Snorkel was this 1972 23m/75ft 6x4 Inc-Co/HUB.*

OTHER MAKES

■ HANOMAG-HENSCHEL

When the two long-established German truck manufacturers Hanomag and Henschel merged in 1968, each company had already built hundreds of water tenders and compact light fire engines. Many of these vehicles had 4x4 drive, including the 1967 Hanomag F45 series. The 1967 Henschel HS100 series 4x4 diesel engine water tender had a 1,500-litres/330-gallons-per-minute pump and a 2,000-litre/440-gallon water tank.

■ HAYES

Daniel Hayes, an American engineer, built the first high-reach wooden aerial ladder mounted on a turntable base in 1868 for San Francisco Fire Department. Requiring the combined efforts of six firemen, his new horse-drawn ladder could be wound up to 26m/85ft. The Hayes aerial heralded a revolution in high-rise firefighting techniques. Before then the maximum height of firefighting ladders had been around 15m/50ft, but these earlier slim-width ladders were often unstable. Hayes disposed of the rights of his ladder design in 1882 to the LaFrance Steam Engine Company, which in 1903 became part of the much larger American LaFrance organization.

INTERNATIONAL

■ BELOW *A 2021 Pierce Tanker, powered by a 400bhp Cummins engine, built on an International chassis for the Henrico Fire Department, Virginia.*

With several manufacturing bases in the USA, International has produced a number of commercial truck chassis that have been used for fire engine construction, including light and standard pumpers and rescue tender applications. For many years, the International chassis included a bonneted-cab layout, and in 1970 a forward-control version was available.

In the 1970s a Ward LaFrance-bodied International T73–250-IHC1800-10 pumper used a 4.3m/169in International Loadstar 1800 chassis powered by a V8 engine and fitted with a 1,135-litres/250-gallons-per-minute pump and a 4,500-litre/1,000-gallon water tank. A number of International-chassied Darley water tenders were built for the newly nationalized New Zealand Fire Service in 1976, and Australian-built International chassis were used for water tenders and turntable ladders by both the South Australian Fire Service and New South Wales Fire Brigade. In recent years, Pierce has built a range of pumpers on International chassis.

■ BELOW *A 1980 International 6x4 tractor provides the pulling power for this Houston Fire Company, Delaware, water tanker.*

■ LEFT *This military firefighting and rescue tender utilizes a heavy-duty International 6x6 chassis.*

■ BELOW *Typical of modern Australian urban fire engines, this International 1800/ACCO water tender belongs to New South Wales Fire Brigade. It is shown here standing at the ready outside Kent Street Fire Station in Sydney.*

■ BELOW *A 1969 International Fleetstar/Superior (USA) of Shoshone County Fire District, Pinehurst, Idaho.*

ISUZU

The Japanese motor manufacturer Isuzu has produced various types of fire engines for many years. Among the first of the modern generation was the TXG20 of the 1960s, which was used for many water tenders. This open-cab vehicle had a 2,250-litre/500-gallon midships-mounted pump, a 3,000-litre/660-gallon water tank and water monitor.

Isuzu chassis are also used for mounting Morita turntable ladders, such as the 40m/130ft model. In the early 1970s Isuzu was also using its low-profile YZ20 tandem-axle chassis, powered by a 10.1-litre, 6-cylinder engine with 195bhp, as a base for the Morita turntable ladders, including the 40m/130ft version. The Chinese Powerstar Trucks company has built a range of fire trucks on Isuzu chassis for many years, and has exported its rescue and pumper trucks around the world.

■ ABOVE *Japanese-built Isuzu chassis are increasingly used for Australian fire engines, such as this heavy rescue tender.*

■ RIGHT *In 2020, the Philippines Bureau of Fire Protection (BFP) took delivery of a total of 84 new fire appliances from Isuzu Philippines, including this aerial truck.*

IVECO

IVECO (Industrial Vehicles Corporation), the commercial wing of Fiat of Italy, became involved with the manufacture of fire engines soon after it acquired the German Magirus-Deutz in 1975. This commercial truck concern was also a long-standing builder of firefighting vehicles and before long the famous Magirus fire engines were bearing the IVECO name.

Magirus has also long been associated with turntable ladders and the IVECO 120, 140, 192 and 256 chassis have all been widely used as a base for Magirus turntable ladders, which continue to appear under the Magirus name.

Today, Magirus uses IVECO trucks as the basis for a wide range of pumpers, rescue, aerial and specialist fire-fighting vehicles, including the GTLF 6x4 pumper, with a 12,000-litre water-tank capacity and a pump capacity of 3,000 litres per minute.

■ LEFT *A 2000 4x4 Iveco Magirus compact hydraulic platform/pump.*

■ BOTTOM LEFT *This IVECO Magirus TLF 3000, with 3,000-litre/660-gallon water tank and 200-litre/44-gallon foam tank, was delivered to the Riga Fire Department in Latvia in 2016.*

■ BOTTOM RIGHT *An Iveco/DAF 19.463 4x4 heavy rescue tender.*

JOHN DENNIS COACHBUILDERS

When in 1984 the British, Hestair-owned Dennis company ceased building complete fire engines to concentrate on producing specialist chassis, John Dennis (grandson of one of the original founders of Dennis Brothers in 1895) decided to set up his own bodybuilding company. Thus in 1986 the infant John Dennis Coachbuilders bodied its first Dennis fire engine chassis, and within two years the company had developed to utilize its first non-Dennis chassis. By 1990 John Dennis's business had grown to the extent that the company had to move into a larger purpose-built factory in Guildford, Surrey, England.

John Dennis built up an enviable reputation for quality. In 1995, the company achieved UK market leadership for the first time, supplying nearly half of Britain's fire brigades. The company built a range of fire engines for the European market, including light water tenders, rescue and emergency tenders, animal-rescue vehicles, multi-purpose refinery vehicles, command and control units, hose layers and operational support units. In addition to traditional water tenders based on Dennis, MAN, Mercedes Benz, Scania and Volvo chassis, John Dennis also built specialist fire engines on other chassis such as Steyr Pinzgauer, Mercedes Unimog and Land Rover. John Dennis Coachbuilders ceased production of new vehicles and closed its doors in February 2019.

DENNIS SABRE	
Year	1994
Engine	6-cylinder diesel
Power	295bhp
Transmission	5-speed automatic
Features	Cummins Euro 3 engine

■ TOP AND ABOVE ***The locker stowage of a typical 1994 John Dennis Coachbuilders/ Dennis Sabre TSD233 water tender was impeccably designed. This vehicle was built for Wiltshire Fire Service, England.***

■ LEFT ***A John Dennis Coachbuilders IVECO Eurocargo-based fire appliance delivered to Kent Fire and Rescue Service, UK, in 2016.***

OTHER MAKES

■ **JAY-FONG**

The Jay-Fong factory in Manchuria, China, has been building large numbers of standard fire engines for use throughout China since the mid-1950s. Based on the Jay-Fong CA-10 bonneted chassis, its standard fire engine came in either a water tender form or a water tanker version.

Jay-Fong water tenders have front or midships-mounted water pumps and a six-man crew cab. Jay-Fong also produces a Chinese jeep-style 4x4, used extensively as light pumps for firefighting in remote rural areas.

■ **J C MOORE INDUSTRIES**

J C Moore Industries is one of the oldest manufacturers and refurbishers of fire engines in the eastern part of the USA. Based at Fredonia, Pennsylvania, the company has a model range that includes pumpers, both urban and mini, tanker pumpers, brush units and other tenders.

J C Moore fire engine deliveries included a pumper tanker on an International chassis, with stainless steel body, 11,350-litre/2,500-gallon tank, and 4,540-litres/1,000-gallons-per-minute pump. Another J C Moore tanker/pumper with a similar body, tank and pumping capacity was mounted on a Mack Granite chassis, although this vehicle had a front-mounted pump.

The company ceased operations in the late 2000s.

■ **JDF TRUCK**

The Chinese JDF Truck company was formed in 2007, and is the specialist vehicle arm of the Dongfeng Group. The company builds a wide range of fire trucks on a variety of domestic Chinese and Isuzu chassis.

■ **JEEP**

The American Jeep chassis is in operational use with a number of fire brigades on both sides of the Atlantic, especially as a fast-response rescue tender. The Jeep 320/40 model has a 3-litre V8 petrol engine, and in the tandem-axle configuration can quickly carry a considerable amount of heavy rescue equipment to the scene of an emergency.

■ BELOW ***A 1968 6x6 Jeep fire and rescue tender on duty in Delaware.***

■ BOTTOM ***This Jeep 4x4 light brush pumper serves with Linfield Fire Company, Pennsylvania.***

Kenworth

■ BELOW *A 1977 Kenworth/King pumper of Squamish Fire Department, BC, Canada.*

Both forward-control and snub-nosed Kenworth chassis are used by a number of American fire engine bodybuilders, including Maxim and Crown for pumpers, rescue tenders, water tankers and custom-built tractors used for drawing 30m/100ft aerial ladders. The Custom Fire Full Response Kenworth T880 pumper has PACCAR 330bhp engine, a 3,800-litre/833-gallon water tank, 76-litre/17-gallon foam tank and 7,500 litre/1,700-gallon-per-minute pump. The Kenworth manufacturing base is in Seattle, Washington, USA.

PIERCE KENWORTH T370 4X4 PUMPER

Year	2020
Engine	PACCAR PX-9
Power	380bhp
Transmission	Allison EV3000 automatic
Features	Hercules Compressed Air Foam System (CAFS)

■ RIGHT *This 2020 Pierce Tanker, built on a Kenworth T800 chassis, was supplied to Wayside Fire Department, Wisconsin.*

■ BELOW *Built in 1963, this Skagit County Kenworth 6x4 tanker has an 18,000-litre/4,000-gallon capacity.*

KME/Kovatch

Founded in 1946, when John 'Sonny' Kovatch Jnr acquired a modest motor repair business on his return from military duty in World War II, Kovatch Mobile Equipment (KME) is based at Nesquehoning, Pennsylvania, USA. A large part of the Kovatch organization comprises KME Fire Apparatus, which is America's largest privately owned fire engine manufacturer.

Today, KME is an industry leader in the production of custom-built special vehicles for a variety of markets across the world. The current range includes pumpers, rescue tenders, wildland vehicles, airport rescue and firefighting trucks, industrial foam tenders, water tankers and a variety of aerial ladders and firefighting platforms.

Customized chassis are constructed to the design requirements of a particular fire department in aluminium, galvannealed steel or stainless steel. Computer-controlled plasma burners and punch presses are an important part of the manufacturing operation. Fire chiefs have a choice of over 300 different configurations of crew cab.

■ LEFT *A 2017 KME 32.6m/102ft AerialCat platform built for Township of Scott Fire Department, Indiana, fitted with a 7,500-litres/1,700-gallons-per-minute pump, plus 1,500-litre/333-gallon water tank and 76-litre/17-gallon foam cell.*

Today, KME is part of the REV Group, along with E-One, Ferrara, Spartan, Smeal and Ladder Tower (LTI). KME still operates independently, and in addition to its main plant in Pennsylvania, it also operates a manufacturing facility at Roanoke in Virginia.

■ LEFT *This KME Pumper/Hazmat unit, with seating for 10 crew members, went into service with the Cuerpo de Bomberos de Tocopilla in Chile in 2020.*

■ BELOW *A 1998 KME mid-mount rear-steer aerial ladder.*

■ BELOW *The Kronenburg MAC (Major Airport Crashtender) CT009 can carry up to 18,000 litres/4,755 gallons of water and 2,000 litres/440 gallons of foam in its 8x8 form, and has a pump capacity of up to 8,000 litres/1,800 gallons per minute.*

OTHER MAKES

■ KARRIER

During the 1950s and 1960s a number of emergency, rescue and salvage tenders were built for British fire brigades by various bodybuilders using the British Karrier Gamecock 2.9m/115in-wheelbase 3–4-ton chassis. These were lightweight derivatives of the Commer commercial chassis range and ultimately all Karrier lightweight vehicles were produced under the name of the parent company.

■ KAWASAKI

The Japanese company is better known for motorcycles, but Kawasaki's engineering skills led to the production of some of the world's smallest fire engines. The Kawasaki Mule, for instance, has been designed with a custom-made body to provide a basic first-aid firefighting response in areas where access for full-sized fire engines is difficult, such as in pedestrianized sectors and old urban centres. The Mule two-seater 2510 model, just 1.3m/4¼ft wide and 2.9m/9½ft long, has 4-wheel drive and carries a portable pump and hose.

■ ABOVE *The Kawasaki Mule fire truck, which can carry a crew of three, was introduced in 2018 in Japan, as a small agile, off-road, first-responder vehicle.*

■ KRONENBURG

Kronenburg BV of Hedel, the Netherlands, has been in the business of manufacturing fire engines since the nineteenth century. In the 1950s and 1960s their water tenders, for urban and rural use, used British or American chassis, including Austin and Chevrolet.

In the late 1960s a typical Kronenburg airfield crash tender utilized a DAF V1600BB358 4x4 chassis with a 6-cylinder, 155bhp engine. It had a 2,000-litre/440-gallon water tank, a 400-litre/88-gallon foam compound tank and a roof-mounted monitor that could be operated from within the cab.

However, to keep up with the increasing size of passenger aircraft, Kronenburg built a large 6x6 crash/foam tender on an FWD 0-153-L6 chassis. Powered by a Waukesha V8 engine with 330bhp, this vehicle had a 6,000-litre/1,320-gallon water tank, a 1,200-litre/264-gallon foam tank and a 2,800-litres/600-gallons-per-minute pump that fed roof-mounted and ground-level monitors.

In 1996 Kronenburg supplied the British Airports Authority Fire Service with 17 6x6 airport foam/crash tenders for service at London Heathrow, Gatwick and Stansted airports.

■ KRUPP

The German truck manufacturer Krupp built a significant number of fire engines both before and after World War II. These included LF16 water tenders, rescue tenders, turntable ladders using both Metz and Magirus ladder mechanisms, and a number of heavy rescue crane trucks. The Krupp name eventually ceased to be associated with fire and rescue vehicles.

■ BELOW *A preserved 1950 LF 16 Krupp water tender.*

■ BOTTOM *A 1940 Krupp heavy pump.*

LAND ROVER

■ ABOVE *Carmichael added the extra trailing rear axle to this 1975 Range Rover 6x4 rescue tender.*

In 1948 the British Rover Motor Company produced its first 4x4 Land Rover, designed primarily for agricultural and utility use. From the earliest days, a number of rural fire brigades around the world purchased Land Rovers to operate as lightweight fire engines, as these were capable of carrying a certain amount of firefighting and rescue equipment over rough terrain. Their operational versatility and functional construction have endured over the years, and hundreds of Land Rovers have seen service as light pumps for both rural and industrial plant use, as rescue and emergency tenders, and as other specialist vehicles.

The first Land Rovers came with a 1.5-litre petrol engine, and in a light fire engine form usually carried a short ladder, a hose reel, a built-in fire pump and small water tank, a hose, and various other firefighting equipment. The first models had a 2m/80in wheelbase and although they were an immediate success, considerable development took place over the following years to widen their performance and scope of work. In 1954, the wheelbase was extended by 15cm/6in, and the rear overhang and body provision was lengthened. A long-wheelbase version was also available with the option of a 1997cc/121.8cu in engine. Land Rover wheelbase options were extended again in 1956 to 2.24m/88in or 2.77m/109in. A year later, the first diesel engine Land Rover was produced. In 1958 the Series II models were introduced. They were slightly wider, had a restyled body and some other cosmetic changes.

Modern Land Rover light fire engines are based on the Defender 110 or 130 chassis. Common firefighting and rescue items include a cab roll cage, a polypropylene water tank with inlet and fill system, a folding-knuckle crane and a powerful winch. A range of modules includes engine-driven soaker or fogging pumps, a hose reel, and a compressed air system that injects air into a water/foam mixture from an on-board compressor.

The Range Rover model was first adapted for British fire brigade operational use in 1972, when in conjunction with Carmichael Ltd an extra trailing axle was added to provide a 6x4 configuration. This enabled a far greater equipment payload to be carried, including hydraulic cutting and lifting gear, heavy rescue tools and generators for tool power and lighting. These Range Rovers were among the first to carry telescopic lighting masts to illuminate the scene of night-time accidents and other emergencies. Powered by a 3.5-litre, V8 petrol engine, many of these high-performance, light fire engines saw service mostly in fast-response rescue/emergency tender guise, especially as motorway and road networks developed. Later Range Rover models are in use with a number of UK brigades, especially in locations where access is difficult.

■ LEFT *This 1968 HCB Angus Firefly 109 light pump was one of many used at the time by UK rural fire brigades.*

■ RIGHT *The Land Rover Defender chassis, in various configurations, has been the basis for numerous designs of rescue and firefighting vehicles over many years, such as this 2012 Angloco light pumping appliance supplied for operations in Laos.*

LEYLAND

Leyland Motors Ltd of Leyland, Lancashire, England, began building fire engines soon after the first motorized fire tender appeared in the early 1900s, supplying its first model to Dublin Fire Brigade in 1910. Before long, fire engine manufacture had become a significant part of Leyland's commercial business alongside its bus and truck division, and it introduced a 6-cylinder, 85bhp petrol engine specifically for fire engine use.

By the end of World War I Leyland, along with Dennis, another English firm, was beginning to dominate the fire brigade market in the UK and throughout the British Empire. The company's fire engines were put into service as far afield as Tasmania and China. Leyland produced several specific chassis for its water tenders and pumps, including the 1920 FE model, followed in 1935 by the FK6 (with a rear-mounted 2,270-litres/500-gallons-per-minute pump) and the FK7 with a 3.5m/138in wheelbase (with a midships-mounted pump). Some FK models were utilized as limousine-type pumps/emergency tenders.

■ ABOVE *This 1939 Leyland FKT 1 pump escape served 21 years in London.*

■ LEFT *This 1935 30m/100ft Leyland/Metz turntable ladder was operational until 1965.*

Until the early 1930s Leyland turntable ladders were mounted on the Leyland LM chassis, but in 1935 the company entered into an agreement with the German turntable ladder manufacturer Metz to supply their ladder mechanisms on a special Leyland chassis. This highly successful 4.4m/174in TLM chassis was available with either an 8.6-litre Leyland diesel or a 6-cylinder, 115bhp petrol engine. The 45m/150ft Leyland/Metz turntable ladder delivered to Hull Fire Brigade in 1936 was at the time the tallest ladder in British fire service use. Some Leyland/Metz turntable ladders had built-in hydraulic jacks. Over 50 Leyland/Metz turntable ladders were manufactured before the outbreak of World War II, which brought this Anglo-German partnership to an abrupt end.

In 1939 London Fire Brigade ordered eleven Leyland FKT dual-purpose pumping fire engines. These pre-war Leyland pumps were powered by a 7.7-litre Leyland 96bhp petrol engine and could carry either a 15m/50ft-wooden wheeled escape ladder or a 10m/35ft extension ladder, and were

■ LEFT *In the 1960s some Leyland chassis were used in India as basic water tenders, such as this Delhi Fire Service vehicle.*

■ LEFT *A preserved 1953 Leyland Comet water tender of Surrey Fire Brigade, England.*

■ LEFT *This 1987 4x4 Leyland/Daf 16/17 water tanker/foam carrier serves with Hampshire Fire Brigade, England.*

■ LEFT *In 1990, Lancashire Fire Brigade, England, commissioned this Leyland Swift/Reeves Burgess coach as a control unit and canteen vehicle.*

some of the first to have all-enclosed crew cabs. During the early stages of World War II, Leyland built over 50 turntable ladders to a government order for National Fire Service use.

After the war Leyland produced its stylish Comet truck chassis with a 5.6-litre diesel engine, and some open-cab water tender/escape ladder versions of this model went to India. The real Leyland fire engine innovation came in 1958, however, with the introduction of the Firemaster chassis. Using Leyland bus and coach parts and powered by an underfloor, midships-mounted 9.8-litre Leyland diesel engine with 150bhp, this chassis allowed the 4,500 litres/1,000 gallons per minute fire pump and its controls to be fitted at the front of the fire engine. Another unusual fire engine feature was the 4-speed semi-automatic transmission via a fluid flywheel and epicyclic gearbox, probably making this one of the first of the two pedal-controlled fire engines.

Two Magirus turntable ladders were built on the Firemaster chassis, but despite its technical features the Firemaster was not a commercial success and only a handful went into operational service.

In 1962 British Leyland acquired the AEC Company and 12 years later absorbed Albion. Various water tenders, emergency tenders and other special vehicles were built in the 1970s and 1980s using Leyland chassis, including the Laird, the Boxer, the Terrier and the Mastiff. British Leyland was acquired by DAF Vehicles in 1987 and since then the Leyland logo has gradually disappeared from fire engines in service.

■ RIGHT *A 1990 Leyland Freighter T45–180 water tender of Greater Manchester County Fire Service, England.*

Liquip

■ LEFT *A Scania 94D 260 heavy pump of the Queensland Fire & Rescue Service.*

Founded 30 years ago, Liquip is an Australian company, based at Smithfield, Sydney, New South Wales. The organization specializes in chemical and bulk liquid distribution vehicles. Since 1996, Liquip have built various specialist rescue vehicles and fire engines for the Asia-Pacific market, including the Queensland Fire Service and South Australian Metropolitan Fire Service, plus a number of custom rescue units for the mining industry, all with steel and alloy bodies. Liquip's range of specialist fire rescue vehicles are available with two- or four-wheel drive, single or dual crew cabs, and water tank/body superstructure in a combination of steels or alloy. The company build a special 4x4 fire tender with 2,000-litre/440-gallon tank for use on sandy islands or other areas where only a 4x4 vehicle can operate.

PUMPER	
Year	1996
Engine	6-cylinder diesel
Power	275bhp
Transmission	automatic
Features	high-output pump

Lowes

■ LEFT *This Mills Tui-built Lowes/Mitsubishi rescue pumper has the capacity to pump 1,800 litres/400 gallons per minute.*

No longer in business, New Zealand-based Lowes Industries was a vehicle manufacturing company that for some years built a number of different fire engines, primarily for New Zealand and Australian fire brigades. The company utilized a number of commercial chassis, including Scania and Mitsubishi, and offered a standard design of light and heavy pumpers, as well as other fire engine types.

A typical 1990s Lowes light pump unit could be found mounted on a Mitsubishi FK160F chassis with a 1,800-litres/400-gallons-per-minute pump and a 2,000-litre/440-gallon water tank.

In 1997, Lowes delivered a rescue pumper bodied on the Scania 93M-250 chassis to the South Australian Metropolitan Fire Service. It featured conspicuous yellow striping, a front-mounted winch and roll-out rescue equipment trays. Two years later, the same brigade received a number of Lowes pumpers on the uprated Scania 94DB-260 chassis. These fire engines were fitted with a Darley 3,800-litres/840-gallons-per-minute pump.

■ RIGHT ***Lowes built a series of pumpers for the South Australian Metropolitan Fire Service on 3 and 4 Series Scania chassis. Darley 3,800-litres/840-gallons-per-minute pumps were standard.***

LTI/LTC

LTI (Ladder Towers Inc) was founded in 1974, and soon developed its own chassis, christened the LTI Olympian. A succession of acquisitions and mergers then took place, with ownership of LTI passing through Simon (owners of the Snorkel brand), and later to American LaFrance. In 2014, LTI was acquired by Smeal, after American LaFrance ceased trading. Smeal itself later became part of the REV group, bringing LTI with it to sit alongside E-One, Ferrara, Spartan and KME. When Smeal acquired LTI, its name was changed to Ladder Tower Corporation (LTC).

Today, LTC produces a range of models, including rear or mid-mounted models, together with tractor-drawn versions. They are available in aerial ladder/articulated boom aerial ladder/water tower and ladder platform configurations. The range includes aerial ladders at 22.8m/75ft, 30.4m/100ft and 33.5m/110ft, plus 30.4m/100ft and 32.0m/105ft tractor-drawn versions. There is also a 28.3m/93ft mid-mount platform.

■ ABOVE ***A 2001 Spartan/LTI tractor-drawn, mid-mount rear-steer aerial ladder.***

■ BELOW ***A 2020 LTC 110ft/33.5m Rear Mount Ladder in service with Dale City Volunteer Fire Department, Virginia.***

LUVERNE

■ ABOVE ***This 1989 Autocar/Luverne pumper has a 6,800 litres/1,500 gpm pump.***

The Leicher brothers acquired the Luverne Wagon Works, of Luverne, Minnesota, USA, in 1896. After the company produced its first car in 1903, it followed up with a number of motorized funeral hearses, and then its first commercial truck. In 1912 the company built the first Luverne fire engine and three years later, its first pumper. Luverne then continued steadily to develop its range of pumpers and other fire vehicles, including 75 fire engines under the Nott name, for small town fire departments.

In 1985, Luverne Fire Apparatus was purchased by Luverne Truck Equipment. This company produced bumpers, grill guards and mirrors for every manufactured truck and van in the United States. Soon after, there followed a move to a new manufacturing facility in Brandon, South Dakota.

In 1997, Luverne was acquired by Spartan Motors, Inc, which in the early 1990s had also purchased the Quality fire apparatus company. In January 2003, Luverne and Quality were amalgamated to form a new fire engine manufacturer, Crimson Fire, on the South Dakota factory site. Crimson Fire was later acquired by Spartan, now part of the REV Group. Fire trucks are still manufactured at the Brandon site under the Spartan name.

■ LEFT ***A Spartan 6x4 chassis forms the base for this Minnesota-based 1994 Luverne pumper/tanker. It features a 9,000-litre/2,000-gallon water tank.***

■ LEFT *This 1954 Mack pumper served in Georgetown Fire Department, Delaware.*

■ BELOW LEFT *Camano Island Fire and Rescue, Washington, run this 1981 6x4 Mack RS/Smiley's 13,600-litre/ 3,000-gallon tanker.*

MACK

Having started life as a maker of truck and bus chassis, Mack was one of the longest established American fire engine manufacturers. Originally founded in 1900 in Brooklyn, New York, the company moved several years later to its base at Allentown, Pennsylvania, where it subsequently became one of America's major truck manufacturers and one of its largest builders of complete fire engines of various types.

Mack produced its first tractor in 1909, designed specifically for towing fire equipment, and built its first pumping fire engine two years later. This was sold to the Union Fire Association of Pennsylvania and was soon followed by a motor-driven hook and ladder truck. Many of the early twentieth-century Mack fire engines were built on the AC model 3½-ton truck chassis, which was soon to be adopted by the US army as the standard military truck. Following World War I, Mack army trucks had a well-deserved reputation for reliability and performance. As a result, Mack vehicles acquired the nickname 'Bulldog', consquently the company adopted the bulldog motif as its insignia. The successful AC model remained in production for over 20 years.

A feature of Mack's early articulated aerial ladders was their length. One was so long that it required the rear axle to be steered by a rear steersman. In 1935 Mack designed and built the first enclosed fire engine in the USA for Charlotte Fire Department of North Carolina. This Sedan model pump incorporated a 3,400-litres/750-gallons-per-minute pump.

After World War II, Mack continued to develop its range of fire engines. A typical early 1950s unit was the Model B95 pumper. With a six-man sedan-type crew cab, it was powered by a Thermodyne 276bhp petrol engine and had a 4,500-litre/1,000-gallon pump. The normal-control B95 lasted in the Mack range for 16 years before being superseded by the R611. This had a 4.3m/169in wheelbase, a three-man cab with a 238bhp Mack diesel engine and a

C95FD PUMPER

Year	1965
Engine	6-cylinder diesel
Power	237bhp
Transmission	2-speed automatic
Features	5-man canopy cab

■ BELOW *A 1981 Mack CF tractor unit pulls a mid-mount 30m/100ft rear-steer aerial ladder in Dover, Delaware.*

■ RIGHT *This 1991 Mack MC/Custom pumper, in service with Savage Fire Department, Minnesota, USA, has a 5,700-litres/1,250-gallons-per-minute pump and a 3,400-litre/750-gallon water tank.*

■ BELOW LEFT *New York Fire Department runs this 6x4 1981 Mack CF/Baker 23m/75ft Aerialscope.*

■ BELOW RIGHT *One of several New York Fire Department c.1980 Mack CF pumpers.*

3,400-litres/750-gallons-per-minute pump. The CF model of the late 1960s went on to become one of the most popular pumps throughout the USA. One of Mack's most powerful pumping units, and probably one of the world's largest fire engines at the time, was the Super Pumper System acquired by New York Fire Department in 1965. This articulated pumping unit had a De Laval pump driven by a 2,400hp Napier Deltic diesel engine that was capable of delivering 33,600 litres/7,400 gallons per minute. It was accompanied by three Mack satellite tenders, each one capable of acting as a hose layer for the 15cm/6in-diameter hose and to provide further massive water monitors.

By this time Mack was also producing 30m/100ft aerial ladders for several fire departments throughout the United States, including New York Fire Department. The company produced its Aerialscope in 1970. This fire engine was mounted on a 3-axle chassis with a 325hp V8 diesel engine driving through a 5-speed gearbox. With telescopic booms and ladder plus a three-man bucket, the Aerialscope had a very wide range of operational ability for rescue and firefighting purposes.

After many post-war years of fire-engine production, Mack ceased production of complete fire apparatus in the mid-1980s and began to sell its chassis to other manufacturers. In 1990, the company became part of the Renault group, and soon after stopped production of the CF chassis.

■ RIGHT *City of Abbotsford Fire Department, British Columbia, Canada, operates this 1985 Mack MC/HUB pumper. It is fitted with a 4,770-litres/1,050-gallons-per-minute pump and a 2,270-litre/500-gallon water tank.*

MAGIRUS

The German firm of Magirus had its origins in 1864 when Conrad Dietrich Magirus founded his company to build fire engines and firefighting equipment. In 1872 Magirus produced a wooden turntable ladder mounted on a horse-drawn carriage chassis. Its wooden ladder sections had to be wound up and rotated by hand, but from this basic start Magirus went on to specialize in and develop rotating turntable ladder technology to become a major international supplier.

In 1932 Magirus built five 30m/100ft all-steel turntable ladders for London Fire Brigade, the first of these new ladders to have been supplied outside Germany.

In 1938 Magirus merged with the engine manufacturer Klockner Deutz and went on to produce a range of commercial truck chassis in addition to fire engines under the Magirus-Deutz badge. After World War II Magirus-Deutz resumed supplying turntable ladders to a number of Europe's fire brigades, often using Leyland or Mercedes chassis as well as its own. In the 1950s the preferred Magirus-Deutz chassis for its 18m/60ft turntable ladder was the C125 fitted with a 125bhp diesel engine. The 2020 Magirus LF-HLF 10 All-wheel is powered by a 251bhp diesel engine, and is fitted with a 2,000-litre/440-gallon water tank, and a pump capable of delivering 2,000 litres/440 gallons per minute.

Although Magirus-Deutz became part of IVECO (Industrial Vehicle Corporation) in 1975, the company has continued to produce fire vehicles under the original Magirus name. Today, Magirus produces a wide range of aerials, pumpers, rescues, airport fire-fighting trucks and specialist vehicles at plants in Germany, Italy, France and Austria, on MAN, IVECO and Mercedes chassis.

250D25

Year	1965
Engine	V12 diesel
Power	250bhp
Transmission	6-speed manual
Features	KW16 crane wagon

■ BELOW LEFT *A 1938 Magirus DL 18m/60ft wooden turntable ladder, originally used by Stuttgart Fire Brigade, Germany.*

■ BELOW RIGHT *This c.1950 Magirus Deutz foam tender served Erdol Refinery Fire Department, Duisburg, Germany.*

■ ABOVE LEFT *A Magirus Deutz c.1990 GFW water rescue unit. This fire engine carries an inflatable boat and various other items of rescue equipment.*

■ LEFT *The 2020 Magirus SuperDragon X8 airport fire engine is powered by a 1,120hp engine and has a pump capacity of 9,000 litres/1,980 gallons per minute.*

MAN

■ LEFT *This 2017 MAN/Angloco Airport Rescue and Fire Fighting Vehicle (ARFFV), was supplied to Waterford Airport in the Republic of Ireland.*

Chassis built by Munich-based MAN have been used in fire engine manufacture across Europe for some years. In the 1960s the Ziegler company provided the bodywork of a number of TLF 16 standardized German water tenders based on the MAN 450 HALF 4x4 chassis, and the HAL 4x2 version. These had a 1,600-litres/350-gallons-per-minute pump. In the UK, MAN chassis were being used on an increasing number of special fire service vehicle applications, including emergency tenders, prime movers and control units. In addition, a number of Metz 30m/100ft turntable ladders mounted on the 12–16-ton MAN 16D series chassis have gone into service.

The most recent MAN TGL, TGM, TGS and TGX chassis are used by a number of manufacturers, including Magirus and Rosenbauer. The Rosenbauer AT HLF20 uses a MAN TGM 4x2 chassis with 320hp engine and MAN TipMatic semi-automatic transmission.

■ RIGHT *This rescue tender was new to Stadt-Bottrop, Germany, in 1960.*

MARION BODY WORKS

Marion Body Works is a long-established family-owned American manufacturer of engineered truck bodies. Founded in 1905 in Marion, Wisconsin, the present ownership and management have been in place since 1980.

The company's comprehensive range of fire engines includes pumpers, rescue pumpers that combine both functions within one emergency vehicle, rescue tenders, hazmat units, and tankers. In addition, Marion also manufactures aerial ladders in conjunction with Aerial Innovations, Inc.

Marion utilize either a commercial or customized chassis, depending on a fire department's specifications. Since 1964, Marion have been building fire engines with all-aluminium bodies. The versatility of Marion-built custom rescue pumpers is well illustrated by the unit that went into operational service with Cooks Volunteer Fire Department of Charlotte, North Carolina, during 2002. This dual-purpose fire engine was built on a Spartan Gladiator chassis powered by a Detroit Diesel Series 60 430hp engine and Allison automatic transmission. The designers at Marion Body Works conceived an all-aluminium body with a six-firefighter crew cab. It has a Waterous CSU 6,810 litres/1,500 gallons per minute water pump with side control panel and a 3,405-litres/750-gallons polypropylene water tank.
In 2014, Marion delivered its 10,000th cab to a custom chassis builder, and celebrated 50 years of building all-aluminium fire apparatus.

Marion built a Rescue Pumper for Marlborough Fire Department, Massachusetts, in 2020, based on a Spartan Gladiator chassis, with a 505hp Cummins diesel engine, 4,313-litres/950-gallons polypropylene water tank, 6,810-litres/1,500 gallons-per-minute water pump and 91-litre/20-gallon foam tank.

■ ABOVE *A 2020 Marion Pumper built on a Spartan MetroStar chassis for the Belltown Fire Department, Connecticut.*

MAXIM

The Maxim Motor Company was founded in the 1900s by Carl Maxim in Middleborough, Massachusetts, USA. He built his first fire engine in 1914 and then produced a range of pumpers and trucks for a number of years before turning its principal production and development efforts towards aerial ladders. Family run for decades, in 1955 Maxim was acquired by the larger Seagrave company, and although the Maxim name continued to appear for some time, after various further ownership changes, the company went out of business in 1989.

■ ABOVE *A 1975 Maxim SLT100 30m/100ft mid-mount aerial ladder.*

■ RIGHT *This 1930 Maxim B50 pumper is fitted with a 2,270 litres/500 gallons a minute pump.*

MERCEDES-BENZ

For several years the world's largest manufacturer of commercial trucks, Stuttgart-based Mercedes-Benz features prominently in the fire brigade market. Since World War II the company has developed many chassis suitable for fire engine use in Europe.

In the 1950s the Mercedes LAF311 4x4 chassis was widely used in Germany for water tenders, while many post-war 30m/100ft Metz turntable ladders used the Mercedes-Benz L315 heavy chassis. In the 1970s the LAF1113 4x4 chassis was extensively used for pump water tenders, with many German Mercedes fire engines being

■ LEFT *A Mercedes Zetros 6x6 fire truck in service in 2017 with the Plawin fire service, attending an incident in Gorzów, Western Poland.*

ATEGO 1328

Year	2003
Engine	6-cylinder diesel
Power	280bhp
Transmission	manual or automatic
Features	disc brakes on both axles

■ LEFT *A rugged-looking Mercedes Unimog 4x4 equipment carrier belonging to Stadt-Bottrop Fire Brigade, Germany, features an HIAB hydraulic arm and front-mounted winch.*

■ FAR LEFT *Stadt-Bottrop Fire Brigade, Germany, use this medium Mercedes as a hose-laying tender.*

■ LEFT *This 1992 Mercedes Unimog 2150 L special incident unit, in service with West Yorkshire Fire Service, England, has all-terrain cross-country capability.*

bodied by Metz. In 1972 the Austrian Rosenbauer company supplied domestic brigades with water tenders using the Mercedes heavy 6x4 2232 chassis powered by a 320bhp diesel engine for service in Austria. These incorporated a 3,200-litres/700-gallons-per-minute pump, a 500-litre/110-gallon foam tank and 9,000-litre/ 2,000-gallon water tank.

More up-to-date, wider Mercedes chassis include the Unimog 1.5-ton, 2150L, 4x4 all-terrain vehicle for forest and rural firefighting, the off-road-capable, heavy-duty Zetros, available in 4x4 and 6x6 versions and powered by a 6-cylinder in-line diesel engine available in a range of outputs up to 510hp and 1,100Nm of torque at 1,100rpm, and the Econic, designed for urban environments.

MERRYWEATHER

For over 130 years the British firm Merryweather was one of the biggest names in fire engines. Its origins can be traced back to 1750 when Adam Nuttall started a company in London, England, building manual fire pumps. Through a series of partnerships, the company became Hadley, Simpkin and Lott in 1792, and was innovative in producing some of the first successful horse-drawn manuals. In 1807, Moses Merryweather joined the firm as an apprentice and by 1839 had complete control of the company. From this time the Merry-weather name became synonymous with reliable fire engines the world over.

FIRE KING	
Year	1902
Engine	2-cylinder steam
Power	30hp
Transmission	chain-driven direct
Features	self-propelling

■ LEFT *A horse-drawn 1880 Merryweather manual pump has folded white pumping handles.*

■ BELOW LEFT *London Fire Brigade once owned this 1902 Merryweather Fire King.*

Merryweather produced its first steam-powered pump in 1861 for the Hodges private fire brigade in Lambeth, London. The Deluge, as it was called, was so successful that, just one year later, Hodges ordered a second, the more powerful 2-cylinder Torrent. These famous steam pumps were instrumental in promoting the excellence of Merryweather's products. At the Crystal Palace National Steam Engine Contest in 1863, Merryweather won first prize, after which the company found its order book full with customers at home and abroad, and went on to construct eleven steam pumps in 1865.

Another Merryweather landmark was the production in 1899 of its first self-

■ RIGHT *With the pump of this Merryweather Fire King already connected to a fire hydrant, firemen set up a hose line ready for action.*

propelled steam fire engine, the Fire King. Capable of providing a firefighting water jet 45m/150ft high at 1,600 litres/350 gallons per minute, it could attain a speed of 32kmh/20mph on the flat. This first model went to India, but before long the Fire King was rapidly superseding horse-drawn steamers in the large city brigades at home. By the turn of the century, Merryweather was also producing a wide range of firefighting equipment, from extinguishers to fire escapes. One novel product was the Quadricycle, consisting of two tandem bicycles between which was suspended a platform for hose and other equipment.

Merryweather was one of the first fire engine manufacturers to utilize the petrol engine. In 1903 it supplied a combination fire escape carrier and chemical fire engine to Tottenham Fire Brigade in north London. Another breakthrough came one year later when Merryweather produced another petrol-driven fire engine for a brigade in Finchley, also in north London. In this model, engine power was also used to drive a built-in water pump. The Finchley fire engine was the precursor of its type, which was soon to be found throughout the world. At this time Merryweather also experimented with a number of battery-electric fire engines, although these needed to carry up to two tons of batteries. With the rapid development of the petrol engine for fire brigade use, interest in electric power soon diminished.

By 1908 Merryweather was taking a serious interest in turntable ladders. In this year it completed a 20m/65ft turntable ladder and innovatively used the vehicle's engine to power the extension and rotation of the wooden ladder sections. The company continued to develop its turntable ladder technology and by the 1930s was incorporating all-steel ladder sections, either on a Merryweather chassis using a Meadows or Dorman petrol engine, or on other suitable commercial chassis. The company's reciprocating water pumps were by then world famous, and it also pioneered the use of foam systems on its pumping fire engines.

Merryweather built a large number of turntable ladders for service during World War II. After the war it continued to focus attention on turntable ladder production, where hydraulic power replaced mechanical power for all ladder movements from the late 1950s. The company also provided bodywork and fire engineering on a range of fire engines for various fire brigades. Merryweather delivered its last turntable ladders in the early 1970s, after which its long-standing name faded from the scene.

■ ABOVE *A number of Merryweather pump escapes were built on an AEC Mercury chassis for the Hong Kong Fire Service in 1961.*

■ LEFT *This AEC Mercury/Merryweather 30m/100ft turntable ladder was delivered to London Fire Brigade in 1965.*

METZ

■ LEFT *This c.1950 Mercedes/Metz is typical of post-WW II German light pumping fire engine design.*

■ LEFT *A Metz turntable ladder built on a Mercedes chassis in service with the Hofgeismar Fire Department in Germany in the early 2000s.*

With its origins going as far back as 1840, the German company Metz has long been associated with the manufacture of firefighting equipment, but is best known for its turntable ladders. Mounted on a variety of suitable commercial chassis, Metz ladders have served for 70 years in the fire brigades of Europe and America. In 1933 Coventry Fire Brigade, in England, took delivery of one of the first Metz all-steel ladders. By 1935 Metz turntable ladders were being offered in 26m, 27m and 30m/85ft, 90ft and 100ft variants. These four-section all-steel ladders were mechanically raised, extended and rotated, although some 1935 models had a hydraulic jacking system. In 1935 Metz entered into an agreement with the British manufacturer Leyland to supply ladders on a Leyland chassis. These vehicles, usually with the 30m/100ft four-section variant, were sold in quantity to brigades in the UK and across the British Commonwealth. In 1936 an unusual 45m/150ft five-section Leyland/Metz turntable ladder was supplied to Kingston-upon-Hull Fire Brigade; at the time it was the tallest ladder in the British fire service, and probably in the world.

Metz re-emerged after World War II to continue developing its turntable-ladder technology, particularly with the addition of a rescue cage at the head of the ladder. With a load capacity of three persons or 270kg/595lb, this incorporates a set of controls allowing the firefighter in the rescue cage to control all the ladder movements. When not in use the cage is carried on top of the ladder. More recently Metz introduced a computerized safety system allowing rapid lifting, extension and rotation to be carried out simultaneously. The computer system also monitors various safety devices on the ladder.

Over the years, Metz has supplied over 2,000 separate aerial fire engines with rescue heights of 18–53m/60–174ft to many fire brigades around the world. These have been mounted on a variety of commercial chassis, including Seagrave, MAN, Mercedes, Scania and Volvo.

In 1998, Metz was acquired by Rosenbauer, and Rosenbauer continues to use Metz technology in its aerial ladders and platforms.

30M/100FT TURNTABLE LADDER	
Year	1937
Engine	Leyland 6-cylinder petrol
Power	115bhp
Transmission	4-speed manual
Features	midships-mounted pump

■ BELOW *A preserved 1954 Dennis F17/Metz 30m/100ft turntable ladder.*

■ LEFT *A Scania G94D-260/Mills Tui standard heavy water tender of the New Zealand Fire Service.*

MILLS-TUI

Based at Rotorua, New Zealand, Mills-Tui has built a number of fire engines for the nationalized New Zealand Fire Service and Australian fire brigades. Its range includes compact rural water tenders based on the Mitsubishi 4x4 chassis, standard water tenders in both 4x2 and 4x4 configurations using chassis such as Scania and Hino, and airport foam and crash tenders on suitable commercial chassis. Mills-Tui has also built combination heavy pumps and aerial ladder units and hazardous material units.

PUMPER

Year	1986
Engine	6-cylinder diesel
Power	185bhp
Transmission	5-speed manual
Features	crew safety cab

■ BELOW *This Mills-Tui/Mitsubishi water tender and aerial ladder is on duty in South Australia.*

MITSUBISHI

■ BELOW *A compact Mitsubishi light pump and rescue tender.*

A commercial Tokyo-based truck manufacturer, Mitsubishi provides a number of suitable chassis for fire service use in Japan and several Asian and Middle Eastern countries. These have included the Japanese fire service MWG 40 T model water tender, which is fitted with a crew cab to accommodate up to six firefighters, a 4,000-litre/880-gallon water tank and a 2,270-litres/500-gallons-per-minute pump.

The Mitsubishi/Fuso Fighter has commonly been used as the basis for fire vehicles, as has the compact Canter 4x4 chassis. In 2020, two Canter-based vehicles developed by Network Rail were delivered to Avon Fire and Rescue Service and South Wales Fire and Rescue Service to assist in dealing with any emergencies in the 4½-mile long Severn Tunnel.

■ LEFT *One of the specially adapted Mitsubishi/Fuso Canters that entered service in late 2020 in the UK.*

■ BELOW *A Hong Kong Fire Service command unit on a Mitsubishi coach chassis.*

OTHER MAKES

■ **MARTE**
Marte Vehicles was established in 1964 in Weiler, Austria, and four years later built its first fire vehicle, a light pump on a Land Rover 110 chassis. The following year, 1969, saw the start of an agency for Ziegler fire engines, and by 1977 Marte had delivered its 100th fire engine.

Steady development continued and in 1982 came an agreement with the German company, Metz, to deliver their turntable ladders to fire brigades in Austria. By 1994, Marte had built and delivered 700 fire engines.

Marte has developed a modular construction system for its fire engine manufacture which utilizes screw-jointed and bonded aluminium components together with special fibreglass reinforced plastics, to resist corrosion.

■ **MCB FIRE**
MCB was founded in 1976 in Iowa, originally to produce ambulances, and they have built a range of custom fire-fighting apparatus on various chassis, including Spartan, Freightliner and Ford F-series. In 2021, the company was sold to Ward Apparatus and moved to New York state.

■ **MIDWEST FIRE TRUCKS**
Based in Luverne, Minnesota, Midwest has produced a range of custom tankers, pumpers and brush trucks since 1987, based on International, Freightliner and Ford F-series chassis.

■ **MOORE ENGINEERING**
Moore Engineering was founded in 1972, and has its manufacturing base near to Adelaide, South Australia. The company builds a range that includes pumps and rescue tenders.

■ **MORITA**
Founded in 1907, Morita is the largest of the Japanese fire engine manufacturers. In recent years, its fire engine models have ranged from water tenders and airport foam/crash tenders, through to aerial ladders and Snorkel platforms. The typical Morita water tender is available on a number of commercial chassis, including Toyota, Hino, Isuzu and Mitsubishi. The 1990s MWG 40T model had a 2,270 litres/500 gallons-per-minute water pump, a 4,000-litre/880-gallon water tank, and a crew cab for six firefighters.

Morita aerial ladders come in heights of 15–56m/49ft–184ft. They are usually mounted with the turntable at the rear of the chassis, European style, and have a fitted rescue cage. In addition most Morita aerial ladders have onboard firefighting water pumps, making them a totally independent unit.

The Morita fire engine range includes platforms mounted on Hino, Isuzu, Mitsubishi or Toyota chassis. Morita's recent MJ series of airport foam/crash tenders includes 4x4, 6x6 and 8x8 versions with foam tanks sizes from 720 litres/158 gallons to 1,680 litres/370 gallons and water tank sizes from 6,000 litres/1,320 gallons to 14,000 litres/3,100 gallons.

■ **MORRIS COMMERCIAL**
Morris Commercial, a British manufacturer of light vans and lorries, never seriously turned its attention to fire engine production and only produced a small number to special order during the years between World Wars I and II. These were mostly built as pumping fire engines using the Morris CS 11/40F chassis powered by a 25hp 6-cylinder petrol engine. They carried an all-enclosed 2,270-litres/500-gallons-per-minute pump mounted on the rear platform of the fire engine body and a 10m/35ft extension ladder. During the 1930s, Morris provided the chassis for some Magirus 30m/100ft turntable ladders.

■ **MOWAG**
Originally a bodybuilding concern, Mowag began manufacturing vehicles in 1951. Based in Kreuzlingen, Switzerland, the company manufactured fire engines alongside a range of military cross-country all-wheel drive vehicles. In addition to its own chassis, Mowag utilized the US Dodge for a number of its fire engine applications. Mowag water tenders of the 1950s were available with a Dodge (Chrysler) 125 bhp 6-cylinder or V8 8-cylinder engine on a 4.5-ton, eight-man crew cab 4x2 chassis. Subsequent versions used a 4x4 Dodge chassis with a 210bhp V8 petrol engine and incorporated a 1,200-litre/264-gallon water tank and a 2,800 litres/600 gallons per minute rear-mounted water pump. Since 2004, Mowag has been part of General Dynamics European Land Systems, and has ceased production of fire engines.

■ LEFT ***A 2016 Morita fire truck built on a Hino chassis for the Nago Rescue department, Okinawa, Japan.***

NATIONAL FOAM

■ ABOVE *The 16.5m/54ft-squirt boom of this 1992 International/National Foam 6x4 foam tender projects foam into oil tanks.*

■ BELOW *Texaco Oil Refinery, Anacortes, Washington, own this 1975 4x4 General Motors/National Foam foam tender.*

National Foam is an American company that specializes in a range of firefighting foam delivery systems and equipment, both fixed and vehicle-mounted. Based in Exton, Pennsylvania, the company is now part of the Kidde FireFighting international organization. National Foam have built a number of foam pumpers, aerials and tankers and are associated with the Feecon company and its airport crash rescue equipment and also with the Wirt Knox firefighting accessories firm. National Foam are an acknowledged world leader in foam-based solutions.

FOAM TENDER	
Year	1975
Engine	V6 petrol
Power	230bhp
Transmission	manual
Features	4x4

NISSAN

The Nissan Company of Kawaguchi, Japan, has provided many chassis for Japanese fire engines, In the early 1950s, the first Nissan F380 truck chassis were used for open-cab pumpers. These had a 6-cylinder, 85bhp, 3.6-litre petrol engine and a manual 4-speed gearbox.

In the 1960s the Japanese fire services used the Nissan Patrol 4x4 as a light emergency-response vehicle, and in the 1980s and '90s Nissan Condor and Resona truck chassis were widely used for fire vehicles.

■ LEFT *This 1950 Datsun fire engine was powered by a 722cc, 4-cylinder engine, the small body allowing it to run through narrow streets.*

■ BELOW LEFT *Used by Dubai's fire service as a fast first-attendance vehicle, this Nissan 4x4 is designed to arrive at an incident before the full-sized fire engines.*

OTHER MAKES

■ **NEEL FIRE PROTECTION APPARATUS**
Established in 1960, in Waco, Texas, Neel Fire Protection Apparatus today produces a variety of custom tankers, pumpers, rescues and wildland trucks on a range of chassis to customer requirements.

OPEL

■ RIGHT *This German Fire Service c.1955 Opel Blitz/Metz light pump carries a front-mounted water pump.*

■ BELOW RIGHT *A 1940 Opel Blitz TSF light pump is painted in wartime livery.*

Opel fire engines have a long history that predates World War II, when the company produced a large number of lightweight pumping and rescue fire engines at its base in Brandenburg, Germany. In preparation for war, Opel manufactured large numbers of special airfield tenders for use by the Luftwaffe, using several 3-ton 4x4 foam tenders and water tanker versions built on the Blitz chassis.

After World War II, Opel was re-established at Russelheim, and in the early 1950s the Blitz series was based on the 1.75-ton 330C model with several subsequent versions. The model introduced in 1960 was based on the first Opel semi-forward control chassis. The 1970 2-ton version with a five-man crew cab with a 2.5-litre, 6-cylinder engine continued this style of lightweight multi-purpose fire engine.

Opel faded from the fire engine scene in the mid-1970s, when it ceased production of light trucks suitable for use as fire and rescue vehicles.

BLITZ

Year	1970
Engine	6-cylinder petrol
Power	2.5-litre
Transmission	4-speed manual
Features	5-man crew cab

OSHKOSH

■ ABOVE *In 2019, this Oshkosh Striker 3000 6x6 ARFF vehicle went into service at the Kennedy Space Center.*

The headquarters of the Oshkosh Truck Corporation is in Oshkosh, Wisconsin, USA. Since its foundation in 1917 Oshkosh has built a range of heavy-duty all-wheel drive trucks. Since World War II, it has tended to specialize in heavy haulage trucks, including those for the military, all designed to operate in extreme weather conditions. So it is not surprising that in their airport foam and crash tenders, Oshkosh manufacture some of the world's largest fire engines for military, municipal airport and civil fire brigade use.

Oshkosh also built a range of aerial ladders and snorkels (boomed hydraulic platforms) based on the Oshkosh A and L series chassis. The L series chassis had a very low overall height of 1.8m/6ft from the road surface, which enabled the ladders to be constructed with a low profile. This allowed them to negotiate low bridges and get to work in streets and within the curtilage of premises where headroom was restricted. The L series had the V6 Detroit Diesel engine developing 335bhp with automatic transmission.

In 1996, Oshkosh acquired Pierce, which is now run as a wholly owned subsidiary.

In 1977, Oshkosh produced the P-15 ARFF, powered by twin Detroit Diesel engines, which provide a massive 990bhp. Twin automatic transmissions provided drive to the eight wheels. The P-15 had a water capacity of 23,000 litres/5,000 gallons, and when the water was combined with foam concentrate, this huge truck could discharge 227,000 litres/60,000 gallons of extinguishing foam.

Oshkosh rapid intervention vehicles

■ LEFT *The 8,200-litres/1,800-gallons-per-minute pump on this giant 1978 Oshkosh M-15 8x8 foam tender draws on 18,000 litres/4,000 gallons of water and 2,300 litres/515 gallons of foam concentrate.*

(RIVs) are fast-response, 110kmh/70mph airport fire engines designed to get to a fire or accident scene ahead of the heavy foam/crash tenders. The latest RIV is the Stinger, based on a Ford F-550 chassis, with a 454–1,136-litre/100–250-gallon water tank, dual handlines and bumper-mounted turret nozzle.

In 2001, Oshkosh introduced the Striker range of airport foam/crash tenders, available in 5,700-litre/1,300-gallon (4x4), 11,000-litre/2,400-gallon (6x6) and 17,000-litre/3,750-gallon (8x8) variants. Updated Striker models were introduced in 2015, and further-revised models were unveiled in 2021. In 2018, the P-19R was produced for the US Marine Corps. This 6x6 vehicle is powered by a 60hp Caterpillar engine, with an Allison 4700SP automatic transmission. The P-19R has a 3,785-litre/833-gallon water tank, and roof- and bumper-mounted turrets capable of discharging a combined 2,800 litres/616 gallons of water up to 305m/1,000ft from a fire. To aid operations and spares support, this vehicle is based on the Marine Corps LVSR and MTVR vehicles, and shares many common components.

■ RIGHT *The 2018 Oshkosh P-19R 6x6 was produced for the US Marine Corps, and shares common components with other Marine Corps vehicles.*

PEMFAB

In 1971, a firm entitled Imperial Fire Apparatus first started to build fire engines on a custom cab in conjunction with another company, Truck Cab Manufacturers of Cincinnati, Ohio. Four years later, Imperial Fire Apparatus was purchased by Pemberton Fabricators, and the name PemFab first appeared on American fire engines. During the next two decades, PemFab constructed a number of fire engines on custom chassis in the Pacemaker series and in the early 1980s, also introduced a new concept of wedge-shaped cab designs subsequently used on PemFab Premier, Royale, Sovereign, and Imperial models. The company ceased trading in 1996.

■ ABOVE *Skagit County Fire Department, Big Lake, Washington, operate this 1981 Emergency One/Pemfab pumper. It incorporates an 8,000-litres/1,750-gallons-per-minute pump and a 2,270-litre/500-gallon water tank.*

PETERBILT

Founded in 1938 by T Peterman, a logger, who was used to adapting and rebuilding army trucks for his own industry, the Peterbilt company grew out of the purchase of the assets of the defunct Waukesha Motor Company, with the primary purpose of custom-building logging trucks. In the first year Peterman delivered 14 trucks and in the second he had increased capacity to 82. During World War II the company supplied government contracts for heavy-duty trucks and was in a prime position to take a share of the market when war ceased. Peterman died in 1945 and the assets were sold to a management group from the company. The company was put up for sale in 1958 when it was acquired by Kenworth, a competitor. In 1960 the company moved to Newark, California, and in 1969 a second plant was built in Tennessee, to cope with demand. In 1975 the Canadian Peterbilt opened for manufacture and in 1983 a further site was opened in Texas.

■ ABOVE ***A 2021 Pierce Tanker built on a Peterbilt chassis, serving with the Odell Fire Department, North Carolina.***

PIERCE

■ BELOW ***This Pierce Ascendant 32.6m/107ft Heavy-Duty Tiller Aerial was delivered to Baltimore County Fire Department, Maryland, in 2021.***

The Pierce Company was founded in 1913 in Wisconsin, USA, when it was first engaged in making a variety of taxis and carriages. It constructed its first fire engine in the late 1940s, and was one of the first manufacturers to use aluminium widely in the vehicle-building process. In the past, the Ford L series, Chevrolet, Dodge and GMC chassis were used for many Pierce mini-pumpers, whilst the Ford C series or Duplex models formed the base for their Suburban series pumpers, which were designed for urban firefighting and rescue. Pierce has built a wide range of pumpers, tankers, rescues and aerials, and currently builds on custom chassis and commercial chassis from Ford, Freightliner, International, Kenworth and Peterbilt.

Recent examples of Pierce builds include the rescue pumper built in 2019 for the Hampden Township Volunteer Fire Company (see below), based on the company's Enforcer chassis, powered by a 450hp Cummins diesel engine, with a 2,840-litre/625-gallon water tank and a 5,680-litre/1,250-gallon-per-minute pump. In 2021, Pierce delivered an aerial to the Baltimore County Fire Department, based on the Pierce Arrow XT chassis with a 600hp Cummins engine and fitted with a 32.6m/107ft heavy-duty ladder. In 1996 Pierce became a wholly owned subsidiary of Oshkosh.

■ BELOW ***A 2019 Pierce Enforcer Heavy Duty Rescue Pumper.***

RESCUE TENDER

Year	1979
Engine	6-cylinder diesel
Power	275hp
Transmission	4-speed automatic
Features	wide range of power tools

PIERREVILLE

The Canadian fire engine manufacturer Pierreville Fire Trucks was founded in 1968 at Saint-François-du-Lac, Quebec. Its origins can be traced to the time when five sons of the Thibault family, which then owned the long-standing Thibault fire engine company, decided to start an independent manufacturing operation not far from the family headquarters.

Considerable success soon followed for Pierreville. Only ten years after its inauguration, when measured by the number of vehicles actually sold and with an order book worth C$8 million, the company could claim to be the largest fire engine builder in Canada. By then it had developed a large factory base and at one stage employed 150 staff building pumpers and aerial ladders, not just for all the major Canadian fire departments and many smaller ones, but for a number of American fire departments as well.

However, Pierreville ceased trading in 1985, but soon afterwards most of its assets and orders were assumed by several members of the Thibault family who formed a company that traded under the name of Camions Incendie Phoenix. This offshoot of Pierreville continued to build a number of various fire engines for eastern Canadian fire departments until 1992 when it too ceased trading and finally disappeared from the fire vehicle scene.

■ **ABOVE RIGHT** ***Vancouver Fire Department, British Columbia, Canada, took delivery of this Imperial/Pierreville pumper in 1974.***

■ **RIGHT** ***The University of British Columbia Fire Department, Canada, operate this 1979 Scot Pierreville 30m/100ft rear-mount aerial ladder.***

PIRSCH

■ **BELOW** ***This 1977 Pirsch pumper served in Blaine, Minnesota.***

Peter Pirsch was a volunteer fireman in the 1880s who took to constructing wooden extension ladders for his own fire department before building some early motorized pumpers. He founded

PUMPER	
Year	1952
Engine	6-cylinder petrol
Power	127bhp
Transmission	4-speed manual
Features	enclosed front cab

■ RIGHT *Carrying 2,270 litres/500 gallons of water, this 1970 Pirsch pump delivers 5,700 litres/1,250 gallons per minute.*

his fire engine company in Wisconsin, USA, in 1900, and the Pirsch name became synonymous with aerial ladders throughout America. The company went on to develop aerial-ladder technology with the pioneering use of aluminium alloys in the construction of ladder sections. It produced the first all-powered American aerial ladder in early 1930.

Pirsch aerial ladders included tractor-drawn versions and had either rear or centre-mounted models. A number of twin-boom Pirsch 26m/85ft Snorkels were also in service in addition to the Pirsch range of pumpers with midships pumps, twin hose reels and top-mounted pump controls. Following a period of financial challenges, Pirsch delivered its last fire engine in 1987.

PLASTISOL

Plastisol BV was a Dutch company based in Wanroij, Holland, which specialized in fibreglass-reinforced polyester construction. The company designed and manufactured crew cabs and bodywork for fire engine use, using a range of commercial chassis including those of Chevrolet, General Motors and Dodge.

In 2002, Plastisol manufactured the tilting one-piece crew cabs and bodywork of 107 new pumping fire engines for the London Fire Brigade. These fire engines were based on a Mercedes Benz Atego 1325F chassis, and a feature of the London pumps was their water and foam tanks which were included in the body core structure. Among some of Plastisol's other fire service general bodywork applications were superstructures for airport rescue tenders, demountable foam containers, and foam trailers with concentrate capacities ranging from 3,000 litres/660 gallons to 16,000 litres/3,524 gallons. Plastisol was declared bankrupt in 2015.

PUMP	
Year	2003
Engine	6-cylinder
Power	326hp
Transmission	automatic
Features	modular locker stowage

OTHER MAKES

■ PRAGA
For many years Praga chassis were used for many fire engines built in former Czechoslovakia for use in East Europe. After World War II the Praga A150 1.5-ton truck chassis was regularly used for light fire tenders. The Praga A150 had a 4-cylinder, 55bhp petrol engine, and, unusually, independent front suspension. The V3S series 6x6 heavy chassis with an air-cooled Tatra diesel engine formed the basis for a number of airfield foam/crash tenders and some pumping fire engines. Many Praga fire engines had bodywork constructed by the Czech Korosa company.

■ PRECISION FIRE APPARATUS
Based in Camdenton, Missouri, Precision Fire Apparatus produces a wide range of custom trucks with bodies in extruded aluminium and stainless steel, on custom and commercial chassis, from companies such as Spartan, Ford F-series and International.

■ ABOVE LEFT *A 9,000-litre/2,000-gallon water tender on a Volvo chassis with Plastisol body.*

■ BELOW *A Scania 124c 420/Carmichael Viper airport foam tender with Plastisol body.*

QUALITY

Founded in 1962, Quality built its first fire engines in 1976 and grew steadily, developing its model range to include a variety of pumpers, rescue trucks and aerial ladders.

The Americana pumper was to be built with up to 50 different equipment compartment configurations and to any length. The Avenger pumper had a short-wheelbase chassis with water tank capacities of 4,500–5,700 litres/1,000–1,250 gallons. The aluminium body of the Colonial model was constructed of only nine extrusions, whilst the Liberty could serve as a rescue pumper with 6cu m/220cu ft of equipment-storage space. The 2002 Volunteer model was an open-cab pumper with a body built of tubular steel and stainless-steel plate.

In 1997, the ownership of the Quality fire engine company was acquired by Spartan Motors Inc, and in 2003 Quality became part of the new Spartan subsidiary Crimson Fire company, at which point vehicles ceased to be manufactured under the Quality brand.

■ ABOVE ***Hayward Fire Department, California, run this 1992 Spartan/Quality pumper with a 9,000-litres/2,000-gallons-per-minute pump.***

■ RIGHT ***This 1999 6x4 Quality/E-One 30.4m/100ft aerial ladder is in service with Marrero Harvey Fire Department, Louisiana.***

RENAULT

French company Renault has had an increasing presence in the European fire engine market, especially since it acquired Dodge (UK) in the 1980s and replaced the Dodge logo on a number of water tenders, emergency tenders and aerial ladders with that of the Renault logo. The Renault G13TC, G16C, G17C, the M230 Midliner and S66C chassis were among those that featured in British fire engine renewal programmes in the early 1990s.

A somewhat unusual Renault application in the UK is that of two railway support vehicles built in 1995 on

■ BELOW ***This mid-1980s Renault turbo water tender serves in Belgium.***

G300 RAIL RESCUE UNIT

Year	1995
Engine	6-cylinder diesel
Power	300hp
Transmission	manual
Features	underslung rail wheels

a G300 tandem-axle chassis to attend emergency calls to the 4½-mile-long Severn Rail Tunnel near Bristol. They carry heavy rescue equipment and have rail wheels that allow them to run on the railway lines in the tunnel.

The Renault 95130, 4x4 heavy-duty, all-terrain vehicle is used in France for forest firefighting, and a number of Renault chassis have been used in Belgium as the base for 30m/100ft turntable ladders. A number of Renault T35 vans have been converted for use as incident support units.

More recently, Renault C-, D- and K-series trucks and Master vans have been used as the basis for a range of fire vehicles from various manufacturers including Magirus and Sides.

■ ABOVE ***Incidents in the UK's Severn Tunnel are attended by this Avon Fire Brigade Renault G800 6x4 rail-rescue unit.***

■ RIGHT ***A Sides Renault 4x4 forest fire tanker, with external cab rollover cage, used by the Dordogne fire service in France.***

REYNOLDS BOUGHTON

Based in Devon, England, Reynolds Boughton has produced a wide range of firefighting and rescue vehicles for service in both the UK and overseas. The company is particularly well known for its work on the Pathfinder airfield crash tender introduced in 1971. This was built on a Reynolds Boughton 6x6 chassis using a General Motors V16 supercharged 2-stroke diesel engine rated in excess of 600bhp. The Pathfinder foam system was developed in conjunction with Pyrene, the British foam specialists. Its remote-controlled roof-mounted monitor could project a foam jet 75m/250ft at 61,300 litres/13,500 gallons per minute.

In 2010, the company was acquired by Skan Group Holdings, and became known as Boughton Engineering Limited, focusing on its core waste-handling equipment business.

■ LEFT ***The high-pressure pump of this British Army Fire Service Reynolds Boughton RB44, 4x4 light pump/foam tender feeds two hose reels. This tender carries 450 litres/100 gallons of water and has a front-mounted winch.***

PATHFINDER

Year	1971
Engine	General Motors V16 diesel
Power	600bhp
Transmission	automatic
Features	Pyrene foam system

Rosenbauer

■ LEFT *A late 1970s Magirus Deutz/Rosenbauer 4x4 water tender on duty with Crete Fire Service.*

■ LEFT *Bruges Fire Brigade, Belgium, operate this Renault turbo/Rosenbauer 6x4 foam/water tender. Lengths of hard suction hose are stored amidships.*

Having built its first fire engine in 1866, Rosenbauer International, based in Leonding, Austria, is a long-established company. Today it is one of the largest global producers of most types of firefighting and rescue vehicles and equipment to fire brigade customers throughout the world. The company has twelve European production plants, which together with five manufacturing centres in America and Asia, plus plants in Russia and Saudi Arabia, currently produce over 14,000 vehicles per year.

Over the years Rosenbauer has used a wide range of chassis makes and types, including Steyr, Mercedes, Renault, OM, Ford, Scania, Chevrolet, Henschel and Faun models. A typical early 1950s Rosenbauer water tender for the Austrian fire service was built on a German V8 4x4 Ford chassis with a 1,500-litre/330-gallon water tank and a front-mounted 1,500 litre/330-gallon-per-minute front-mounted pump. The crash/foam tender delivered to Vienna Airport in the same period was mounted on a Saurer 6GAFLL 4x4 diesel engine chassis with a 4,000-litres/880-gallons water tank.

In the 1960s Rosenbauer produced a number of light water tenders on the semi-forward-control Opel Blitz 1961 chassis for service in Germany. Their basic firefighting equipment included a light portable 800-litres/176-gallons-per-minute pump. In 1972 Rosenbauer built a 26m/85ft 3boom hydraulic platform on a Steyr 1,290 chassis with a 230hp diesel engine. In 1974 it pioneered a demountable equipment pod system using flatbed lorries as prime movers.

The current model range is divided into municipal, aerials and airport vehicles. The RT is a hybrid vehicle, fitted with high-capacity batteries to enable external electrical devices to be operated with a combined power

■ BELOW *A 1988 Oshkosh/Rosenbauer 8x8 foam tender at a Wisconsin airport, USA.*

■ BELOW *This Rosenbauer turntable aerial, built on a Mercedes chassis, was in service at Heidelberg Airfield, Germany, in 2018.*

■ RIGHT *Stationed at Padderborn Airport, Germany, this MAN F2000/Rosenbauer Buffalo 9000 6x6 airport foam tender is powered by a V10 600hp turbo diesel engine.*

consumption of up to 18kW, in addition to providing emissions-free short-range operation for the vehicle itself. The RT uses touch-screen control technology, and its software suite even includes integration with drones for aerial analysis of an incident.

The AT range provides a wide range of chassis options, with wheelbases of 3.0– 5.5m/12–18ft), water tank sizes of 500–5,500 litres/132– 1,453 gallons, and crew capacity from five to nine firefighters, including the driver.

The ET series rescue truck is designed for urban operations and is available on MAN, Mercedes-Benz, Volvo, Scania and Renault chassis, with various wheelbases. Bodies are built from reinforced aluminium sheeting, providing a self-supporting structure, and a range of optional pump equipment can be fitted.

The CT range provides a series of more compact vehicles for urban operations, with two crew-cab options to seat five or nine crew members, with a wide range of optional equipment.

The compact CBS water tender range is built using a modular system, providing high flexibility to suit customers' individual requirements. The most current range of airport firefighting vehicles includes the Panther, the latest version of which is available in 6x6 and 8x8 forms, the Buffalo for rapid intervention and off-road use, and a series of rescue-stair systems. The company also produces a range of aerial ladder and platform units.

■ BELOW *A Rosenbauer Panther 6x6 airport firefighting vehicle at Maizuru Air Station, Japan, in 2015.*

OTHER MAKES

■ RK AERIALS

RK Manufacturing was founded by Rob and Pam Kreikemeier in Fremont, Nebraska, USA, in 1988 with a modest 465sq m/5,000sq ft building and three employees. Since then, the company has grown rapidly. Within eight years, RK's manufacturing area had quadrupled, producing an annual output of 12 aerial ladders. Within two years, the production facility had doubled to cover 3,700sq m/40,000sq ft, and the staff was up to 35. In January 2000, RK Aerials joined the Rosenbauer America Group enterprise.

Under the Rosenbauer name, RK Aerials now builds ladders in 18m/60ft, 23m/75ft and 33.2m/109ft lengths. The aerial platform models come in 26m/85ft and 31.7m/104ft versions.

■ RMA SV

RMA Special Vehicles is based in Thailand, with manufacturing facilities in Thailand, Myanmar, Turkey, Dubai and Australia. The company offers a range of compact emergency vehicles, including a fire truck with a 1,000-litre/264-gallon water tank based on a Ford F-series chassis, and a Ford Transit van-chassis-based rescue unit.

S&S Fire Apparatus

■ ABOVE *A 1997 Peterbilt/S&S tanker of Hempfield Fire Department, Pennsylvania.*

American company S&S Fire Apparatus began operating in the early 1980s as an independent fire engine manufacturer. It had offices in Fairmount, Indiana, and Keller, Texas.

The company was an innovative and pioneering leader in the use of stainless steel for fire vehicle construction. It steadily developed its fire vehicle range, and the range included the Indure stainless steel pumpers, SST and Infinity III (elliptical) series tanker/pumpers, and Highland mini-pumpers. S&S acquired the Attack 1 fire apparatus product line including high-strength lightweight bodies, and the resulting S&S Quick Attack light brush fire engines. Hundreds of S&S off-road fire engines operated with the US Forest Service and Bureau of Land Management and their severe-duty vehicles were well proven in their wildland and brush fighting capacity.

In 2005 the company was acquired by Texas-based SNF Industries, and S&S operations ceased in 2008.

■ BELOW *Frankford Fire Department's, Delaware, Ford/S&S light pumper.*

Saulsbury

The American fire engine builder Saulsbury Fire Rescue Company built up an enviable reputation for the design and manufacture of rescue tenders, both compact models and those mounted on bigger chassis. Saulsbury rescue tenders carry a vast range of high-powered lifting, cutting and other specialized equipment needed to deal with a variety of non-fire emergencies.

Rescue tenders were built to the specific needs of individual fire departments, one example being a tandem-axle heavy rescue model providing the facility of a mid-chassis-mounted 13ton crane with hydraulically extended arms.

The Saulsbury Fire Rescue Company was acquired by Emergency One in 1998, the Saulsbury name continuing to appear on fire apparatus, but the company ceased operations in 2004.

6x4 HEAVY RESCUE TENDER	
Year	1992
Engine	6-cylinder diesel
Power	350hp
Transmission	4-speed automatic
Features	heavy-duty rescue equipment

■ ABOVE *A Delaware-based 1999 Saulsbury heavy rescue unit stands by.*

■ LEFT *Hockessin Fire Company, Delaware, own this smart 1999 Saulsbury tanker.*

Saviem

In the years following World War II, Saviem, based in Seine, France, constructed a number of chassis for fire engines widely used throughout France, including water tenders, industrial foam tenders and airport foam/crash tenders.

SM10 FOAM TENDER	
Year	1971
Engine	6-cylinder diesel
Power	170bhp
Transmission	4-speed manual
Features	remote-controlled monitor

These included the JL23 chassis for heavy water tenders with a pump output around 2,270 litres/500 gallons per minute, and a typical airport tender built in the early 1960s on the Saviem TZ21-N 6x6 chassis. This model had a 6-cylinder 180bhp petrol engine, but, unusually at the time, the fire-water pump was powered by a separate Chevrolet power plant, nowadays a common feature on airport fire tenders. In later years, Saviem fire engines became progressively part of the expanding Renault commercial vehicle division.

■ ABOVE *A Renault/Saviem 6x4 rear-mount hydraulic platform is ready for the next call-out.*

Saxon Sanbec

One of the UK's major fire engine bodybuilders, Saxon Sanbec's manufacturing base was located at its Sandbach premises in Cheshire, England. The company began operation in 1982, soon after the demise of the Cheshire Fire Engineering Company, formerly part of the fire engine bodybuilding division of ERF.

Saxon Sanbec grew impressively, to design and supply a large number of fire engines throughout the UK's fire brigades. They included water tenders, rescue tenders, aerial ladders, control units and a number of other special-use vehicles.

Saxon Sanbec fire engines were based on a variety of commercial chassis, including those of Dennis, Dodge, Mercedes, Scania and Volvo.

After a period of difficult trading conditions, the company closed in 2005.

RESCUE PUMP	
Year	1990
Engine	diesel
Power	6-litre
Transmission	5-speed manual
Features	range of rescue equipment

■ BELOW *One of the London Fire Brigade's stylish 1990 Volvo FL6.14/Saxon rescue pumps idles in a park.*

■ BELOW *A pair of Saxon water tenders – on the left, a Mercedes 814L and on the right, a Mercedes 1124F.*

SCAMMELL

■ BELOW *This odd-looking three-wheeled 1939 Scammell pulled a 2,160-litres/475-gallons-per-minute Scammell trailer pump.*

■ BOTTOM *A British Royal Air Force Scammell/Carmichael 4x4 foam tender attends a fire engine rally.*

Scammell Motors of Watford, UK, was already a significant builder of commercial trucks and military vehicles when it built its first of a series of fire engines in 1933. This was for the local fire brigade and was based on their F7B chassis with 4-cylinder, 85bhp petrol engine, an 1,800 litres/400 gallons-per-minute midships pump and a 180-litre/40-gallon water tank. An unusual feature of this Scammell was the fitting of an electric heater in the engine cooling system to keep the water sufficiently warm to ensure immediate starting in cold weather conditions.

A completely different kind of fire engine was the wartime 6-ton Utility MH6 mechanical horse three-wheeled model introduced in 1939. This carried a two-man crew and had a 1,600-litre/350-gallon water tank, a transverse-mounted 110-litres/25-gallons-per-minute pump, a hose and a short ladder. After World War II, Scammell heavy 4x4 and 6x6 chassis were used for a number of overseas foam tenders going into service in Venezuela.

In 1955, Scammell became part of the Leyland group, and in the late 1980s, Leyland was bought by DAF, which led to the end of Scammell production in 1988.

MOUNTAINEER 4X4

Year	1950
Engine	8-cylinder petrol
Power	150bhp
Transmission	4-speed manual
Features	foam tender

SCANIA

■ RIGHT *A 1999 Scania 94F 260/John Dennis Coachbuilders water tender of Cambridgeshire Fire and Rescue Service, England.*

Scania is one of the world's largest manufacturers of heavy trucks and buses, having no fewer than 11 factories in five countries. Founded originally in Sweden in 1891, Scania celebrated its millionth truck off the production line in 2000. Originally trading as ScaniaVabis, the company merged in 1969 with Saab to become SaabScania. From then on the truck and bus division simply became known as Scania.

Scania fire engines came into widespread general use outside Scandinavia during the 1970s. Until then the standard ScaniaVabis Swedish water tender had a 3,000-litre/660-gallon water tank with a pump capable of maximum output of 2,500 litres/550 gallons per minute. In 1970 Scania also provided the chassis for some of the first of the modern-style emergency tenders for the Swedish fire service. These used the normal control L80 chassis with the Scania DS8 6-cylinder 190bhp turbocharged diesel engines. Some of these emergency tenders were among the first to incorporate a hydraulic lifting arm, now a relatively normal fitting on fire engines used for a range of non-fire rescue work.

Once the first Scania chassis started to be used for fire engine construction in Europe, the Scania badge rapidly became visible in many fire brigades. The first Scania fire engines in the UK were turntable ladders in the early 1980s, and were soon followed by the first Scania water tenders, mostly on the G92M 4x2 chassis.

In the early 2000s, the Scania P94 and P124 chassis were used extensively for fire vehicles, including a 4x4 version, the P124 CB model, available with the DSC12 diesel engine producing 400bhp. The P-series Crew-Cab is still in widespread use for a variety of fire engines, including emergency/rescue tenders, foam tenders and turntable ladders. Scania chassis are used by a number of specialist manufacturers, including Rosenbauer and Angloco, and in 2019, Angloco began delivery of 33 new appliances to the Lincolnshire Fire and Rescue Service in the UK. These trucks were based on the P320 4x2 chassis with 320hp engines, 1,800-litre/475-gallon water tank and 100-litre/26-gallon foam tank and a pump rated at 3,400 litres/898 gallons per minute at low pressure.

L80

Year	1971
Engine	8-cylinder diesel
Power	190bhp
Transmission	5-speed manual
Features	normal control cab

■ RIGHT *This 2019 Scania/Bronto Skylift/Angloco aerial ladder platform, supplied to the UK's Humberside Fire & Rescue Service, featured the first new generation low-level Scania CL20L cab in the UK. The specially-commissioned livery is particularly striking.*

SEAGRAVE

■ BELOW *The coiled hose draped across the bonnet of this preserved 1933 Seagrave 6B pumper is ready to connect to a street hydrant. This fire engine was owned by Gustine Fire Department, California.*

One of the best-known American fire engine manufacturers, Seagrave is particularly renowned for its long experience and expertise with aerial ladder design. The company was founded in Michigan by Frederick Seagrave in 1881 to build simple ladders for fruit-picking work, but before long Seagrave was approached by a local fire department to try his hand at constructing a wheeled firefighting platform for transporting ladders to fires. Soon Seagrave was building considerable numbers of horse-drawn wooden ladders and the company moved to larger premises at Columbus, Ohio.

The largest of the Seagrave aerial ladders reached up to 26m/85ft, but required considerable hand-winding efforts by at least four men. Driven by competition from other fire engine builders, notably American LaFrance, in around 1900 Seagrave developed a successful system using coiled springs to assist the extension of the aerial ladder. In 1935 it produced the world's first all-welded alloy-steel ladder and soon after, the first fully hydraulically operated aerial ladder, where all operations were powered by oil pressure.

Meanwhile Seagrave also began building motorized pumpers for many US fire departments, and by the start of World War I had pioneered a number of technical developments. These included the centrifugal water pump, which was more efficient than rotary and piston types, and engine cooling systems, which are vital when pumping for hours at a time. Seagrave continued to develop

■ BELOW *A 2014 Seagrave Marauder II with Apollo 2 32m/105ft rear-mount, 4-section tower, operating with City of Bridgeton Fire Department, New Jersey.*

■ **BELOW** *This 2013 Seagrave Marauder Heavy Rescue serves with St. Charles Fire Department, Illinois.*

■ **BELOW MIDDLE** *A 6x4 1988 Seagrave JE pumper of Truckee Meadows Fire Department, Nevada, stands at the ready in the station yard.*

aerials and pumpers, with the distinctive Seagrave-snout bonnets being a feature of their post-war fire engines.

In 1964 Seagrave was acquired by the FWD Corporation, makers of heavy-duty trucks for both public and military use, and soon afterwards Seagrave moved to FWD's headquarters at Clintonville, Wisconsin, where Seagrave continued to develop a range of aerials, ladders and pumpers. Some longer tractor-drawn articulated aerials came with a rear-steer axle controlled by a tillerman.

Today, FWD Seagrave produces a comprehensive range of custom apparatus including pumpers, pumper-tankers, rescue pumpers, heavy rescue units, aerial ladders, aerial platforms and tractor-drawn aerials. Vehicles are built on Seagrave's own custom chassis, with stainless-steel safety cage built into the cab, or on commercial chassis, depending on customer requirements.

■ **BELOW** *Newark Fire Department, Delaware, operate this colossal 1987 Seagrave 30m/100ft mid-mount rear-steer aerial ladder.*

SHAND MASON

■ LEFT *A preserved 1890 Shand Mason steamer complete with horses and crew wearing brass helmets.*

The origins of Shand Mason can be traced back to 1774, when James Phillips, a London engineer, started building manual pumps. His company was acquired by the larger engineering firm of WJ Tilley, and in 1851 the growing business adopted the name of Shand Mason. By then the London-based company was building some solid and reliable horse-drawn manual pumps, but in 1856 it produced the first steam-driven fire pumper.

At the 1862 fire engine trials held during the Great Exhibition in London's Hyde Park, England, a Shand Mason easily won the small fire engine class, while its great rival, Merryweather, won the large class. Shand Mason steam engines used a shorter stroke in both their single and later 2-cylinder models and were generally more technically advanced than those of Merryweather. The company won significant orders from both the UK and abroad, and produced large numbers of fire engines from its London factory at Blackfriars. In 1863, Shand Mason's output was 17 steam fire engines, of which two were destined for the London Fire Engine Establishment, while the remaining 15 went overseas to fire brigades in New Zealand, India, Russia and Poland. Soon after self-propelled steam fire engines first appeared in America in 1867, both Shand Mason and Merryweather produced similar models. Shand Mason's attempts at a self-propelled steam fire engine were never successful, however, leaving Merryweather to capitalize on and steadily monopolize the steam fire engine scene. Despite the arrival of the petrol engine for fire brigade use in the early 1900s, Shand Mason doggedly stuck to steam power. The company's inevitable decline came in 1922, when the remnants of the once proud world-leading fire engine manufacturer were acquired by Merryweather, its long-standing competitor.

STEAM PUMP

Year	1890
Engine	2-cylinder steam
Power	15hp
Transmission	horse-drawn
Features	1,589lpm/350gpm output

■ LEFT *An 1876 Shand Mason in use in the early twentieth century at Manchester Square Fire Station in London's West End.*

■ RIGHT *A London fireman stokes the firebox of a preserved Shand Mason steam pump during a display in the late 1930s.*

SHELVOKE AND DREWRY

Shelvoke and Drewry of Letchworth, England, was originally a builder of municipal vehicles for local authority use. In the 1970s the company turned its attention to the fire brigade market with a range of chassis types. These included the CX 4x4 for airport fire and rescue use, using the Rolls-Royce B81 235bhp engine with automatic gearbox. Until 1986 the company also built a number of water tenders and turntable/aerial ladders for various UK fire brigades. These Shelvoke and Drewry fire engines were based on the WX and heavier WY chassis but despite their innovative crew cab, few fire trucks of this make have survived in active operational service with fire brigades, the company ceasing trading in 1991.

■ ABOVE *A young boy enjoys being in a 1980 ex-London Fire Brigade Shelvoke and Drewry SPV WX water tender with four-door crew cab.*

SIDES

The French Sides company originated in 1951 and has steadily grown to become a very large manufacturer of fire engines for all types of operational use, including municipal, industrial and aviation fire brigades. The company has its manufacturing base at Saint Nazaire, where 73 per cent of fire engine output is destined for export.

The vehicle range includes first-attack units, pump water tenders, forest fire tenders, rescue tenders, industrial fire engines which use dry powder, foam and gases, and airport tenders both large and small. A typical water tender is the VPI first-attack unit, built on a Toyota Landcruiser chassis. It carries 600 litres/158 gallons of water and has a pump capacity of 500 litres/132 gallons per minute.

Sides airport fire engines are in service at over 200 airports worldwide. One of the largest is the Sentinel 8x8 major foam crash tender model, mounted on a Mercedes Actros 8x8 chassis, and powered by twin engines, it has a 17,000-litre/4,490-gallon water tank, together with 500kg/1,100lb of dry powder. The water pump has an output of 7,200 litres/1,900 gallons per minute, while the roof-mounted dual monitor has a discharge rate of 7,000 litres/1,849 gallons per minute with a maximum reach of up to 100m/328ft. The Sentinel also features a portable foam nozzle with a flowrate of 450 litres/119 gallons per minute.

■ LEFT *In service with the French military, this Sides 6x6 airport foam tender stands by on the taxiway of an air force base in France.*

6x6 AIRPORT FOAM TENDER

Year	1963
Engine	8-cylinder petrol
Power	330bhp
Transmission	6-speed manual
Features	high-output foam capacity

■ LEFT *A Sides Sentinel S3X, built on a MAN 6x6 chassis, with a 4,500-litres/1,189-gallons per minute roof monitor, in service at Bordeaux Airport, France.*

■ OPPOSITE *Norwich Airport, England, have this Gloster Saro/Simon Javelin 6x6 foam tender in operational use.*

■ BELOW *A 1990 Simon/Duplex/Grumman tanker in service with Odessa Fire Company, Delaware.*

SIMON

In 1963 Simon Engineering of Dudley, England, built the first British hydraulic platform for firefighting and rescue use. Simon's early platforms differed substantially from those of contemporary American makes through the use of three elevating booms rather than two. For more than two decades, the company delivered platforms to many British and overseas fire brigades.

The first Simon hydraulic platform, a SS65 model (20m/65ft) mounted on a Commer chassis, went into service in Monmouthshire Fire Brigade in 1963. Later Simon models included the DS50 (15m/50ft), SS70 (21m/70ft), SS85 (26m/85ft) and the SS263 (27.7m/91ft). Simon also produced a 15m/50ft telescopic arm mounted on a turntable with a high-discharge water monitor at the top. Known as the Simonitor, this could deliver up to 3,600 litres/800 gallons per minute at its head. The monitor could be remotely controlled from the ground or from the top of a

■ LEFT *The British Defence Fire Services have been supplied with several c.1980 Gloster Saro/Simon 4x4 Mk 10 foam/crash tenders, such as this example.*

■ LEFT *Derbyshire Fire and Rescue Service, England, run this 1990 Dennis F127/Saxon/Simon ST240-S 24m/78ft aerial ladder platform.*

narrow ladder slung above the telescopic booms. Simon later developed an aerial ladder platform, which combined a telescopic boom with a hydraulic platform and a ladder that ranged alongside the variable length of the main boom. This series included the ALP 340 model, which was mounted on a suitable 3-axle chassis.

The Simon company was acquired by IVECO Magirus of Germany in 2000, after which the Simon aerial fire engine range was marketed under the Magirus name alone.

340 AERIAL LADDER PLATFORM

Year	1996
Engine	6-cylinder diesel
Power	310bhp
Transmission	automatic
Features	34m/111ft working height

■ ABOVE ***In the 1990s Simon introduced a new aerial ladder platform, known as the 340. This demonstration model is built on a Mercedes 2435 6x4 chassis.***

■ BELOW ***This magnificent 1988 Simon-Duplex/LTI 30m/100ft 6x4 rear-mount aerial ladder is in service with Fletcher Fire Department, North Carolina, USA.***

Skilled Equipment Manufacturing (SEM)

In 1996, the established Australian company Skilled Equipment joined forces with the Victoria Country Fire Authority, which had traditionally built its own fire engines for more than 40 years. The outcome was a joint arrangement to build fire engines, and one year later, Skilled Equipment Manufacturing (SEM) was inaugurated. Since then, the company has constructed a wide range of fire engines for various Australian fire brigades and a number of overseas customers.

In 2000 the company acquired the interests of the Australian Fire Company and although production continued for a time at the latter's South Australian plant, from 2002 all manufacturing operations were concentrated at Skilled Equipment's premises at

■ ABOVE *One of a number of American LaFrance/Skilled Equipment Manufacturing pumpers delivered to Queensland Fire & Rescue Service in 2001.*

■ BELOW *In 2001 Western Australia Fire and Rescue received their second Scania P124G 360/Bronto F32/Skilled EM 8x4 32m/105ft aerial ladder platform.*

■ **RIGHT** ***A Freightliner FL80/ Skilled Equipment Manufacturing 6x4 Australian heavy pumper of the Metropolitan Fire Brigade.***

■ **BELOW RIGHT** ***This Category 7 Mitsubishi light tanker is one of 20 built by Skilled Engineering Manufacturing for Australia's New South Wales Fire Service.***

Ballarat. In 2011, SEM itself was acquired by Varley.

Apart from using a range of commercial chassis, SEM has produced fire engines for the Australian Fire Service for operational use in city centres and at incidents in the remote outback regions. In 2001 SEM delivered pumpers to Queensland Fire and Rescue built on an American LaFrance chassis, quite an unusual combination. In the same year, the company also delivered 20 light tankers, built on a Mitsubishi Canter 4x4 chassis, for the New South Wales Rural Fire Service; and a much larger fire engine – a Scania P124 360/Bronto 32m/104ft aerial ladder platform, that was delivered to Western Australia Fire and Rescue.

■ **BELOW** ***A Mitsubishi/Skilled Equipment Manufacturing 4x4 light pump with rear crew cab.***

124 8x4 ALP

Year	2001
Engine	diesel
Power	360bhp
Transmission	automatic
Features	32m/105ft height

SMEAL

■ LEFT *A 2020 Smeal Enclosed Top Mount Custom Pumper built on a Spartan MetroStar chassis.*

■ BELOW LEFT *Skagit County Fire District, Allen, Washington, own this 1988 Ford C8000/Smeal 4,500-litres/1,000-gallons-per-minute pumper.*

The Smeal Fire Apparatus Company began life in Snyder, Nebraska in 1964, when welder Don Smeal, a volunteer firefighter, was asked to repair the local fire department's fire engine. Don suggested that the fire board buy a new chassis so that he could build a unique fire engine. The resultant vehicle had an enclosed six-man crew cab, water tank, and 12.8m/42ft, two-section, hydraulically operated ladder. The new fire engine was so successful that the interest it generated heralded the birth of the Smeal company.

Nowadays, Smeal is recognized for its excellent engineering and workmanship across its wide range of pumpers, aerials and platforms, and is part of the REV Group, along with Spartan and Ladder Tower.

During 2003, Smeal delivered an interesting order for more than 20 multi-functional pumpers for Riverside County, California. These were to fulfil both urban and rural operational use and are based upon the Spartan Sierra chassis/cab with Cummins ISL 370hp engine and Allison automatic transmission. Water tanks with 2,270-litre/500-gallon capacity are fitted and a 9,080-litres/2,000-gallons-per-minute pump provides a powerful firefighting attack with a 113-litre/25-gallon foam concentrate supply.

The range today includes the S180 series of pumpers built on the company's MetroStar chassis with engines from 350–450hp, 2,800–3,785-litre/616–833-gallon water tanks and 5,688 litres 1,250 gallons-per-minute pumps.

A full range of aerials and platforms is available, with ladder heights ranging from 16.7m/55ft to 38.1m/125ft.

PUMPER

Year	2003
Engine	8-cylinder diesel
Power	370 bhp
Transmission	automatic
Features	combined urban/rural use

■ BELOW *Vancouver Fire Department's 2001 Spartan Gladiator 6x4/Smeal 30m/100ft aerial ladder.*

SNORKEL

■ BELOW *A 1988 Mack CF/Pierce pumper carrying a 15m/50ft Snorkel serves with Tacoma Fire Department, Washington.*

Snorkel aerial fire engines first made an appearance on the American scene in 1968. Having noticed the locally-used small fruit-picking trucks, which had two elevating booms with a small basket at the top for the fruit picker, Chicago Fire Department commissioned the Missouri-based Pittman Manufacturing Company to build a 16.8m/55ft version. Based on a General Motors chassis for firefighting duties, it had a working platform at its head that was able to take several firefighters. The 5cm/2in diameter nozzle was capable of delivering water into the upper floors of a burning building at a rate of 5,500 litres/1,200 gallons per minute.

The prototype platform was so successful that Chicago Fire Department ordered more of the same. Before long the Snorkel Fire Equipment Company had been formed at Elwood, Kansas, to manufacture hydraulically operated firefighting and rescue platforms 16.8–26m/55–85ft high. In some cases these were mounted on a suitable pumper chassis to produce a combination fire engine, able to pump water and work at height.

28M/85FT SNORKEL	
Year	1972
Engine	V8 diesel
Power	350bhp
Transmission	manual
Features	6x4

With a continual decline in demand for its products, production of the Snorkel aerial fire engines ceased production in the early 2000s, but in 2014 the company was acquired by Ladder Tower, which is now itself part of the REV Group, with Spartan and Smeal, and a 16.7m/55ft version of the Snorkel is now offered.

■ RIGHT *This 1987 23m/75ft Snorkel is based on a Spartan MS20/Van Pelt/FMC 6x4 chassis. It belongs to the City of Arroyo Grande Fire Department, in California.*

SPARTAN EMERGENCY RESPONSE

Spartan Emergency Response was formerly part of Spartan Motors – a US specialist-vehicle design and manufacturing company formed in 1976. The business quickly grew, and after manufacturing fire-engine chassis for several years, Spartan acquired Luverne and Quality in the mid-1990s. This business later became Crimson Fire, and was itself rebranded as Spartan ERV in 2012. In 2017, Spartan ERV acquired Smeal and Ladder Tower, and in 2020, Spartan ERV became part of the REV Group.

Over the years, Spartan has built a range of fire vehicles based on a number of custom and commercial chassis, including

■ TOP *Storey County Fire Department, Nevada, operate this blue and white 1992 Spartan/HiTech pumper.*

■ RIGHT *This Delaware-based 1990 Spartan/4-Guys 6x4 tanker sports a highly polished stainless steel water tank.*

■ BELOW *A 1992 Spartan Gladiator/ Darley 6x4 pumper of Point Roberts Fire Rescue, Washington, has a 6,800-litres/ 1,500-gallons-per-minute pump and 9,000-litre/2,000-gallon water tank.*

■ BELOW *The 2021 Spartan 23m/75ft Aerial has a 4.3m/14ft-reach outrigger system and up to 2,271-litre/500-gallon water-tank capacity.*

■ BELOW *A 1990 Spartan/Darley foam tender is on duty at the Arco Refinery, Ferndale, Washington. It is operated by Cherry Point Fire and Rescue.*

the company's own custom Gladiator and MetroStar designs. The Gladiator heavy-duty chassis, introduced in 1983 and still in production today, is one of the company's longest-serving designs. Powered by Cummins diesel engines from 400–600hp, and fitted with Allison automatic transmissions, a wide variety of optional specifications is available for the Gladiator, with 4x2, 4x4 and 6x4 chassis, two- and four-door crew cabs, and raised roof options. The chassis has been widely used for custom pumpers, rescues, aerials and tankers.

■ ABOVE RIGHT *The 2021 Spartan Transformer multi-function pumper/rescue vehicle is available with water tank capacities from 1,893–5,678 litres/416–1,250 gallons.*

■ RIGHT *A 2019 Spartan Gladiator-based Walk-In Heavy Rescue built for the Philadelphia Fire Department.*

STEYR-DAIMLER-PUCH

Steyr was one of Austria's main fire engine manufacturers, having for many years built fire vehicles of both heavy and light types. One of the best-known Steyr fire engines was the cross-country all-terrain Pinzgauer series. These rugged models were first introduced in 1971 and developed directly from the smaller 4x4 Haflinger 700AP series that was first produced in 1959. The latter had a rear-mounted, air-cooled, flat twin engine and independent suspension. The larger Pinzgauer featured a centre tube chassis incorporating the 4-speed automatic transmission, and the unitary body frame was then mounted to the chassis tube to provide an exceptionally rigid base. The Pinzgauer was available in 4x4 or 6x6 options, powered by a 5-cylinder, 2.5litre, turbocharged diesel engine.

Another commonly seen Steyr fire engine was the Type 4000/220 water tender of the 1970s and 1980s, based on the Steyr 790 4x4 chassis. This had a 170bhp diesel engine, an 18,000-litres/4,000-gallons-per-minute pump, and a 4,000-litre/880-gallon water tank.

In 1990, Steyr's truck production was taken over by MAN, though Steyr-branded vehicles continued to be produced in Austria until 2003.

■ ABOVE *This Steyr fire truck, seen here fitted with snow chains, was in service with the Vorderweissenbach fire service in Austria in the mid-2000s.*

PUMPER

Year	1973
Engine	Ford gas turbine
Power	375hp
Transmission	n/k
Features	experimental vehicle

■ LEFT *A Rosenbauer hydraulic platform, belonging to the fire brigade of the City of Lienz, in the Austrian province of East Tyrol. Traditional Austrian fire helmets are visible through the windscreen.*

SUPERIOR

The Superior Emergency Equipment company of Canada began life in a small plant in Red Deer, Alberta, in 1973 and grew steadily to become Canada's largest manufacturer of fire engines.

Its first fire vehicle, manufactured in 1973, was an industrial pumper built on an International Cargostar tilt-cab chassis. This had a midships-mounted 2,840-litres/625-gallons-per-minute pump. A benchmark in Superior's commercial progress was Calgary Fire Department's order for three pumpers built on a Hendrickson chassis.

In the early days, all Superior fire engines were manufactured of steel fabrications, but from 1978 the company began to use all-aluminium construction. In the late 1970s, Superior formed a subsidiary company called CamAm Fire Apparatus, Inc, to market Superior fire engines in order to widen sales in northwest America. A number of Superior vehicles were supplied to American fire departments through this company.

A further new division, known as Superior Fire Trucks Ltd, was formed in 1980. Based in Kingston, Ontario, this was primarily to serve Superior users in eastern Canada. Around this time, the parent company entered into an agreement with the American

■ ABOVE RIGHT *A 1981 Ford C800/Superior pumper of Lovelock Fire Department, Nevada, carries 6,800 litres/1,500 gallons of water and pumps 4,500 litres/1,000 gallons per minute.*

■ BELOW *This 1989 General Motors Corporation/Superior pumper has a roomy crew cab, carries 3,200 litres/700 gallons of water and the pump delivers 4,770 litres/1,050 gallons per minute.*

■ LEFT ***Parkland County Fire Department, Stoney Plain, Alberta, USA, took delivery of this International S4900/Superior long-wheelbase pumper in 1999. It features high-level storage for suction hoses and a 4,100-litre/900-gallon water tank.***

■ ABOVE LEFT ***This 1994 Spartan/Superior 6x4 pumper delivers 4,770 litres/1,050 gallons per minute. The ample bodywork conceals a 7,500-litre/1,650-gallon water tank and plenty of stowage.***

manufacturer of hydraulic platforms, Simon Snorkel, to build this equipment on Superior chassis, but the real springboard for the years ahead came in the mid 1980s with the demise of the large Canadian fire engine builders, Pierreville and King Seagrave. From then on, the commercial fortunes of the company continued apace. In 1987 there were separate agreements with Pierce, Snorkel and Smeal for Superior to have exclusive marketing rights for these makes of fire engine in Canada.

Then in 1992, Emergency One purchased the Superior Emergency Equipment company and a new firm, Superior Emergency Vehicles, emerged as a subsidiary of Emergency One. Superior went on to produce more than 300 fire engines per year and during 2003 delivered its 3,000th emergency vehicle.

For some years, Superior built all initial attack and light rescue fire engines for the Emergency One Group. These vehicles included the Wildland units, Grizzly tankers and Lynx mini pumpers on GMC 3500 chassis, and the Super Lynx midi-pumpers on the Ford F550 chassis. Light rescue tenders come in various length walk-in units on Ford Super Duty and Medium Duty chassis.

Once Canada's largest builder of domestic fire engines, Superior exported fire and rescue vehicles to diverse countries, including Saudi Arabia, Qatar, the Philippines, Colombia, Venezuela, Argentina, Belgium and the Netherlands.

In 2006, Emergency One Group began to wind down manufacture at the Red Deer plant, and the final truck to leave the production line was an E-One Cyclone II custom pumper.

■ LEFT ***This International 4300/Superior pumper went new in 2002 to Mnjikaning Fire and Rescue, Ontario, Canada.***

Sutphen

■ TOP *Jefferson Fire Department, Pennsylvania, run this 1986 Sutphen Deluge pumper.*

■ MIDDLE *This compact Sutphen 23m/75ft mid-mount aerial ladder was delivered to Oak Bay, British Columbia, in 2002.*

■ BOTTOM *A Sutphen SP70 Aerial Platform, powered by a 450hp Cummins diesel engine, delivered in 2020 to Douglas Fire Department, Georgia.*

The Sutphen Corporation is an old family-owned organization with a very long association with firefighting. Its founder, C H Sutphen, built his first steam fire pump back in 1890 in Columbus, Ohio. Sutphen's son Harry later took his place in the business and grandsons Thomas and Robert joined after World War II. The sixth generation of the family are now working in the business, making the more than 130 years of continuous operation unique in fire truck manufacture.

Since those early days, when the first fire engine was built in the garage of one of its employees, the Sutphen corporation has produced a large number of custom-built pumpers at its Ohio headquarters. The corporation has five factories, specializing in different types of trucks. The first manufactures aerial platforms and aluminium pumpers; the second takes orders for boom aerials, platforms and climbing ladders with stainless steel bodies. The third plant assembles the components on the custom chassis, the fourth plant manufactures

■ LEFT *The 1980 Seagrave PS/Sutphen 6x4 long-wheelbase pumper incorporates a 10,000-litre/2,200-gallon tank.*

■ BELOW LEFT *South Bowers Fire Company, Delaware, run this 1994 Sutphen high-volume pumper.*

stainless steel and aluminium pumpers for sale throughout the north-east USA. Repair and refurbishment are carried out at the newest plant, located next to the custom-chassis plant.

It is probably best known for its front and midships-mounted, telescoping aerial tower ladders. These models use a box-style trussed construction for building an aerial ladder of great strength. Combined with two sets of outrigged jacks, with a total overall spread of 4.5m/15ft, this construction provides maximum stability while the fire engine is working in an elevated and extended position on the fireground.

Apart from dedicated high-rise fire engines, Sutphen also builds a large number of combination firefighting vehicles. These are aerial ladders mounted on a suitable pumper base to allow the fire engine to either pump firefighting water or operate at upper floor level, or both.

■ LEFT *This 2021 Sutphen Custom Pumper was built for Indian River County Fire Department, Florida.*

■ BELOW *This Sutphen 6x4 26m/85ft mid-mount aerial ladder went to Bismarck Fire Department, North Dakota in 1976.*

OTHER MAKES

■ SAURER
The Saurer firm, one of the longest-established Swiss manufacturers of commercial trucks, has supplied chassis for many of the country's heavier fire engines, including water tenders, airport foam/crash tenders and turntable ladders. Besides building fire engines for Swiss fire brigades, Saurer also export fire vehicles to Austria and other European countries.

Some of the earliest Saurer fire engines were built in 1914 with wooden 18m/60ft Magirus turntable ladders, one of which remained in operational service until 1964. After World War II, the 2DM Saurer 4x4 chassis with a 160bhp diesel engine was used for many standard-pattern Swiss water tenders. These had a rear-mounted pump and a 2,000-litre/440-gallon water tank. In 1958 Saurer delivered a 50m/165ft Magirus turntable ladder to Vienna Fire Service. One of the highest in Europe at the time, this Saurer/Magirus turntable ladder used the 8G-2HL 4x2 chassis powered by a 180bhp V8 diesel engine.

■ SILSBY
The Silsby Manufacturing Company was formed in 1845 to build steam fire engines for the increasing number of US fire departments. Like a number of fire engine companies, Silsby made its base at Seneca Falls, in New York State, and was soon supplying steam pumps to fire departments from coast to coast. In 1891 Silsby became one of the principal constituents of the American Fire Engine Company, which in 1903 evolved into American LaFrance.

■ SILVANI
Since its foundation in 1938, Silvani Anticendi has become a major manufacturer of fire engines along with a wide range of other firefighting and fire-protection equipment. Based in Bareggio, Milan, Italy, the Silvani product range includes water tenders, foam tenders and dry-powder units for specialized industrial fire risks, including some heavy vehicles on 6x6 chassis.

Silvani also builds trailer-mounted large-capacity water and foam monitors. Other important features of the Silvani product range are its maritime pump and water fittings for firefighting tugs, and its modular firefighting airborne system for aircraft and helicopters, used in aerial attacks on wildland and forest fires.

■ SKODA
In 1925 this Czechoslovakian car and van manufacturer merged with its rival Laurin and Klement and went on to produce a number of commercial truck chassis, which have been used for fire engines across Eastern Europe. Skoda is now based at Miladá Boleslav in the Czech Republic. In 2000, Skoda became a wholly-owned subsidiary of the Volkswagen Group.

Typical Skoda fire engines have included the compact light water tender based on the DVS12L/A Skoda light van chassis with a 1.2litre, 50bhp engine. This had a crew complement of four firefighters and carried a light portable pump and hose. Skoda also produced a number of ASC25 water tenders using the 706 RTHP 4x4 chassis. This heavier vehicle has a 6cylinder, 160bhp diesel engine, carries a crew of eight and has a 3,500-litre/770-gallon water tank and carries 200 litres/44 gallons of foam compound.

More recently, Skoda Karoq and Kodiaq cars have been widely used as emergency-service fast-response vehicles, and in 2020, Skoda UK delivered 35 Kodiaqs to the West Sussex Fire and Rescue Service, with four-wheel drive, and powered by a 2.0-litre, 150hp diesel engine.

■ SOUTHEAST FIRE APPARATUS
Southeast Fire Apparatus is based in Corbin, Kentucky, and acquired the apparatus division of Wynn Fire Equipment in 2012. The company builds a range of pumper, tankers and rescue trucks on custom and commercial chassis.

■ SPENCER MANUFACTURING
Spencer Manufacturing was founded in 1986, and manufactures a wide range of custom pumpers, rescue-pumpers, tankers, pump-tankers and wildland vehicles on a variety of chassis for customers throughout the Midwest.

■ STAR
For many years fire engines built on the Polish-manufactured Star chassis formed a large part of the pumping vehicles used by Poland's firefighters. The Star water tender, built on the A-26P 4x4 chassis, had a 2,000-litre/440-gallon water tank and carried 120 litres/26 gallons of foam to provide a first-aid foam firefighting attack. A portable pump was carried in addition to the fire engine's integral fire pump.

Some Star military-type chassis were also utilized for fire service use. A number of the 660 6x6 all-terrain chassis, for instance, were used for all-terrain emergency tenders. In the late 1970s Star was one the first East European fire engine builders to incorporate the use of alloy roller shutters for equipment lockers into its water tender design.

■ STONEFIELD
The short-lived British Stonefield Vehicles Ltd manufactured a number of fire engines in both 4x4 and 6x4 configurations that were unusual for their chassis-less construction. From 1978 six Stonefield emergency tenders, powered by 5.2-litre V8 petrol engines with an automatic gearbox, went into service with English and Scottish fire brigades. Others were supplied to airport fire brigades.

■ SUMMIT FIRE APPARATUS
Summit Fire Apparatus was formed in 1975 in Edgewood, Kentucky. In 1994 the company doubled its plant size to 2,880sq m/31,000sq ft, and today its line of apparatus includes heavy rescue trucks, mini-rescues, hazmat units, brush trucks, pumpers, tankers and an innovative 'air and light' vehicle designed to support crews on-scene by refilling air bottles and providing lighting rigs.

■ SVI TRUCKS
SVI began building custom fire apparatus in 1971. The fourth-generation family-owned company is now based at Fort Collins, Colorado, and has produced over 1,000 emergency-service vehicles of all types for fire-services throughout the US and for export customers.

TATRA

Tatra started manufacturing cars in Kopprivnice, now in the Czech Republic, in 1919 and since then has also been a principal supplier of chassis for fire engines, many being delivered to other East European countries, including Poland and former East Germany. Many vehicles have bodywork fitted by Korosa, another Czech company. The Tatra 138 and the later 148 6x6 series were typical heavy chassis used for foam tenders.

Today, Tatra builds a range of fire trucks on 4x4 and 6x6 chassis – pumpers, rescues, airport tenders, aerial and platforms – to suit customers' specifications.

■ ABOVE RIGHT *A 2019 6x6 Tatra airport crash truck, powered by a 435hp Tatra Euro 5 engine.*

■ RIGHT *A 6x4 Tatra rescue tender of Prague Fire Brigade.*

THIBAULT

The Thibault name is synonymous with Canadian-built fire engines. The company originated in the early twentieth century, when its founder, Charles Thibault, first built manual pumps, then horse-drawn fire engines, before completing his first motor fire engine, a Ford, in 1918.

Charles's son, Pierre, assumed command of the developing business in 1938 when the company relocated to Pierreville, Quebec. Throughout World War II, Thibault produced a range of government firefighting vehicles and equipment, but at the end of hostilities, returned to building fire engines for Canada's fire departments.

■ LEFT *This Shell-owned 1956 Ford F/Thibault foam tender served at Shellburn Refinery No.1, Burnaby, in British Columbia. It carried 3,800 litres/840 gallons of foam concentrate.*

Supplying both pumpers on custom chassis and, from 1960, aerials, Thibault went from strength to strength. Its aerials were particularly successful, with many ladder sections being supplied to American fire engine manufacturers for incorporation into their own products. By then, Thibault fire engines were in widespread operational use across Canada and export orders were delivered to fire brigades in the West Indies and South America.

When the founder's grandsons started their own independent fire engine manufacturing operation under the Pierreville name in 1968, Thibault began to suffer commercially, and was declared bankrupt in 1972. It was sold on, only to suffer the same fate again five years later. The Thibault name eventually re-emerged as Camions Pierre Thibault, Inc.

When the nearby Pierreville operation closed down in 1985, most of the company assets were assumed under the Thibault name before Camions Pierre

LIGHT PUMPER	
Year	1975
Engine	V6 petrol
Power	6-litre
Transmission	5-speed manual
Features	4x4

Thibault, Inc, went bankrupt in 1990. A new Canadian company, Nova Quintech Corporation, acquired the Thibault assets and continued the manufacture of pumpers and aerials. In 1995, however, it decided to concentrate its activities on aerial fire engines, and two years later the American fire engine company Pierce acquired the Nova Quintech aerial ladder business.

The Thibault family link was maintained by several family members who continue building pumpers, tankers, and other items of firefighting and rescue equipment in Canada today, on the original Pierreville site, under the Carl Thibault Emergency Vehicles name.

■ ABOVE ***A Thibault utility lighting vehicle with open rear cab of Neptune Rose Fire Company, Burlington, New Jersey, USA.***

THORNYCROFT

■ RIGHT ***A c.1970 Thornycroft Nubian Major/ Dennis Mk 9 6x4 crash tender originally supplied to the British Royal Air Force Fire and Rescue Service.***

Thornycroft chassis were first used for fire engines in the 1930s, but the company's name is best remembered for its airport and airfield crash tenders, built in considerable numbers in the 1950s and 1960s. Thorneycroft was based at Basingstoke in England, but the Basingstoke factory closed in 1969, and production of specialist vehicles transferred to Scammell.

The company supplied 4x4 and 6x4 Nubian variants for military and civil use. With roof-mounted foam monitor jets, the Nubians were fitted with either the Rolls-Royce B80 or B81 5.7litre, 8-cylinder petrol engines developing 140bhp, giving a Nubian a top speed of 60mph/95kmh. These airport tenders weighed in at 14 tons, but with ever-larger passenger jets, the demand for greater aviation firefighting capacity continued to increase, so in 1964 Thornycroft introduced the Nubian Major. This much more powerful 6x6 aviation fire engine was powered by a V8 Cummins diesel engine with 300bhp through a 5-speed semi-automatic gearbox. Firefighting foam output was rated at 31,800 litres/7,000 gallons per minute.

NUBIAN MAJOR 6X4 (20-TON)

Year	1966
Engine	V8 diesel
Power	300bhp
Transmission	5-speed semi-automatic
Features	66kmh/41mph in 41 secs

■ LEFT ***A Thornycroft Nubian Major/HCB Angus 6x4 foam tender in service at Dubai International Airport, in the United Arab Emirates.***

Toyne

Toyne is an American manufacturer based in Breda, Iowa. It was here that in 1942 founder blacksmith Gilbert 'Gib' Toyne built his first fire engine body based on a Model T Ford chassis for a local fire department in the city of Schleswig, Iowa. Toyne expanded his fire engine business, delivering front-mounted pumpers equipped with 2,270-litre/500-gallon water tanks. The company steadily built up a well-founded reputation for quality and heavy-duty construction, especially in off-road rural firefighting.

In 2017, Toyne celebrated its 75th anniversary, and today manufactures a wide range of pumpers, rescue pumpers, tankers and aerials, with bodies constructed of heavy-duty aluminium, stainless steel or Toyne's exclusive bolted/brushed stainless steel design. The pumpers can be customized or commercial and include the Metrocat heavy-duty aluminium body, severe-duty custom chassis, or polished unpainted stainless steel.

The tanker range includes heavy-duty vehicles with varying capacities (7,570–15,141 litres/1,665–3,330 gallons) and front- or midship-mounted pumps, or portables. Aerial ladders include a 23m/75ft along with 31.4m/103ft rear-mount ladder units. These aerials are available in a choice of formed stainless steel, aluminium or bolted/brushed stainless steel construction.

Toyota

The Tokyo-based Japanese car manufacturer Toyota has built a large number of chassis suitable for fire engine use. These have included many with bodies (pumps, aerial ladders and platforms) built by Morita, another Japanese company. In the early 1960s, Toyota still produced an open-bodied pump for urban Japanese fire brigades. This was based on the FC80 chassis that was powered by a six-cylinder petrol engine of 145bhp with four-speed manual gearbox.

Toyota chassis are particularly used for the MWG 40T pump, which incorporates a 2,270 litres/500-gallons-per-minute water pump, a 4,000-litre/880-gallon water tank and a crew cab that accommodates six firefighters. This model has been exported to fire brigades in Asia and the Far East. ToyoAce, Hilux and Landcruiser chassis have also been extensively used for fire vehicles around the world.

BJ 4x4

Year	1955
Engine	6-cylinder petrol
Power	3.3-litre
Transmission	manual
Features	all-terrain light pump

■ ABOVE *A c.1980 Toyota Dyna control unit of the Delhi Fire Service, India, carries a folded telescopic radio aerial on the roof. The red and white chequered markings are traditionally used to identify the central control point at a fire. Usually, they are applied to the upper half of a vehicle, but in this case no half measures have been taken.*

OTHER MAKES

■ TEMAX

Founded in 1965, Temax SA operates from its Athens production base, building a range of firefighting and rescue vehicles for Greek fire brigades, the armed forces, the civil aviation authority, the forestry departments and industrial companies.

Many Temax fire engines have been built on commercial chassis, including Chrysler, Mercedes-Benz, Scania, and Volvo, but today the company's vehicles are based primarily on Mercedes chassis. Temax pumpers are available with pumping capacities varying from 400 litres/88 gallons per minute to 6,000 litres/1,320 gallons per minute, and water tank capacity options from 500–12,000 litres/110–2,640 gallons.

The Temax range of firefighting tenders can be configured according to a fire brigade's precise needs. Some of the options available for airport fire tenders include manual or remote-controlled roof-mounted monitors, manual or automatic foam systems, ground-sweep nozzles, remote-control facilities, and manual or electric-rewind hose reels.

VARLEY

■ LEFT *In 2000, Queensland Fire and Rescue Service, Australia, bought this Varley urban pumper built on a Scania 94D 310 chassis.*

Varley Specialised Vehicles was formed in 1999 as an offshoot of the Australian parent company, Varley, which is involved in manufacturing, defence, power, and ship-repair activities.

The new division was formed with the intention of building fire engines utilizing special-purpose components, Rosenbauer pumping technology and Magirus firefighting equipment. Initially, two mainstream designs were developed – the Trident airport crash tender and the Firepac pumper. Both these models drew on combined bus and coach chassis manufacture and are in widespread use throughout Australian fire brigades.

The Firepac 4-door urban pumper has greater crew cab space than normal, together with a tilt cab that gives excellent access to the Caterpillar 250hp diesel power unit. The unique cab design of the Firepac provides rollover protection and allows easy exit from and access to the cab for a crew, especially when wearing breathing sets.

More recently, the Varley Commander cab chassis has been used extensively for building custom pumpers, normally powered by a 374hp Cummins diesel engine and with pump outputs of 3,500–5,500 litres/924–1,453 gallons per minute In 2011, Varley acquired the SEM business, which is still run independently of Varley Specialised Vehicles.

TYPE 5 COMMANDER

Year	2002
Engine	6-cylinder diesel
Power	274bhp
Transmission	automatic
Features	urban pumper

VOLKAN

■ BELOW *This 2021 Volkan Lion 8x8 airport crash truck is powered by twin 625hp Mercedes engines.*

Based in Izmir, Turkey, Volkan has been manufacturing fire engines since 1974, offering a bodybuilding design and supply service for urban, rural, airport, petrochemical and industrial fire brigades vehicles. The range includes water tenders, pumps, foam tenders and turntable ladders using chassis which include Mercedes and IVECO.

FOAM TENDER

Year	2002
Engine	6-cylinder diesel
Power	326bhp
Transmission	manual
Features	4x4

VOLKSWAGEN

Volkswagen light vehicles have been used for many years by European fire brigades, both as light fire tenders and for the general firefighting and rescue transportation of equipment, including light portable pumps and hose, and for the movement of personnel. The Volkswagen Combi and the LT31 series have been used regularly in various first-aid firefighting roles in support of major fire engines. Volkswagen is based in Wolfsburg, Germany.

■ LEFT *This c.1960 Volkswagen utility vehicle was used as a staff car by Stadt-Bottrop Fire Brigade, Germany.*

VOLVO

Volvo produced its first commercial trucks in 1928, just a year after its first cars rolled off the production line in Gothenburg, Sweden. One of the earliest Volvo fire engines built in that first year used an LV45 chassis and was built for the City of Gothenburg. The demand that followed was such that Volvo started to produce a chassis specifically for fire brigade use.

There then followed a series of Volvo chassis fitted with a 6-cylinder, 4-litre engine. Approximately 1,700 Volvo LV70s with a 4-litre, 6-cylinder engine were built between 1931 and 1936, most of which were used for fire engine or bus applications. The LV70, along with the LV68, was one of the first Volvo truck models to run on fuel other than petrol, when the Hesselman engine, which was able to run on several different fuels including fuel oil, was introduced in 1933. Volvo used this engine from 1933 until 1947 when it completed the design of its first diesel engine.

■ ABOVE *In 1928 the first Volvo truck to be used as a fire engine had a 28hp 2-litre petrol engine. It carried rolled hose.*

■ BELOW *By the 1930s the Volvo LV90 fire engine boasted a front-mounted pump and wheeled 15m/50ft escape ladder.*

FL10 ALP

Year	1997
Engine	6-cylinder diesel
Power	340bhp
Transmission	automatic
Features	32m/105ft working height

■ LEFT *A 1988 Volvo FL6 17/Metz 30m/100ft turntable ladder on duty with Hampshire Fire Brigade, England.*

■ BELOW LEFT *This Minnesota-based 1987 Volvo N12/Hills 6x4 tanker has a 15,900-litre/3,500-gallon water capacity.*

Outside Scandinavia Volvo initially tailored two models, the FL616 and the FL617, to cover the bulk of its fire applications. The FL614 chassis was introduced primarily for use as a water tender, with the heavier FL617 being used for hydraulic platforms and as a prime mover for demountable bodies. Although Volvo commercial vehicles were available in the UK from 1967, it was not until the FL6 truck series was introduced in the mid-1980s that Volvo fire engines started to appear in the UK. Today, Volvo fire engines are in service in most of the UK's fire brigades.

Volvo's success in the UK firefighting arena is reflected by orders for more than 300 vehicles from over half of Britain's 60 public fire brigades. The first large order for the FL614 came in 1990, when London Fire Brigade, the UK's largest fire authority, requested 34 water tenders. The capital's brigade had already taken delivery of six Volvo FL10 8x4 Bronto 33m/109ft aerial ladder platforms. At that time, these were the tallest aerials in service with any UK fire brigade.

In 1992 the FL617 was replaced by the FL618 and joined by a higher-powered alternative, the FS7. This 7-litre diesel-engine version of the well proven FL6 provided an 11 per cent improvement in power and a 33 per cent increase in torque over the most powerful 6-litre unit then standard in the FL6. In 1995 Volvo introduced a new turbocharged 6-litre engine, which had been designed specifically to meet fire brigade demand for a higher-powered, compact engine to boost performance. It produced 19 per cent more power and 18 per cent more torque than the existing engine.

Volvo has developed chassis for specific operating needs. For instance, Hampshire Fire and Rescue Service, in England, has an FL618 with a specially

■ BELOW *A 2019 Volvo FL/Angloco compact rescue pumping appliance for the South Yorkshire Fire and Rescue Service.*

■ RIGHT *This long-wheelbase Volvo Autocar tanker is operated by Selbyville Fire Department, Delaware.*

low cab height and Metz turntable ladder. The vehicle is 212mm/8¼ in lower than standard in order to provide access to the inner courtyard of Winchester Cathedral via a low arch. Volvo FL and FE crew-cab chassis are widely used for fire vehicles, and Greater Manchester Fire Service was one of the first customers for the FL816 appliance, powered by a Euro 6 280hp engine matched to an Allison 3000 automatic transmission, with bodywork by Emergency One (E-One) and an 1,800-litre/475-gallon-capacity water tank. FE chassis are popular as the basis for water tankers and aerial platforms in 4x2 or 6x2 configurations, with 250hp, 280hp or 320hp engine options. In 2020, seven 12-tonne Volvo Medium Rescue Pumpers (MRPs) were delivered to West Sussex Fire and Rescue Service.

OTHER MAKES

■ VAN PELT/FMC

American fire engine builder Van Pelt started business in 1925 in Oakdale, California. The company built up a customer base on the Pacific coast with a range of custom-built pumpers and aerial ladders.

After World War II, Van Pelt ceased to make its own chassis, offering instead a range of fire engines built upon suitable commercial alternatives such as Duplex, Ford and Spartan. In 1984, the Van Pelt Company was acquired by the FMC (Food Mechanical Corporation), one of the world's largest manufacturers of military and agricultural caterpillar vehicles. At that time, FMC also had a fire engine division originally formed in 1965 by its acquisition of the John Bean Company. This latter manufacturer was one of the pioneers of the use of high-pressure firefighting water pumps for fire engines.

The enlarged company produced the Quick Attacker short-bodied pumper range with various pumping capacities available from 1,125–6,800 litres/250–1,500 gallons per minute. These pumpers also had an impressive 2.43cu m/86cu ft of inboard storage. In addition, the Van Pelt/FMC range included the Roughneck series budget pumper, tankers with capacities of up to 11,300 litres/2,500 gallons and various aerial ladder configurations.

■ ABOVE *This 1971 Duplex/Van Pelt was acquired by Ukiah Fire Department, California in 1989 from Redwood City.*

Apart from its fire engines for American operational use, numerous types of Van Pelt/FMC fire engines were built for service in more than 30 countries. The company finally ceased fire vehicle production in 1990 to concentrate on manufacturing aviation equipment.

■ VOGT

Based at Oberdiessbach in Switzerland, VOGT build a range of pumpers, foam tenders and airport crash tenders for the international market. The fire engines are often based on MAN, Mercedes, Scania and Volvo chassis among others with 4x4, 6x4, and 8x4 configurations. Foam tenders are available with multi-compartments for up to four different types of extinguishing media plus a dry powder unit.

The company is noted for its use of electronic pump controls. VOGT fire engines can be fitted with a programmable logic controller that has complete control of the vehicle's water pump delivery, up to 6,000 litres/1,320 gallons per minute. Hose lines and outlets are operated via electropneumatic valves, which monitor water pressures to ensure that maximum operating levels are not exceeded. Precise amounts of foam concentrate can also be controlled. This system allows the firefighter at the hose branch to control the settings of water and foam as well as to operate the pump via a radio link.

WARD LAFRANCE

The Ward LaFrance fire engine company was founded in Elmira Heights, New York, in 1918 by A Ward LaFrance, who soon became a principal force in the American firefighting equipment industry. It has no connection with American LaFrance, which was founded earlier by another family member.

The company produced large numbers of fire engines leading up to World War II, and in 1937 introduced a restyled range of open-cab bonneted pumpers with midships-mounted pumps and incorporating a fire crew standing area in the rear body. These designs contributed to the developing shape and design of American fire engines of that time.

Ward LaFrance continued to produce the Fireball pumper range in the 1950s, following it with the 1960s Fire Brand models. A further new arrival in the range was the P80 Ambassador pumper, which was powered by a 6-cylinder Waukesha F817G petrol engine with 280bhp and a 5-speed manual gearbox. Offered as part of this new pumper in 1968 was the Ward LaFrance command tower – a vehicle-width, 6.7m/22ft elevating platform, raised by hydraulic rams. Fitted with a vertical access ladder, the tower carried a 4,500-litre/1,000-gallon monitor and could be used as a lighting platform or aerial command control point.

Ward LaFrance also produced some 23–30m/75–100ft aerial ladders, both rear and midships-mounted, together with hydraulic platforms up to 26m/85ft. All these aerials were available on two or tandem-axle chassis, depending on weight factors. The company has also built several compact pumpers and other fire engines, together with a number of telescopic-boomed water towers, on 4x4 chassis.

The company closed its doors in 1979.

■ BELOW *Los Angeles County Fire Department, Pearblossom, California, took delivery of this new Ward LaFrance Ambassador pumper in 1972. It has a 4,500-litres/1,000-gallons-per-minute pump and 2,270-litre/500-gallon water tank.*

■ ABOVE *A 1973 Ward LaFrance pumper of Orbisonia-Rockhill Fire Department, Pennsylvania.*

■ BELOW *A 1976 International 2010A Ward LaFrance pumper with a 4,500-litre/1,000-gallon water tank and pump.*

WESTATES

■ ABOVE *A 1985 Ford L8000/ Westates pumper of Snohomish County Fire District, Getchell, Washington.*

■ LEFT *A 1984 Duplex D350/ Westates pumper based in Antloch, California.*

In 1956 the Westates Truck Body Company began trading in Redwood City, California. After building a number of commercial truck bodies, Westates began to manufacture fire engine bodies for the California State Division of Forestry. During the early 1960s, the company delivered its first heavy rescue unit and from then on Westates regularly built fire engines for many American municipal fire departments.

Westates relocated to new premises in Menlo Park, California, in 1969 and in 1983 moved to Woodland, California. In 1977, Westates designed the original through-the-tank ladder tunnel arrangement, and the company continued its strong technological leadership. In 1996 an industrial laser-cutting machine, which worked to European standards, was installed at the premises, and one year later, a laser-cut stainless steel fire engine body became a Westates standard.

In 2009, Westates ceased trading, and its assets were acquired by the American Truck and Trailer Body Company, though production of fire vehicles ceased.

PUMPER

Year	1986
Engine	6-cylinder diesel
Power	350bhp
Transmission	manual
Features	6,810lpm/1,500gpm pump

■ LEFT *Skagit County Fire District, LaConner, Washington, operate this 1983 Ford C/Westates pumper with a 4,500-litres/ 1,000-gallons-per-minute pump and a similar capacity water tank.*

■ LEFT *A 1986 International S2674 chassis provides the base for this Westates 6,800-litres/1,500-gallons-per-minute pumper with a 3,400-litre/750-gallon water tank.*

WESTERN STATES

■ BELOW *A 1989 Autocar Western States pumper of Lebanon Fire District, Oregon, carries a front-mounted 6,800-litres/1,500-gallons-per-minute pump.*

This American fire apparatus company started life as the Neep Fire Equipment of Cornelius, Oregon. Neep sold firefighting equipment and developed this work into the building of their first fire engine in 1941. This was followed by a number of other fire department vehicles and in the 1940s, Gloyd Hall acquired the interests of the Neep company and the brand name was changed to Western States Fire Apparatus, Inc.

Trading under this new title, the company continued its steady output of fire engines, building mostly a range of pumpers, including front-mounted, midships, and Intra-Cab models, and various other types of pumper tenders, until going out of business in 2003. The company delivered over 1,200 fire engines to fire departments throughout the American northwest, and in Texas, California, Colorado and Wyoming. Some Western States pumpers were also exported to Kuwait.

■ ABOVE RIGHT *Front-mounted pump controls and inlets/outlets are a feature of this 1975 Seagrave/Western States 6x4 pumper.*

■ RIGHT *Portland Fire Bureau, Oregon, operate this 1981 Spartan pumper with a typical Western States front-mounted pump.*

■ ABOVE *A 1962 Ford F800/Western States light pumper of Skagit County Fire District, Birdsview, Washington.*

WHITE

The White brothers, Thomas, Rollin, Walter and Windsor built their first steam engine in 1900, building on the success of their father's sewing machine business. Productivity increased year on year, and the range of vehicles expanded to include buses, police patrol wagons, fire apparatus and later, sightseeing buses. Petrol-powered engines made their first appearance in 1909 and in 1916 the company was reorganized under the name White Motor Company.

The company eventually merged with Freightliner Trucks after having acquired Sterling in 1951 and Autocar in 1953. By 1975 the newly named White Truck Group had also acquired Diamon Reo, but by 1981 the company was bankrupt and bought out, and it disappeared in 1995.

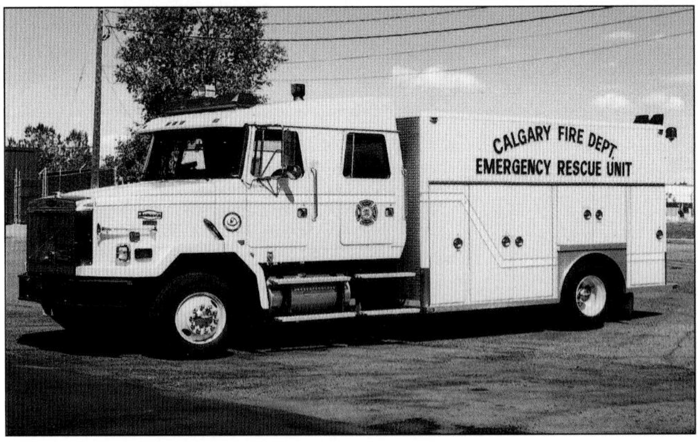

■ ABOVE *A 1991 White/General Motors/Anderson pumper in British Columbia.*

■ LEFT *A 1990 rescue unit based on a White/General Motors/Autocar/ Computerlog arrangement.*

OTHER MAKES

■ WATEROUS
The Waterous Company was founded in St Paul, Minnesota, USA, in 1886 by the two Waterous brothers, to manufacture horse-drawn steam fire engines and other firefighting equipment. Waterous fire engines were soon in use across America and in 1898 the company had pioneered a petrol-driven water pump pulled by horses. In 1906 Waterous produced a petrol-powered pumper with separate engines for road traction and water-pump power. One year later it produced a pumper that used a single petrol engine for both road propulsion and pump power.

Waterous ceased to build complete fire engines in 1929 in order to concentrate on developing firefighting water-pump technology, which it offered to other fire engine builders worldwide. Today Waterous fire pumps are the most frequently specified types in North America, and a number are in operational service around the world.

■ WAWRZASZEK
The Wawrzaszek Special Engineering Company, based in Bielsko-Biala, Poland, builds a varied range of firefighting and rescue vehicles. These include pumps and aerial ladders and platforms, hazardous material incident units and support vehicles for a variety of high-risk fire protection industries. Suitable commercial chassis are used according to payload and specification.

■ WELCH FIRE EQUIPMENT
Based at Marion in Wisconsin, Welch Fire Equipment was formed in 1964 to sell fire equipment. After a few years, the company began building rescue units, tankers and pumpers, and has now built over 1,500 fire and emergency vehicles for customers throughout the USA and Mexico.

■ WYNN FIRE EQUIPMENT
This company was formed in 1986 in Corbin, Kentucky, and built a range of pumper, tankers and rescue trucks on custom and commercial chassis. In 2012, the apparatus division was sold, and became Southeast Fire Apparatus, while the original company continued as a fire-equipment and used apparatus dealer.

YOUNG

Allen Case founded his American fire engine-building company in 1932. It was known as Cayasler before it assumed the title of Young Fire Equipment Company in 1944. Until it ceased trading in 1991, Young built over 2,000 fire engines at its production plants around Buffalo, New York State. In later years it produced 22.5mm/73ft 8in hydraulic platforms built on the Young Crusader chasses, and a number of pumpers were built with folding rear crew-cab doors operated by a compressed-air mechanism.

■ ABOVE *Mt Jackson Fire Department, Shenandoah County, Virginia, operates this 1989 Young Crusader II pumper, which incorporates a roomy rear crew cab compartment. The mid-mounted pump has a capacity of 5,700 litres/1,250 gallons per minute, while the water tank holds 2,270 litres/500 gallons.*

ZIEGLER

■ BELOW *A 2002 MAN/Ziegler 8x8 airport foam tender at Stuttgart Airport, Germany.*

Albert Ziegler founded his hose-manufacturing company in 1890 in Giengen, Germany, and although it steadily expanded its range of firefighting equipment, it did not build a fire engine until 1953. The first was a KFL6 water tender constructed on an Opel Lightning 1.75-ton chassis. From then on, a range of Ziegler engine types were developed, using diesel engines for the first time in 1963. Some of the early vehicles went to European brigades.

In 1969 Ziegler's first airport crash tender went into service in Copenhagen. By this time the company was supplying an ever-expanding range of water tenders, rescue tenders, aerial ladders, airport foam/crash tenders and other firefighting vehicles, as well as continuing to develop its fire pump and equipment side of the business.

Today, Ziegler is Germany's largest firefighting equipment manufacturer and supplies very large numbers of fire

■ ABOVE LEFT ***This Ziegler pumper, built on a MAN chassis has a 9,000-litre/2,378-gallon water tank and was delivered to Czech Republic in 2019.***

■ ABOVE RIGHT ***A c.1970 Opel Blitz/Ziegler rescue tender of the Bad Nauheim Fire Brigade, Germany.***

engines and components to fire brigades in over 70 countries. Current Ziegler fire vehicles range from the small VRW quick-response light rescue vehicles, to the huge 8x8 FLF 60/Z8 airport foam tender. The Ziegler VRW is based on various commercial chassis, including the Mercedes-Benz 412D 4x2 with a 5-cylinder 122 bhp engine, and the Chevrolet Suburban K 2500 4x4 with a V8 engine with 250bhp. It is equipped either with a light water unit or a complement of rescue tools and electrical power.

At the other end of the Ziegler range is the FLF 60 Z8 airport foam tender, which weighs just over 38 tons and carries a crew of three. This uses a MAN 38.1000 8x8 chassis with a 12-cylinder, 1,000bhp engine with automatic transmission, which provides a 0–80kmh/50mph performance in approximately 20 seconds. The FLF 60 Z8 carries 12,000 litres/2,666 gallons of water, 1,500 litres/330 gallons of foam concentrate, and 500kg/1100lb of dry powder. The Ziegler fire pump has a maximum output of 7,000 litres/1,540 gallons per minute, the roof-mounted monitor delivers 5,000 litres/1,100 gallons per minute and 1,000 litres/220 gallons are delivered through the front-mounted monitor. Both monitors are remotely controlled from the driving cab.

Ziegler also supplies the DLK 23/12 turntable ladder on the Mercedes Benz Atego 1528 or the MAN 15.264 chassis, and the Bronto Skylift F32 MDT aerial platform ladder on the Mercedes Benz Atego1828 or MAN 18.264 chassis.

VLF 24/12

Year	2002
Engine	6-cylinder diesel
Power	240hp
Transmission	automatic or manual
Features	quick-response pumper

■ LEFT ***Lüdenscheid Fire Brigade, Germany, use Ziegler-bodied fire engines, such as this Mercedes 1019/Ziegler rescue tender.***

OTHER MAKES

■ ZIL

From 1942 onwards the UAZ Moscow truck and van factory built a number of small first-aid fire engines for Russian fire brigades, using the UAZ 450A 4x4 van chassis. After 1956, however, all standard Russian-built fire engines were constructed under the ZIL badge and a vast number of ZIL fire engines went into service right across the Soviet bloc. These included the ZIL 130 and 150 series 4x2 water tenders of the late 1950s, which were powered by a 6-cylinder, 95bhp engine. Both series had an 1,800 litres/400 gallons per minute pump, but the ZIL 130 had a 2,100-litre/460-gallon water tank, while the 150 series had the slightly larger 2,150-litre/470-gallon version. Some ZIL 130 models also included a 500-litre/110-gallon foam-concentrate tank to provide a firefighting attack at oil refineries and petrochemical plants.

ZIL also produced a heavy chassis known as the 131 6x6 series, designed for a Soviet-manufactured AL30 30m/100ft turntable ladder. ZIL water tenders and turntable ladders have found their way to a number of countries outside the Soviet Union, including Iran and Egypt, as well as several African countries.

ZIL was declared bankrupt in 2013.

GLOSSARY

Apparatus Generic American term for a fire engine.

Aerial Ladder A telescopic steel ladder made up of sections, which rotates around a turntable mounted either at the rear or middle of a fire engine chassis. It has either a crew bucket or cage at top able to provide rescue and project a water jet into buildings at upper levels. In USA, some aerial ladders are tractor-drawn articulated units with a steered rear axle.

Aerial Ladder Platform (ALP) Fire engine with cage for high-rise firefighting and rescue with several folding telescopic booms which rotate through 360 degrees. Has an auxiliary ladder alongside booms.

Air Masks and Bottles US term for compressed air or oxygen breathing sets, and air/oxygen cylinders.

Airfield Crash Tender Powerful high-capacity foam tender with all-wheel drive designed for aviation and airport firefighting and rescue.

Brake Horsepower (bhp) The power developed by an engine as measured by a dynamometer.

Branch The nozzle end of a firefighting hose line.

Breathing Apparatus European term for breathing sets.

Chemical Incident/Hazmat Unit Fire engine which carries protective suits and equipment for dealing with nuclear/biological/chemical spills, leakages and subsequent decontamination.

Control/Despatch Centre Geographically centralized, computer-controlled communications base that handles all emergency calls, mobilizes fire engines and has overall control of major incidents.

Control Unit Fire engine designed to operate as mobile command centre at fires and other emergency incidents.

Emergency Tender Fire engine which carries a wide range of cutting, lifting, and heavy rescue equipment, virtually a travelling workshop with self-contained power supplies for tools and lighting.

Engine US term for a fire engine with the primary purpose of pumping water and providing hose lines. Also known as a pumper.

Fire Engine Generic term for all types of firefighting and rescue vehicles.

Fire Station/Firehouse Building which houses fire engines, has accommodation for firefighters and some training facilities.

Foam Tender Fire engine which produces and projects large quantities of foam on to liquid fires involving fuels and petrochemicals.

Forward Control/Cab Over Engine A cab directly over the engine unit.

Hazmat Denote hazardous materials including those of a toxic, corrosive or irritant nature.

Hose Usually in 22.8m/75ft lengths and with either snap-together or screw couplings. Is stowed coiled or flaked on fire engines.

Hose Layer Fire engine capable of laying out up to a mile of pre-flaked hose at speed during major firefighting operations, from a major water source to the scene of the fire.

Hose Line Lengths of hose joined together taking water from a fire engine to the scene of the fire.

Hose Reels Small, 2.5cm/1in diameter, rubber hose, coiled on circular drums on each side or at the rear of most pumps/water tenders. Fed from an onboard water tank and used to provide an immediate attack on a small fire.

Hydraulic Platform First-generation, high-rise fire engine consisting of several folding, hydraulically operated booms with a cage at the top.

Pump European term for a fire engine which carries crew of six, pumps water, carries breathing sets, ladders and firefighting and rescue gear. Also the term for the separate inbuilt machinery that pressurizes and propels water from the fire engine through hoses to the fire.

Pumper US equivalent of pump.

Pump Escape European term for Pump which also carries a 15m/50ft wooden, wheeled escape ladder with the primary purpose of performing a rescue.

Rescue Truck US term for Emergency Tender.

Special Service Call Any non-fire emergency such as a road or rail crash, accident, chemical spill or leak, animal rescue, or humanitarian duty.

Steamer Fire engine with coal-fired boiler producing steam to drive the water pump to produce a water jet.

Thermal Imaging Camera Hand-held electronic device which allows fire crews to see clearly through smoke.

Tiller Long-wheelbase, USA aerial-ladder fire engine with a rear-axle steering position to assist the vehicle to negotiate tight corners.

Tower Ladder A US aerial ladder with a fitted cage at its head with fixed hose.

Truck US term for apparatus (fire engine) which carries ladders, forcible entry and other heavy gear.

Turntable Ladder European equivalent of US aerial/tower ladder able to rotate 360 degrees around a turntable base.

Water Carrier/Tanker Fire engine with large-capacity water tank used to ferry firefighting water in rural areas.

Water Fog Finely atomized water mist produced at hose branch to protect firefighters from the intense, radiated heat of a fire.

Water Tender A rural, pumping fire engine with 13.5m/45ft ladder.

INDEX

Page numbers in *italic* type refer to picture captions; **bold** numbers refer to A–Z entries.

ACKNOWLEDGEMENTS

Picture Credits
The publishers would like to thank the following for their kind permission to reproduce their photographs:
Key: b: bottom; c: centre; l: left; m: middle; r: right; t: top.

AKG 12t. **Alamy** 7b, 34–35, 55m, 63 tr, 81b, 82t, 85tr, 115t, 122t, b, 123, 152m, and 188b. **Andrew Henry** 54 b, 136, 137t, 147b, 148t and br, 152t, 155t, 159t and cr, 163t, 166bl, 184t, 187t, 194b, 206c and br, 208b, 213c and b, 214b, 216c, 219t, 234b, 240t, 241c and b, 242b, 252c. **Bob Dubbert** 48c, 141t, 142c, 153 second from tr and second from br, 167bl, 185b, 210b, 230c and b, 237c and 248 second from b. **Bridgeman Art Library** 12bl and br, 13tr and b, 16bl and br, 17b, 18tl, 19b, 20b, 21br, 22tl, 24t, 40b and 112t. **Code Red** 8, 9, 29tl, 31bl, 60b, 78b and 95b. **Corbis** 17tlt, 91t. **Dan Goyer** 130b, 131cr, 132cr, 160c, 183b, 210t, 216b, 231t, 233tr, 235b, 240b and 249t. **Dave Stewardson** 32tr, 131tr, 148bl, 150b, 169 t and b, 175t, second from t and br, 177t, 184c, 197b and bc, 199t, 212b, 213t, 223c, 232t, 236b, 238b, 245c and 250b. **Firepix International** 28t, 60tlt and tc, 76tr, 77br and bl, 79t, 80t, 86, 88t, 92bl, 95t, 98b, 100t, 102br, 103b, 110b, 113tc, 114 tl, tr, 116bl, 117b, 119tl, 120b and 121b. **Gary Chapman** 94t and b. **Iveco** 33b, 65cb, 187 bottom three pictures. **Jerry Hepworth** 126b, 127t, 129t, 139 tr, 145t and b, 149c, 156br, 176t, 195b and bc, 203 second from b, 205b and 226b **Jerry Sires** 4, 49b, 53b, 63tl, 65b, 101t, 109bl, 130c, 158 c and b, 160t, 163b, 173 t and c, 177b, 178b, 179t, 181t, c and b, 186 second from t, 189b, 191b, 197t, 198t and b, 214c, 218 all, 223b, 226t, 232c, 238 second from t, 241t and 246t. **Keith Wardell** 1, 51tr, 126t, 129c, 138tr, 139cl and cr, 149bl and br, 154t, 156c, 157tr, 162t, 165t, c and b, 166cr and br, 167tl and cr, 168tl, 174 tr, 192 second from bl, 194c, 195t and tc, 200tc, tr and c, 201c, 202b, 203tl, 204bl, 205t, 209t and c, 21t, 220b, 244t, 245t and 252tr. **NASA** 209b. **National Motor Museum** 6l, 43tr, 44t, 46b, 47b, 50b, 58bl, 166cl and 221t. **Neil Wallington** 2, 5, 6 br and tr, 10–11, 14 all, 15t, 16t, 17tr, 19tr, 21tr, c and bl, 22tr and b, 23t and b, 25t and b, 26t, 27t, 29b, 30bl and br, 31t, 32tl and br, 33tl and tr, 36br, 39bl and br, 41tl and b, 44b, 45b, 46t, 47c, 48t and b, 51b, 57cr, 59tl and bl, 60tr, 61b, 62b, 69tl, second left from t and br, 70–71, 72t, 73t, 74t and b, 75 all, 76tl and b, 77t, 78t, 79bl and br, 80b, 82b, 83b, 84l and r, 85b, 87b, 88b, 89, 90, 92t and br, 93t, 97t and b, 98t, 102t and bl, 104t and b, 105t and b, 106tl and tr, 107bl, 108t, 109t, 111b, 112b, 113tl and b, 115bl, 116t and br, 118tr, 119b, 120t, 121t, 129b, 133b, 137b, 138 second from b and b, 139tl and br, 146b, 154c and b, 155bl and br, 156t and bl, 159cl, 162b, 167tr and cl, 176c, 183bc, 194t, 199tcr and tclt, 203tr, 204t, 215t and b, 217tr, 219blt, 224 all, 226c, 227tr, 251b. **Roger Mardon** 239. **Shane Mackichan** 52t and b, 53t, 131tl and b, 132ct, 140 all, 141c and b, 144, 147t and tc, 150t and third from t, 153 second from tl, 160b, 161t, 167br, 171c, 172t, 174tl, 175bl, 176b, 177c, 178t, 182t and c, 183t, 185t, 186bl, 190b, 198c, 199b, 208t and tcr, 212t, 232b, 236t and c, 238t, 247t, 248t and b, 249c, bl and bt, 250t and c. **Shaun Ryan** 3, 127c, 130t, 143t and b, 147 second from b, 150 second from t, 153br, 157b, 158t, 168t and second from t, 171b, 174c and b, 181t and b, 184b, 202t and second from t, 214t, 222t, 227b, 231b, 235t, 237t, 246c, 247c and b, 248 second from t and 251t. **Simon Rowley** 202 second from b and 219 br. **Shutterstock** 66, 83t, 113tr, 114b, 115br. **Spectrum** 51tl. **Steven Schueler** 125, 128b, 134 all, 135 all, 170b, 189t and c, 196t, c and b, 206t and tcr, 228 all, 229 all, 243t. **S W Stevens-Stratten** 126c, 128t, 138tl, 139bl, 145c, 149tl, 155c, 167tr, 193c, 204brt, 220t. **Terry Yip** 13 t and b, 168b, 173b, 190t and 212c. **Travel Ink** 15 bottom, 108bl and r, 109br, 110t and 118 tl. **TRH** 18tr and b, 19tl, 20t, 24b, 26b, 27b, 28b, 29trt, 30t, 31br, 32cl, 36t and bl, 37t and b, 38t and b, 39t, 40t, 41tr, 42t and b, 43tl and b, 45t, 47t, 49t, 50tl and tr, 56t and bb, 57t, bl and br, 58t and c, 59tr and br, 6rl, 62t, 65tl, 67b, 68 all, 69br, 72b, 73b, 91b, 96, 100b, 101c and bb, 107br, 117tl, tc and tr, 119tr, 149tr, 166t, 193t, 203b, 225c, 227tl and 244c and b. **Wikimedia Commons** 67t, 87t, 93b, 111t, 146t, 157tl, 164b, 172b, 187 second from t, third from t, 192bl, 200b, 202bc, 205m, 207b, 215c, 217tl, b, 222b, 223t, 225t, b, 234t, 240m, 252tl.

Page 1: London Fire Engine, 2020. **Page 2:** Fire engines attend a fire scene in Tokyo, Japan. **Page 3:** 1926 American LaFrance pumper. **Page 4:** A specialized ERF foam tender in action. **Front Endpaper:** Bronto Skylife F54HDT front aerial platform. **Back Endpaper:** Seagrave Marauder II.

Acknowledgements
The author wishes to thank the following for their assistance and technical advice during the preparation of this book: Martin Aust (Angloco Limited), Ron Bentley, Eric Billingham, Gary Chapman, Maurice Cole, Detlef Gerth, Mike Hebbard, Andrew Henry, Jerry Hepworth, Chris Jackson, Simon Rowley, S W Stevens-Stratten, Keith Wardell, Duncan White. Thanks to the Chief Officers and uniformed personnel, including photographers of many fire bridgades including: British Airports Authority, Cheshire, Cleveland (UK), Cornwall, Devon, Dorset, Essex, Greater Manchester, Hampshire, Humberside, Kent, Lancashire, Leicestershire, Lincolnshire, London, Mid and West Wales, New Orleans (Captain Chis Mickel), Wiltshire, Network Rail, West Midlands Fire Service (Edward Ockenden) and West Yorkshire Fire Service (Brian Saville and Andrew Henson). Eurotunnel, and The UK Fire Protection Association. The librarians of the London Fire Brigade Library and the Fire Service College Library, England. Simona Hill of Anness Publishing for all her editorial guidance. And lastly my wife Susie, who has given unstinting amounts of help and encouragement throughout the marathon compilation of this book.

The publishers would like to thank the following for their generous assistance: Shane Mackichan, Andrew Henry, Shaun Ryan, Steven Schueler and Jerry Sires, plus many of the fire engine manufacturers listed in this book.

This edition is published by
Lorenz Books
an imprint of Anness Publishing Ltd
info@anness.com
www.lorenzbooks.com
www.annesspublishing.com

Publisher: Joanna Lorenz
Editorial Director: Helen Sudell
Project Editor: Simona Hill
Additional Text: Steve Rendle
Designer: Mike Morey
Cover Designer: Nigel Partridge
Production Controller: Ben Worley

A CIP catalogue record for this book is available from the British Library.